Intelligent Continuous Security

AI-Enabled Transformation
for Seamless Protection

Marc Hornbeek
Foreword by Jimmy Xu

O'REILLY®

Intelligent Continuous Security

by Marc Hornbeek

Published by O'Reilly Media, Inc., 1005 Gravenstein Highway North, Sebastopol, CA 95472.

O'Reilly books may be purchased for educational, business, or sales promotional use. Online editions are also available for most titles (*http://oreilly.com*). For more information, contact our corporate/institutional sales department: 800-998-9938 or *corporate@oreilly.com*.

Acquisitions Editor: Simina Calin	**Indexer:** BIM Creatives, LLC
Development Editor: Corbin Collins	**Cover Designer:** Susan Brown
Production Editor: Elizabeth Faerm	**Cover Illustrator:** José Marzan Jr.
Copyeditor: Audrey Doyle	**Interior Designer:** David Futato
Proofreader: Piper Content Partners	**Interior Illustrator:** Kate Dullea

June 2025:　　　　　First Edition

Revision History for the First Edition
2025-06-09:　　First Release

See *http://oreilly.com/catalog/errata.csp?isbn=9798341615915* for release details.

979-8-341-61591-5

[LSI]

Table of Contents

Foreword

With over two decades working in technology across public and private sectors—as a developer, systems engineer, network administrator, security engineer, consultant, solutions architect, advisor to VCs and founders, and now as a technology executive of security vendor Cycode—I've witnessed firsthand the ongoing struggle to balance speed and security. Over the past 10 years, I've helped lead multiple DevSecOps transformations for Fortune 500 organizations and seen the profound impact of integrating security into software development lifecycles. Currently, I work with Cycode's product APSM, a single platform that discovers and manages all security tooling and data across the entire software development lifecycle.

I've known Marc Hornbeek for eight years, dating back to when I led DevSecOps efforts while he championed DevOps. We often collaborated to bridge the very silos this book addresses: DevOps and SecOps. Back then, we knew our efforts could shape industry best practices. Today, achieving that vision is more urgent than ever.

Software development has undergone seismic shifts: the Agile movement, the rise of DevOps and cloud native practices, and now the AI and generative development era. With AI code assistants and "vibe coding" on the rise, we're seeing faster delivery—along with new and complex risks. AI-generated code isn't inherently secure, and even the assistants themselves can be compromised. As the pace of software innovation accelerates, our security approaches have not evolved fast enough to match.

Two core challenges consistently block progress. First: organizational friction. While much has been said about Dev versus Ops or Dev versus Sec, the increasingly fraught relationship between DevOps and SecOps remains largely unspoken. In large enterprises, these teams often compete for control rather than collaborate toward shared goals. Second: technology overload. Rapid innovation, market saturation, and security feature sprawl have created confusion. In some cases, teams lag behind; in others, they overinvest in tools without addressing fundamental process and culture issues.

It's time for a paradigm shift. We don't need to debate shift left versus shift right anymore. What we need is Continuous Security—unifying DevOps and SecOps and leveraging AI to build intelligent, adaptive defenses across the lifecycle.

In *Intelligent Continuous Security*, Marc offers just that: a bold, practical blueprint for embedding AI-driven security into every stage of software delivery. This book isn't just about improving security; it's about transforming how teams work, think, and respond. For leaders and practitioners alike, this is essential reading to meet the demands of modern software development.

Read it. Apply it. The future of security depends on it.

— Jimmy Xu
Field CTO, Cycode

Preface

Security in software development and operations has long been treated as a discrete function—something to be bolted on to applications and infrastructure rather than designed into them from the start.

The shift toward DevSecOps was meant to address this, bringing security earlier into the development lifecycle. But even with this progress, security remains fragmented, with DevSecOps focusing on securing the pipeline and SecOps dealing with threats after deployment. This divide has left organizations struggling to implement security as a truly continuous and intelligent discipline—one that spans from code inception to runtime protection. This book introduces Intelligent Continuous Security (ICS) as a solution to this challenge, integrating AI-driven automation, continuous monitoring, and adaptive security models into a cohesive strategy that unifies security across the entire software lifecycle.

The need for ICS has never been greater. Cyber threats are evolving at an unprecedented pace, outpacing traditional security controls and response mechanisms. AI-powered attacks, supply chain compromises, and regulatory complexities require security teams to rethink their approach. ICS does not simply layer security controls on top of existing workflows; it embeds security as code, as automation, and as intelligence, making it a core enabler of both resilience and business agility. By leveraging AI-driven automation, predictive threat detection, and continuous compliance validation, ICS helps organizations move beyond static security models toward adaptive, self-healing defenses that keep pace with emerging risks.

This book is designed for security professionals, DevOps engineers, IT leaders, and decision makers who want to move beyond incremental security improvements and adopt a holistic, AI-assisted approach to cybersecurity. Throughout the chapters, I outline the principles, strategies, and real-world implementations of ICS, including how to break down silos between DevSecOps and SecOps, how to measure and optimize security effectiveness, and how AI can transform everything from security operations to regulatory compliance. The book also addresses the human and organizational challenges of ICS adoption, recognizing that technology alone is not enough—it requires a shift in culture, skills, and governance.

As you embark on this journey, I encourage you to approach ICS not as a destination but as a continuous evolution. The security landscape will keep changing, but by embracing automation, intelligence, and collaboration, organizations can stay ahead of the curve. My hope is that this book will serve as both a guide and a catalyst—empowering you to build security architectures that are not just strong, but also intelligent and adaptive in the face of an uncertain future.

Conventions Used in This Book

The following typographical conventions are used in this book:

Italic
> Indicates new terms, URLs, email addresses, filenames, and file extensions.

> This element signifies a general note.

O'Reilly Online Learning

For more than 40 years, *O'Reilly Media* has provided technology and business training, knowledge, and insight to help companies succeed.

Our unique network of experts and innovators share their knowledge and expertise through books, articles, and our online learning platform. O'Reilly's online learning platform gives you on-demand access to live training courses, in-depth learning paths, interactive coding environments, and a vast collection of text and video from O'Reilly and 200+ other publishers. For more information, visit *https://oreilly.com*.

How to Contact Us

Please address comments and questions concerning this book to the publisher:

O'Reilly Media, Inc.
1005 Gravenstein Highway North
Sebastopol, CA 95472
800-889-8969 (in the United States or Canada)
707-827-7019 (international or local)
707-829-0104 (fax)
support@oreilly.com
https://oreilly.com/about/contact.html

We have a web page for this book, where we list errata, examples, and any additional information. You can access this page at *https://oreil.ly/intelligent-continuous-security*.

For news and information about our books and courses, visit *https://oreilly.com*.

Find us on LinkedIn: *https://linkedin.com/company/oreilly-media*.

Watch us on YouTube: *https://youtube.com/oreillymedia*.

Acknowledgments

My sincere gratitude goes to the O'Reilly editing and publishing team for helping to bring this book to reality, and especially to the technical reviewers:

- Debashis Bhattacharyya, director and principal architect, Opus Technologies
- Victorio Mosso Zempoalteca, CEO and founder, Analytica MTY
- Dominic Monn, founder, MentorCruise

.

CHAPTER 1

Introduction to Intelligent Continuous Security

The growing complexity and frequency of cyber threats demands a more unified and intelligent approach to security. Traditional DevSecOps and SecOps models have been effective in their respective domains—DevSecOps in integrating security into development pipelines and SecOps in maintaining operational security. However, the increasing sophistication of attacks, progressively driven by AI, necessitates an evolution in the management of security across the entire software lifecycle. This chapter introduces the concept of *Intelligent Continuous Security* (ICS), a framework that bridges the gap between development and operations by applying AI to transform siloed DevSecOps and SecOps toward more automated and enhanced security practices throughout the value stream.

Intelligent Continuous Security unifies DevSecOps and SecOps into a single, cohesive model that continuously adapts to emerging threats. By leveraging AI, any organization may enhance its ability to detect vulnerabilities early in the development cycle, automate compliance checks, and respond swiftly to incidents in production environments. This approach eliminates silos between development and operational teams, enabling real-time collaboration and a more resilient security posture. It provides a proactive model where security is embedded at every phase, from code inception to production, ensuring end-to-end protection.

This chapter explains the foundational principles of Intelligent Continuous Security and why transforming from traditional siloed DevSecOps and SecOps practices to end-to-end Continuous Security is critical in today's fast-paced and evolving cybersecurity landscape. It covers the limitations of traditional DevSecOps and SecOps models, explains the role of AI in addressing these gaps, and sets the stage for leveraging AI to transform to an AI-driven Continuous Security model. By the end of this chapter, you'll have a clear understanding of the necessity of this shift and the key benefits AI can offer in transforming to Continuous Security.

Definition and Overview

Intelligent Continuous Security is an advanced security framework that integrates AI to unify and enhance the security practices of DevSecOps and SecOps. It goes beyond the traditional, siloed approaches by automating key security functions across the entire software lifecycle, from development to operations. By applying AI to automate routine tasks, detect anomalies, and continuously monitor security, organizations can improve both the speed and effectiveness of their security operations while reducing human error and resource constraints.

This approach is particularly critical in today's digital landscape, where cyber threats are increasingly sophisticated and attackers use AI-driven methods to evade detection. Intelligent Continuous Security allows organizations to stay ahead of these threats by continuously learning, adapting, and evolving their security protocols.

This section defines the core elements of Intelligent Continuous Security, describes its key capabilities, and explores why it is an essential evolution from traditional security models. The following subsections dive deeper into the history of DevSecOps and SecOps and the role AI plays in transforming Continuous Security for a more secure future.

As indicated in Figure 1-1, Intelligent Continuous Security is defined as applying AI-augmented security practices across the entire software development lifecycle and production operations. In DevSecOps, the goal is to prevent vulnerabilities during planning *and* engineering, and in the Continuous Integration/Continuous Delivery (CI/CD) pipelines, ensuring that security is integrated from the start. Once we move into SecOps, the focus shifts to defending against exploits and attacks in production environments.

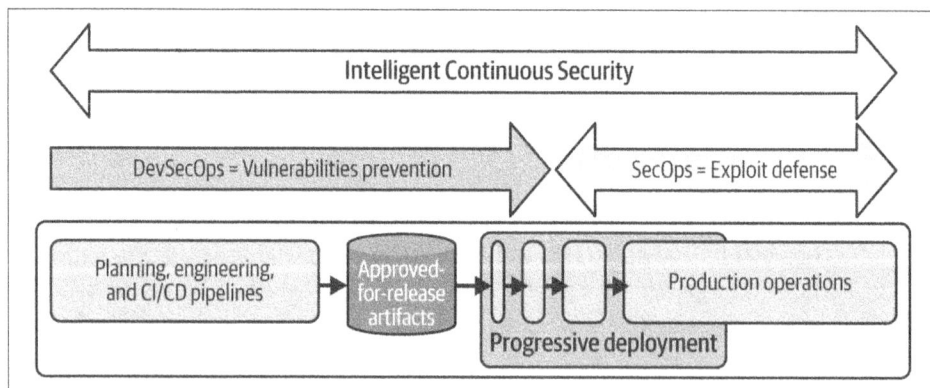

Figure 1-1. Intelligent Continuous Security

What makes Intelligent Continuous Security powerful is its ability to provide real-time threat detection, automated security testing, and seamless integration of security measures across both development and operations. This ensures that as we progress from development to production, security remains a constant, proactive element.

History of DevSecOps and SecOps

DevSecOps and SecOps emerged and evolved as critical practices in the world of modern software development and IT operations. While both practices have helped mitigate risks in their respective domains, they often operate in silos, leading to a fragmented security posture. The challenges posed by misaligned goals, incompatible tools, and insufficient communication between teams have created gaps that leave organizations vulnerable to attacks.

Timeline of SecOps evolution (2000–2025)

SecOps focuses on operational security once applications are deployed. It prioritizes monitoring, incident detection, and response within live production environments. SecOps teams are responsible for maintaining system integrity and protecting data while ensuring compliance with industry or any other regulations.

Here are some of the key milestones indicating how SecOps has evolved over the past 25 years:

- 2000: Rise of Security Operations Centers (SOCs)
  - The concept of centralized SOCs emerged, focusing on real-time monitoring and incident response.
  - "SOCs became vital for real-time monitoring, focusing on the identification and resolution of security incidents as they arise."
    —RSA Conference, 2000
- 2003: Introduction of security information and event management (SIEM)
  - SIEM tools became a core component of SecOps, allowing for the centralized collection, analysis, and response to security events across networks and systems.
  - "The adoption of SIEM transformed security operations by allowing for centralized event logging, correlation, and real-time analysis."
    —Spafford, 2003
- 2005: Emergence of incident response teams
  - The formalization of incident response teams became essential for handling security breaches, focusing on rapid detection and remediation.

- "Incident response teams became the backbone of security operations, focusing on identifying and neutralizing breaches as quickly as possible."
—Baker, 2005

- 2010: Proliferation of advanced persistent threats (APTs)

  - SecOps teams shifted to more proactive threat-hunting strategies as APTs became a significant challenge, requiring enhanced defense capabilities.

  - "The rise of APTs forced organizations to move from reactive security to proactive threat hunting and defense."
—Mandiant, 2010

- 2012: Integration of automation in SecOps

  - Automation tools were introduced to reduce the burden of manual threat detection, improving the speed and efficiency of SecOps.

  - "Automation has become a key component of security operations, enabling faster responses to security threats and reducing human error."
—Accenture, 2012

- 2015: Rise of cloud and multicloud environments

  - SecOps had to adapt to cloud services and distributed systems, leading to new approaches for monitoring, incident detection, and compliance in hybrid environments.

  - "SecOps had to evolve as cloud environments introduced new complexities and risks that required continuous monitoring and compliance."
—AWS Security Best Practices, 2015

- 2017: Use of AI in threat detection

  - AI and machine learning (ML) began to be used to automate anomaly detection, improving the ability of SecOps teams to handle sophisticated cyber threats.

  - "AI has enhanced security operations by automating anomaly detection, significantly improving the speed of identifying potential threats."
—Darktrace, 2017

- 2019: VUCA (Volatility, Uncertainty, Complexity, and Ambiguity)

  - VUCA was introduced to SecOps to help teams manage the unpredictable and rapidly changing threat landscape, characterized by sophisticated attack methods and complex IT environments.

  - "Security teams must now operate in a VUCA world—where volatility, uncertainty, complexity, and ambiguity define the evolving threat landscape."
—Gartner Security & Risk Management Summit, 2019

- 2019: Introduction of Security Orchestration, Automation, and Response (SOAR)

  — SOAR platforms enabled SecOps teams to automate and orchestrate responses to security incidents, integrating multiple tools and workflows for more effective defense.

  — "SOAR solutions bring automation and orchestration to security operations, allowing for faster and more coordinated responses to cyberattacks."
  —Splunk, 2019

- 2021: Zero Trust security model gains traction

  — The Zero Trust model reshaped how SecOps managed access and identity, focusing on continuous verification instead of perimeter-based security.

  — "Zero Trust has redefined SecOps, emphasizing continuous authentication and monitoring instead of traditional perimeter-based security models."
  —Google Cloud security white paper, 2021

- 2023: AI-driven incident response and threat hunting

  — AI-driven tools became essential for real-time incident response and predictive threat modeling, allowing SecOps to be more proactive and efficient in threat mitigation.

  — "AI-driven tools for threat hunting and incident response have become crucial for SecOps teams combating sophisticated, fast-evolving cyber threats."
  —Hornbeek, 2023

- 2024: SecOps and DevSecOps integration under Intelligent Continuous Security

  — SecOps and DevSecOps practices unified under Intelligent Continuous Security, providing real-time security integration across both development and operational environments.

  — "Intelligent Continuous Security has unified SecOps and DevSecOps, ensuring consistent, real-time security across the entire software lifecycle."
  —Hornbeek, 2024

Timeline of DevSecOps evolution (2008–2025)

DevSecOps, which integrates security into the DevOps pipeline, aims to shift left by embedding security into development and delivery processes. This approach ensures that security is treated as a foundational element rather than an afterthought. It arose from the need to address the rapid pace of software delivery and the increasing complexity of modern IT environments. By automating security checks and integrating them into CI/CD pipelines, DevSecOps enables teams to catch vulnerabilities early, reducing the risk of security breaches in production.

The following timeline enumerates some of the key milestones, indicating how DevSecOps has evolved since the birth of DevOps in 2008:

- 2008: The emergence of DevOps

  — The term *DevOps* was coined at the first DevOpsDays conference in Belgium, emphasizing collaboration between development and operations for faster, more reliable software delivery. Security was not a primary focus at this stage.

  — "The term DevOps emerged in 2008 to describe a culture of collaboration between software developers and IT operations professionals."
  —Fowler, 2008

- 2012: Early integration of security into DevOps

  — Organizations began realizing the need to integrate security into the DevOps pipeline, coining the term *DevSecOps*. The goal was to shift security left, embedding it early in the software development lifecycle.

  — "Security must be baked into DevOps from the beginning and not bolted on later."
  —Rogers, 2012

- 2014: Rise of Continuous Integration (CI) and Continuous Delivery (CD)

  — DevSecOps gained traction as CI/CD pipelines became mainstream, requiring security automation and early detection of vulnerabilities within fast-moving development cycles.

  — "With continuous delivery, security must shift left and be integrated into every step of the pipeline."
  —Humble and Farley, 2014

- 2016: Official definition of DevSecOps

  — By 2016, DevSecOps had become more formalized, with widely accepted frameworks focusing on embedding security into all stages of the DevOps lifecycle.

  — "DevSecOps extends the principles of DevOps to include security, ensuring that it is not an afterthought but part of the entire lifecycle."
  —Gaudreau, 2016

- 2017: Adoption of security automation tools

  — The integration of automated vulnerability scanning, static code analysis, and compliance checks into CI/CD pipelines accelerated the adoption of DevSecOps practices.

  — "Security automation is the key to integrating continuous security checks within CI/CD workflows."
  —Sharma, 2017

- 2019: Widespread adoption of DevSecOps practices

  — DevSecOps reached a tipping point of adoption across industries such as finance, healthcare, and technology, where security and compliance are critical.

  — "DevSecOps is no longer optional; it's a critical practice for organizations with stringent security and compliance needs."
  —Gartner, 2019

- 2020: Emergence of AI in DevSecOps

  — AI-driven tools began enhancing DevSecOps practices by automating threat detection and vulnerability management and improving incident response times.

  — "AI is transforming DevSecOps by enabling the real-time detection of threats and automating complex security tasks."
  —NIST AI-DevOps Report, 2020

- 2022: DevSecOps becomes a strategic imperative

  — DevSecOps was recognized as a strategic requirement for modern businesses aiming for faster software delivery while maintaining high security standards.

  — "The need for integrated security in DevOps pipelines has made DevSecOps a core business requirement for many organizations."
  —Forrester, 2022

- 2024: Intelligent Continuous Security emerges

  — AI-driven Continuous Security practices unified DevSecOps and SecOps under a broader Intelligent Continuous Security model, making automated security a business-critical function.

  — "Intelligent Continuous Security has become essential for businesses combating advanced cyber threats in a dynamic environment."
  —Hornbeek, 2024

This historical divide between DevSecOps and SecOps highlights the need for a more integrated, continuous approach to security that spans development and operations. The rise of AI in security offers the potential to bridge this gap, creating a seamless, end-to-end security framework.

Figure 1-2 illustrates the history of key milestones for SecOps and DevSecOps. Both SecOps and DevSecOps have evolved over the years in terms of practice, scope, automation, and use of AI technology.

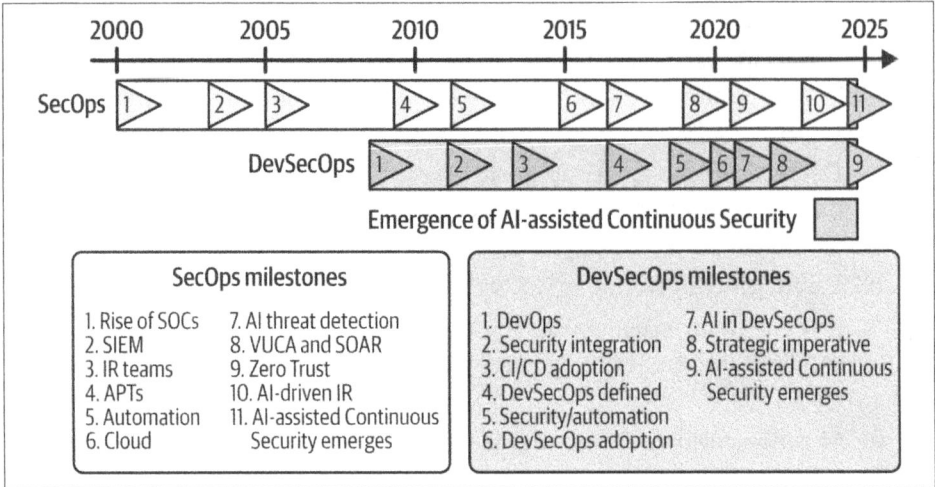

Figure 1-2. History of SecOps and DevSecOps

The emergence of Intelligent Continuous Security is a logical evolution that leverages the integration of siloed SecOps and DevSecOps practices and tools. AI assistance simplifies the transformation to a more integrated security solution.

Definition of Intelligent Continuous Security

Continuous Security is an approach to ensuring that security practices are integrated, automated, and maintained throughout every stage of the software lifecycle. Rather than treating security as a one-time or periodic activity, Continuous Security embeds security controls into both the development (DevSecOps) and operational (SecOps) processes. This ensures that vulnerabilities are detected early, compliance is maintained, and threats are continuously monitored and mitigated in real time.

With Continuous Security, security measures are applied in an ongoing manner, from the initial stages of code development through testing, deployment, and into production. It incorporates automated security testing, real-time threat detection, and continuous monitoring, ensuring that systems remain secure as they evolve. The goal is to shift from reactive, after-the-fact security measures to a proactive model that continuously defends against threats.

AI plays a critical role in Continuous Security by enabling the automation of complex tasks such as vulnerability management, compliance checks, and incident response. By leveraging AI-powered tools, organizations can enhance the speed and accuracy of security operations, reduce manual intervention, and improve their overall security posture. This approach ensures that security remains a constant and adaptive element of the development and operations cycle, reducing risks and improving resilience against evolving cyber threats.

Figure 1-3 compares the traditional approaches of DevSecOps and SecOps with Intelligent Continuous Security. In DevSecOps, the focus is on shifting security left, integrating security measures into the development and CI/CD pipelines, and ensuring that vulnerabilities are caught early. SecOps, on the other hand, is concerned with in-production security, focusing on monitoring and protecting live systems from exploitation. Intelligent Continuous Security goes a step further by applying end-to-end security practices, continuously securing every phase, from development through to production, by leveraging AI and ML.

Aspect	DevSecOps	SecOps	Intelligent Continuous Security
Focus	Security integrated into DevOps	In-production security operations	End-to-end Continuous Security
Primary objective	Shift security left in development	Monitor and protect live systems	Secure every phase, continuously
Key practices	Automated security in pipelines	Incident detection and response	Integration of lifecycle security practices leveraging AI and ML

Figure 1-3. Intelligent Continuous Security comparison

Intelligent Continuous Security

Here is the definition of Intelligent Continuous Security as I use it in this book:

Intelligent Continuous Security applies AI-augmented security practices continuously across the entire software development lifecycle and operational environment. It leverages AI to ensure real-time threat detection, automated security testing, and seamless integration of security across development and operations.

Importance of Intelligent Continuous Security in the Modern Threat Landscape

The digital threat landscape is rapidly evolving, driven by advancements in both technology and the methods employed by cybercriminals. As organizations increasingly adopt cloud services, microservices architectures, and CD models, their attack surfaces have grown significantly. Simultaneously, the emergence of AI-driven threats such as autonomous malware, deepfake-based fraud, AI-enhanced phishing attacks, and others detailed in this chapter has intensified the challenge for cybersecurity teams. These developments highlight the limitations of traditional security models, which often struggle to keep up with the speed and sophistication of modern threats.

In this context, Intelligent Continuous Security becomes critical. As discussed in Chapter 5, AI can process vast amounts of data in real time, detecting subtle anomalies that would be difficult for human analysts to identify. It can also automate repetitive tasks, such as vulnerability scanning and compliance checks, ensuring that security processes are both efficient and scalable.

This section explains the importance of adopting a Continuous Security model in response to the growing cyber threats faced by modern enterprises. It also covers the specific risks associated with DevSecOps, SecOps, and Continuous Security, illustrating why traditional approaches are no longer sufficient in addressing the current and future threat landscape.

DevSecOps Risk Landscape

DevSecOps introduces significant advantages by integrating security earlier in the development lifecycle, yet it also faces unique challenges. As development teams prioritize speed and efficiency, they are pressured to deploy code quickly, sometimes at the expense of thorough security testing. This creates the risk of vulnerabilities slipping through undetected, especially in fast-moving CI/CD pipelines. Additionally, developers may lack the necessary security expertise, leading to gaps in secure coding practices.

Another risk associated with DevSecOps is the reliance on automated tools that may not always catch the latest or most sophisticated threats. While automated testing can improve efficiency, it can also lead to overreliance on static scans that fail to detect dynamic vulnerabilities. Furthermore, the rapid pace of DevOps often leads to a focus on functionality and feature delivery, leaving security measures as a lower priority. This can result in code being deployed without adequate security assessments, increasing the likelihood of security incidents once in production.

To mitigate these risks, Intelligent Continuous Security enhances DevSecOps by integrating real-time, AI-driven threat detection and vulnerability management into the development pipeline. As explained in Chapter 5, AI can provide developers with automated insights, flagging security concerns early in the development process and offering proactive solutions to address them before the code reaches production.

As I stated before and have illustrated in Figure 1-4, there are stark differences between DevSecOps and SecOps and the challenges they face due to their cultural and operational silos. DevSecOps prioritizes rapid software delivery, focusing on CI/CD automation, while SecOps emphasizes stability, risk, and compliance, with a focus on monitoring, detection, and incident response in production environments. The lack of a cohesive security strategy between these teams is often caused by misaligned goals, fragmented tools, and key performance indicators (KPIs) that don't overlap. This disconnect is further exacerbated by legacy structures, insufficient training, and the slow adoption of integrated security tools. For organizations to truly secure their environments, we need to bring these teams together, aligning their tools, data, and communication strategies under one cohesive security framework.

Figure 1-4. DevSecOps and SecOps security landscapes

SecOps Risk Landscape

SecOps, which focuses on maintaining security in production environments, faces its own set of risks. In the operational phase, the primary challenge is monitoring for and responding to real-time threats. SecOps teams are often overwhelmed by the sheer volume of data and alerts generated by modern infrastructures, leading to alert fatigue and the risk of missing critical security incidents. Moreover, traditional SecOps practices are often reactive, focusing on responding to incidents after they occur rather than proactively preventing them.

A major risk in SecOps is the slow response time to emerging threats. Security teams may not have the tools or resources to detect *zero-day vulnerabilities* (software flaws or security gaps that are unknown to the vendor or developer and have not yet been patched) or APTs quickly enough to mitigate damage. Additionally, the growing complexity of IT environments, including multicloud and hybrid setups, introduces further risks due to fragmented security controls and inconsistent policies across environments.

Intelligent Continuous Security enhances SecOps by providing continuous monitoring, AI-driven incident detection, and automated responses. This enhancement is enabled by AI's use of advanced algorithms to analyze large volumes of real-time data, identifying anomalies and threats faster than manual methods, while automating responses to reduce reaction time and human error, enabling SecOps teams to maintain robust, proactive security. AI can help reduce alert fatigue by filtering out false positives and identifying genuine threats more quickly, allowing SecOps teams to focus on critical issues. Furthermore, AI enhances the ability of SecOps to respond to threats proactively, automating the identification and patching of vulnerabilities before they can be exploited in production environments.

Continuous Security Risk Landscape

Continuous Security combines the efforts of both DevSecOps and SecOps to ensure that security measures are maintained consistently across the entire software lifecycle. However, like any model, it has its risks. One of the primary challenges is the complexity of integrating security into every phase of development and operations, especially for organizations that are not already following DevSecOps or SecOps best practices. The transition to a Continuous Security model requires significant cultural, process, and tool set changes which can be met with resistance or resource constraints.

Another risk is the potential for security automation to create blind spots. While automation is a core component of Continuous Security, overreliance on automated tools without proper oversight can lead to vulnerabilities being missed, particularly if the tools are not updated to handle the latest threats. Additionally, security teams may become complacent, assuming that automated processes will handle all potential risks, which can lead to gaps in manual oversight and incident response readiness.

Intelligent Continuous Security addresses these risks by creating a more dynamic and proactive security environment. AI enhances the accuracy and efficiency of security automation, ensuring that vulnerabilities are detected and addressed in real time across all stages of the software lifecycle. This continuous adaptation and improvement makes Intelligent Continuous Security more resilient to evolving threats, providing organizations with a comprehensive, end-to-end security solution.

As illustrated in Figure 1-5, many companies today are facing a new wave of cyberattacks where AI is playing a central role. Criminals are using AI-driven phishing attacks that dynamically adapt and improve, making them harder to detect. Polymorphic malware, such as DeepLocker, uses AI to change its behavior and evade traditional security measures. We are also seeing the rise of AI-generated fake media, such as deepfakes, which are being used for fraud and extortion.

Additionally, ransomware attacks are becoming more sophisticated, with AI helping to evade detection by continuously altering attack patterns. Criminals are also leveraging botnets with AI for command-and-control operations, making these attacks more coordinated and harder to shut down. Organizations need Intelligent Continuous Security to match these advanced AI-based threats and ensure that they are well protected. Chapter 8 explains in detail how this is done for these and other use cases.

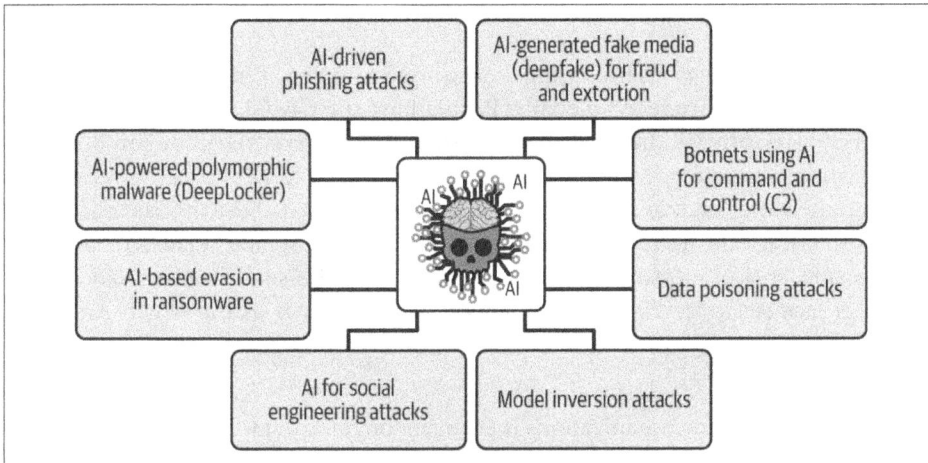

Figure 1-5. Cybercriminals are increasingly using AI

Regulatory and Compliance Landscape

Today, regulatory and compliance requirements are becoming increasingly stringent, especially for industries dealing with sensitive data, such as finance, healthcare, and government sectors. Organizations are under immense pressure to meet security standards and avoid severe penalties for noncompliance. The rise of data protection laws, such as the General Data Protection Regulation (GDPR) in the European Union, and the California Consumer Privacy Act (CCPA) and Health Insurance Portability and Accountability Act (HIPAA) in the United States, have elevated the importance of maintaining robust security frameworks throughout the software lifecycle.

The challenge, however, is that traditional DevSecOps and SecOps practices often treat compliance as an afterthought, typically managed in silos and addressed during specific stages of development or production. This fragmented approach can result in compliance gaps, leading to financial penalties, legal challenges, and reputational damage. As the threat landscape evolves, organizations need a continuous, proactive strategy that embeds compliance within every phase of their operations. Intelligent Continuous Security provides this capability by automating compliance checks and real-time monitoring, ensuring that regulatory requirements are met consistently and efficiently across development and production environments.

This section explores the significance of regulatory and compliance considerations in modern security practices. It also examines the specific regulatory requirements that impact DevSecOps and SecOps, and how Intelligent Continuous Security addresses these needs through automated compliance monitoring and real-time audit readiness.

Regulatory Landscape

The regulatory landscape is becoming increasingly complex as new cybersecurity laws and standards are introduced globally. Regulations such as GDPR and CCPA mandate strict data privacy and security controls, with severe penalties for breaches. Organizations operating in financial services are subject to additional requirements under frameworks such as the Payment Card Industry Data Security Standard (PCI DSS), while those in healthcare must comply with HIPAA and related regulations. Additionally, critical infrastructure operators in industries such as energy and transportation face strict security requirements under such laws as the North American Electric Reliability Corporation's Critical Infrastructure Protection (NERC CIP) standards.

The challenge for many organizations is ensuring ongoing compliance with these varied and evolving regulations. Traditional approaches to regulatory compliance are often reactive, relying on periodic audits and manual reviews, which can lead to lapses in security controls and delayed responses to compliance violations. With the increased complexity of modern IT environments—ranging from multicloud setups to microservices architectures—managing compliance manually is both time-consuming and prone to error.

Intelligent Continuous Security can help with regulations such as GDPR and CCPA by automating compliance checks throughout the software lifecycle. AI-powered tools can continuously monitor systems to ensure that they meet the necessary regulatory requirements, flagging any deviations in real time. This allows organizations to maintain compliance without interrupting their development or operational workflows, significantly reducing the risk of regulatory breaches and associated penalties.

Compliance Landscape

The compliance landscape is closely tied to the regulatory frameworks that govern how organizations handle sensitive data, manage security risks, and protect consumer privacy. Meeting compliance requirements often involves adhering to a complex set of industry standards, such as ISO/IEC 27001 for information security management, System and Organization Controls 2 (SOC 2) for service organizations, and NIST's Cybersecurity Framework for critical infrastructure protection. These standards require organizations to implement rigorous security controls, audit processes, and incident response protocols, which can be difficult to manage using traditional, manual methods.

One of the key challenges in maintaining compliance is the need for real-time audit readiness. Many organizations struggle with providing continuous proof of compliance, especially when faced with unexpected audits or investigations. Without an automated system in place, security teams may find themselves scrambling to gather documentation and evidence of compliance, increasing the risk of fines or penalties for noncompliance.

Intelligent Continuous Security offers a proactive solution to these challenges by automating compliance monitoring and auditing processes. AI can ensure that security controls are consistently enforced across all systems, automatically generating audit trails and compliance reports. AI-assisted automation eliminates the need for manual intervention and ensures that organizations are always audit ready, helping to reduce both the cost and risk associated with compliance management.

Real-Time Compliance and Security Audits

In addition to ensuring regulatory compliance, Intelligent Continuous Security enhances an organization's ability to conduct real-time security audits. Traditional security audits are often conducted periodically and retrospectively, making it difficult to address issues in real time. This reactive approach leaves organizations vulnerable to security gaps that may remain unaddressed until the next audit cycle.

Summary

This chapter provided the foundation for understanding how AI revolutionizes traditional security practices, addressing the limitations of DevSecOps and SecOps. The chapter emphasized the importance of Intelligent Continuous Security, which bridges the gap between development and operations by automating security measures across the entire software lifecycle. This model enhances vulnerability detection, automates compliance checks, and strengthens incident response through AI-driven insights. Key takeaways highlight the need for a proactive, unified security framework capable of adapting to the evolving cyber threat landscape.

The chapter also provided a definition and overview of Intelligent Continuous Security, discussing its ability to streamline security tasks and reduce operational silos. This approach allows organizations to respond to cyber threats more quickly and efficiently. A historical context of DevSecOps and SecOps illustrates how both domains have evolved to address specific security challenges but remain siloed. The chapter outlined how AI resolves these silos by offering a continuous, real-time security solution that spans development and operations, ensuring consistent protection throughout the value stream.

Next, the chapter explored the importance of Continuous Security in modern IT environments, particularly in light of emerging AI-driven threats. With cyberattacks becoming more complex and pervasive, organizations must move beyond reactive security models. Intelligent Continuous Security equips organizations with the tools to stay ahead of these threats by automating routine security tasks and providing real-time threat detection and mitigation. The chapter also discussed the specific risk landscapes of DevSecOps, SecOps, and Continuous Security, illustrating how AI addresses their unique challenges.

Finally, the chapter examined the regulatory and compliance landscape, highlighting the growing complexity of cybersecurity laws and standards. Organizations are under increasing pressure to meet compliance requirements such as GDPR and HIPAA, which often necessitate rigorous, ongoing audits. Intelligent Continuous Security simplifies this process by automating compliance monitoring, ensuring real-time audit readiness, and reducing the risk of noncompliance penalties. This proactive model allows security teams to focus on more strategic tasks while ensuring continuous adherence to regulatory requirements.

Later chapters will explain in depth how Intelligent Continuous Security is a revolution beyond current siloed DevSecOps and SecOps practices. But first, Chapter 2 will explain how Intelligent Continuous Security unifies SecOps and DevSecOps into a more cohesive, end-to-end security framework.

From DevSecOps and SecOps to Intelligent Continuous Security

This chapter examines how integrating DevSecOps and SecOps into a unified approach addresses the gaps left by traditional security practices. Siloed methods often create vulnerabilities in both development and operational environments. By uniting these practices through Intelligent Continuous Security, organizations eliminate fragmentation and improve the speed and accuracy of threat detection and response. AI-driven automation enhances scalability and ensures that security remains seamless across the entire software lifecycle.

AI-driven security tools play a critical role in optimizing vulnerability detection, compliance checks, and real-time incident response. Integrating security across both development and operations creates a continuous, adaptive security framework. This approach strengthens an organization's ability to proactively defend against modern cyber threats and adapt to the rapidly evolving threat landscape.

Limitations of Separate DevSecOps and SecOps Practices

To understand the need for an integrated security approach, it's essential to first examine the inherent limitations within DevSecOps and SecOps when they are applied independently. DevSecOps, which emphasizes embedding security early within the development cycle, can struggle with complex security requirements in fast-moving Continuous Integration/Continuous Delivery (CI/CD) pipelines. Challenges such as insufficient developer training in security practices and overreliance on automation leave vulnerabilities that may go undetected. Additionally, the primary focus of DevSecOps is on pre-deployment security, which limits its effectiveness in managing real-time threats in production environments.

Similarly, SecOps, which is dedicated to maintaining security in live production environments, faces its own set of challenges. With a focus on monitoring and incident response post-deployment, SecOps often lacks visibility into vulnerabilities that originate from development. This disjointed approach can lead to delays in identifying security issues that originated earlier in the lifecycle. Furthermore, SecOps teams frequently face alert fatigue and struggle to keep up with real-time threat intelligence, often reacting to incidents after they have already caused damage. The next two sections explain these limitations in depth, providing context for understanding why separate security frameworks may leave significant security gaps.

Limitations of the DevSecOps Approach to Software Security

DevSecOps primarily focuses on integrating security throughout the development process rather than managing security in live production environments. The practices aim to ensure that security is embedded at every phase of development, from requirements gathering through testing and deployment.

The term *DevSecOps* can be misleading because it implies that *security (Sec)* is fully integrated into both *development (Dev)* and *operations (Ops)* processes. However, in practice, DevSecOps primarily focuses on embedding security into the development phase, from initial requirements through deployment preparation, without directly managing security in production environments. By focusing mainly on pre-deployment security, DevSecOps aims to ensure that secure code and configurations are delivered to production, but it leaves much of the operational security—such as continuous monitoring, real-time threat detection, and incident response—to SecOps or other operational security teams. Thus, a more accurate term for this practice would be *DevSec*, emphasizing that it secures the development pipeline up until deployment, rather than covering the full span of operational security. Figure 2-1 identifies the DevSec(Ops) pillars of practice.

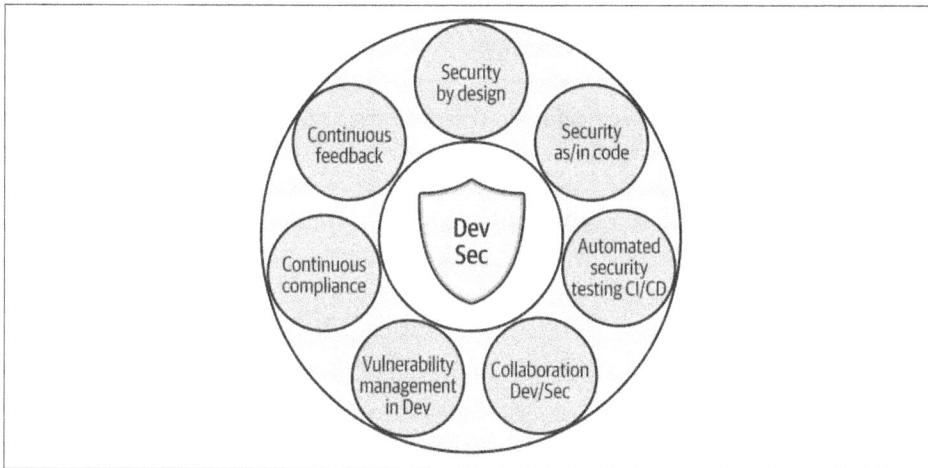

Figure 2-1. DevSec(Ops) practices

Here's a bit of background information about each of the DevSec pillars of practice:

Security by design

Often described as "shifting left," security by design elevates security to a first-class consideration from the earliest stages of the software development lifecycle (SDLC). Instead of treating security as an afterthought or a bolt-on feature, this approach integrates security requirements into the design and planning phases. By embedding security directly into the architecture, organizations can address potential vulnerabilities before they become deeply entrenched in the system. This proactive strategy not only minimizes the risk of security flaws later in the lifecycle but also reduces the cost and complexity of fixing issues discovered during testing or post-deployment.

For instance, during the requirements gathering phase, teams might conduct comprehensive threat modeling exercises to identify and mitigate potential risks. This early focus ensures that security considerations are aligned with the application's goals and functionality, setting a solid foundation for resilient development practices. By treating security as a fundamental design principle, the entire development process becomes more robust, efficient, and secure.

Security as Code (SaC)

Codifies security practices and policies into the same version-controlled systems that govern application development. Access controls, network policies, and security configurations are defined as part of the codebase, making them consistent, repeatable, and scalable across environments. Consider a DevSecOps team using Infrastructure as Code (IaC) tools such as Terraform or AWS CloudFormation to define firewall rules and access controls. With these tools, security policies can be automatically applied during deployment, ensuring that environments are secure by default. By treating security as an integral part of the infrastructure, teams eliminate the inconsistencies and manual errors that often plague traditional security practices.

Security in code review

Security in code review processes offer a critical opportunity to incorporate security into the development lifecycle. By embedding security considerations into peer reviews, teams add an additional layer of scrutiny to identify vulnerabilities that automated tools might miss. For instance, during a routine review, a developer might notice that a newly written API endpoint lacks proper input validation. By flagging this issue early, the team prevents a potential attack vector from reaching production. These peer reviews not only catch vulnerabilities but also reinforce a culture of security-minded development.

Automated security testing

Integrates seamlessly into the CI/CD pipeline, ensuring that every piece of code is scrutinized for vulnerabilities as part of the development workflow. Rather than treating security testing as a separate or post-development activity, this approach embeds it into the heart of the software lifecycle. With each new code commit or build, static and dynamic security tests automatically run, identifying issues before they have a chance to progress further. Consider a team leveraging static application security testing (SAST) and dynamic application security testing (DAST) tools during their CI/CD processes. These tools proactively scan code for potential vulnerabilities during both the build and pre-deployment phases, catching problems early when they are faster and cheaper to fix. By incorporating automated security testing, development teams can confidently maintain the rapid pace of modern software delivery without causing delays.

Collaboration between development and security teams

Lies at the heart of modern security practices. In this approach, security becomes a shared responsibility rather than a siloed afterthought. By working together, developers and security professionals can embed security considerations into every stage of the software lifecycle. Imagine a DevSecOps team conducting hands-on security training and workshops for developers, teaching them secure coding practices and empowering them to identify and mitigate risks on their own. This cultural shift not only increases security awareness but also reduces the bottlenecks traditionally associated with security teams handling issues in isolation. The result is a development environment where security is a collaborative, continuous effort.

Vulnerability management

Ensures that potential weaknesses in code, dependencies, or third-party libraries are identified and addressed as part of the development process. This proactive approach minimizes the risk of vulnerabilities reaching production, where remediation is more challenging and costly. For example, tools such as Dependabot or Cycode integrate directly into development workflows, continuously scanning codebases for known vulnerabilities in dependencies. When an issue is identified, these tools alert developers with actionable recommendations to resolve it. By making vulnerability management an integral part of development, organizations strengthen their applications against a wide array of threats long before deployment.

Continuous compliance

Distinct from traditional workflows in which compliance has often been treated as a separate, manual task completed late in the development process—or even in post-deployment. Continuous compliance turns this paradigm on its head, automating compliance checks and integrating them directly into the CI/CD pipeline. For instance, a healthcare organization subject to Health Insurance Portability and Accountability Act (HIPAA) regulations might use automated tools to validate that its code adheres to security and privacy standards. By embedding these checks into the development process, teams ensure that compliance is no longer an afterthought but a continuous activity, significantly reducing the risk of regulatory violations while maintaining the pace of innovation.

Continuous feedback and improvement

The cornerstone of adaptive and resilient security practices. By establishing feedback loops between development and security teams, organizations create an ongoing process of learning and improvement. This approach ensures that security practices don't remain static but instead evolve alongside new threats, vulnerabilities, and lessons learned from real-world experiences. Take, for example, a post-incident retrospective following a security breach. A retail company detects a vulnerability in its web application that allows unauthorized access to sensitive customer data. After containing the incident, the team conducts a detailed post-mortem review to understand what went wrong. They uncover that the vulnerability stemmed from a misconfigured API introduced during a rushed deployment. Armed with this knowledge, they implement stricter security checks in their CI/CD pipeline and provide targeted training for developers on secure API design. The insights gained not only address the immediate issue but also inform broader improvements in their security practices.

Beyond incident response, continuous feedback extends to routine development processes. Security teams might review the results of automated testing or code reviews to identify recurring vulnerabilities or areas where developers need more support. For instance, if a pattern of insufficient input validation emerges across multiple projects, the organization might prioritize integrating validation frameworks into its coding standards or offer workshops on secure coding techniques. This iterative approach ensures that feedback is actionable and directly impacts future development cycles.

Retrospectives also play a key role in fostering collaboration and transparency between teams. By openly discussing what worked, what didn't work, and what can be improved, organizations create a culture of accountability and shared ownership of security outcomes. These retrospectives aren't about assigning blame. They're about uncovering systemic issues and finding opportunities to strengthen the organization's overall security posture.

Ultimately, continuous feedback and improvement transforms security from a reactive function to a proactive, evolving discipline. By integrating lessons learned at every stage—from automated testing to incident response—organizations ensure that their security practices remain agile and effective in an ever-changing landscape. This continuous refinement not only enhances resilience but also builds trust among teams and stakeholders, making security an integral part of the organization's DNA.

DevSecOps emphasizes the integration of security throughout the development process, from initial design to deployment, by automating security testing, enforcing compliance, and fostering collaboration between development and security teams. It does not directly address production security, but rather ensures that code deployed to production is secure, reducing the risk of vulnerabilities making it into live environments.

Thinking deeply about the DevSec pillars of practice, you can understand where the deficiencies for security occur:

Overemphasis on automation and tooling
> While DevSecOps emphasizes automation in security testing (e.g., static code analysis, vulnerability scanning), there is often an overreliance on these tools. Automated tools may not catch complex or evolving threats such as logic flaws or vulnerabilities in third-party dependencies. For example, in 2021, the SolarWinds hack exposed a major vulnerability in software supply chains. Attackers inserted malicious code into updates, bypassing automated security checks. The attack went unnoticed for months, highlighting the limitations of automated tools in detecting sophisticated threats hidden in trusted components.

Security as a secondary priority

The pace of development often takes precedence over comprehensive security measures. The desire to meet tight deadlines and deliver rapidly can lead to security testing being deprioritized, creating an environment where vulnerabilities are introduced and left unchecked. This prioritization gap was painfully evident in the case of Log4Shell (CVE-2021-44228), a critical vulnerability in the Log4j logging library that emerged in 2022. Despite the widespread adoption of CI/CD pipelines, many organizations failed to identify and patch this vulnerability promptly. The urgency of rapid deployment overshadowed thorough assessments of third-party libraries, leaving thousands of systems exposed to significant risk. This example highlights the need to treat security as a core element of development, not as an afterthought.

Lack of deep security expertise

This emphasizes the shared responsibility of security, expecting developers to incorporate security practices into their workflows. However, this expectation often collides with a reality where many developers lack the necessary depth of knowledge in secure coding and infrastructure management. The Capital One breach of 2019 underscores this challenge. An attacker exploited a misconfigured firewall in a cloud environment, exposing the personal data of over 100 million users. While automated tools are valuable, they cannot fully compensate for the absence of robust security expertise. Integrating training programs and fostering close collaboration between security experts and developers is essential to bridge this knowledge gap and prevent such misconfigurations.

Challenges with continuous monitoring

While DevSecOps excels at embedding security during development and deployment, production environments often fall into a blind spot. Continuous monitoring in production is frequently neglected, leaving vulnerabilities unnoticed until they are exploited. The Equifax breach in 2017 is a stark reminder of this oversight. A failure to apply a patch for a known vulnerability allowed attackers to exploit the system for months, leading to the exposure of sensitive information for millions of individuals. Continuous monitoring tools, backed by AI-driven anomaly detection, are critical to maintaining vigilance and ensuring that post-deployment environments remain secure.

Misaligned goals between development and security teams

DevSecOps promises seamless integration of security into the development lifecycle, but cultural barriers often undermine this ideal. Development teams prioritize speed and innovation while security teams focus on risk mitigation—two goals that can feel inherently at odds. This disconnect contributed to the Uber breach of 2016, where poor collaboration allowed hackers to exploit vulnerabilities in internal systems, resulting in the theft of personal information for 57 million users. Breaking down these silos requires fostering a culture of collaboration where security is viewed as a shared objective and not a competing priority. Shared tools, clear communication channels, and joint accountability can help align these teams toward common goals.

Limited visibility into third-party components

Modern DevSecOps pipelines rely heavily on third-party libraries and APIs, but the lack of visibility into these dependencies creates significant risks. When vulnerabilities in external components go undetected, they can compromise entire systems. The Magecart attack of 2018 demonstrated this vividly, as attackers injected malicious code into third-party JavaScript libraries used on ecommerce sites. High-profile companies such as British Airways and Ticketmaster fell victim, exposing customer payment data. To mitigate these risks, organizations must adopt dependency scanning tools and enforce strict policies for evaluating and managing third-party components. Regular audits and automated alerts for vulnerabilities can significantly reduce the attack surface.

Difficulty scaling security in large organizations

As organizations grow, scaling DevSecOps practices across multiple teams and projects becomes increasingly challenging. Maintaining a consistent security posture while coordinating across diverse pipelines and environments is a daunting task, and vulnerabilities can slip through the cracks. The Microsoft Exchange Server vulnerability in 2021 revealed how complexity and scale can hinder timely patching, leaving organizations globally exposed. Addressing this challenge requires centralizing security policies, automating compliance checks, and investing in scalable tools that can adapt to organizational complexity. A federated model, where centralized guidance is combined with team-level autonomy, can strike the right balance for effective security at scale.

As you can see, DevSec(Ops) is an effective approach to integrating security into the SDLC, but it has notable limitations, especially in environments with complex architectures or where speed is prioritized over thorough security practices. High-profile exploits such as the attacks on SolarWinds, Log4Shell, and Equifax highlight the importance of continuously improving security practices, tools, and expertise within DevSec(Ops) frameworks.

Limitations of the SecOps Approach to Software Security

The key pillars of practice for SecOps revolve around ensuring comprehensive, real-time security for live production environments. These pillars, illustrated in Figure 2-2, are designed to safeguard infrastructure, data, and applications while responding proactively to cyber threats.

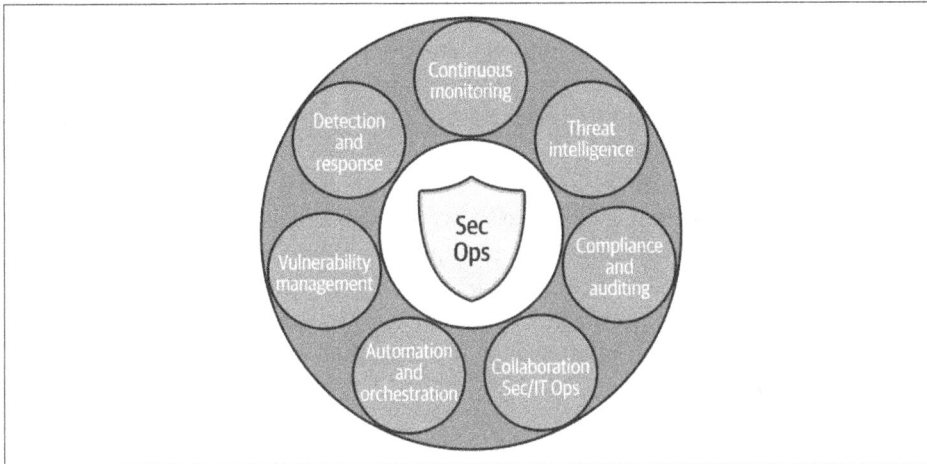

Figure 2-2. SecOps practices

Let's take a closer look at the most recognized pillars of SecOps practices:

Continuous monitoring
> Continuous monitoring serves as the vigilant eyes and ears of an organization's security infrastructure, tracking network traffic, user behavior, and system activities in real time. Unlike static checks, this approach ensures that anomalies and suspicious activity are identified as they occur, enabling rapid detection and intervention. Picture a security information and event management (SIEM) system in action, continuously collecting and analyzing data streams from thousands of endpoints. When unusual login patterns or sudden spikes in data transfer are detected, the system generates alerts for the security team, allowing them to address potential threats before they escalate. This ongoing visibility across the infrastructure is the cornerstone of effective threat prevention and mitigation.

Threat intelligence integration
> Staying ahead of attackers requires a deep understanding of the ever-evolving threat landscape. Threat intelligence integration enables organizations to incorporate both external and internal data feeds into their security operations, keeping defenses sharp and current. Imagine a SIEM system enriched with real-time threat intelligence that identifies malicious IP addresses, phishing domains, and emerging malware signatures. When a phishing campaign targets the organization, the system automatically blocks emails from known malicious sources and flags suspicious links for review. This proactive use of intelligence ensures that the SecOps team is always prepared to defend against the latest threats.

Compliance and auditing

For many organizations, meeting regulatory and industry compliance standards is not just a legal requirement; it's a cornerstone of trust with clients and partners. Compliance and auditing processes ensure adherence to frameworks such as the General Data Protection Regulation (GDPR), HIPAA, or Payment Card Industry Data Security Standard (PCI DSS), while also reinforcing robust security practices. Take a healthcare provider that uses automated tools to log access to patient records and flag any unauthorized attempts. These logs are not only essential for internal reviews but also serve as evidence during external audits, demonstrating the organization's commitment to safeguarding sensitive information. Automation reduces the burden of manual compliance checks and ensures that no detail is overlooked.

Collaboration between security and IT operations

This is essential for balancing security requirements with the need to maintain system performance and uptime. Misalignment between these teams can lead to inefficiencies or even security gaps. Consider a scenario where a major patch needs to be applied to address a critical vulnerability. Without coordination, IT operations might delay the patch to avoid disrupting business services, while the security team prioritizes immediate action. Regular communication, shared tools, and joint workflows bridge this gap. By aligning priorities and understanding each team's constraints, organizations can secure their infrastructure without sacrificing operational efficiency.

Security automation and orchestration

With the growing complexity of cybersecurity, manual workflows can no longer keep pace. Security automation and orchestration streamline repetitive tasks, such as alert management, incident response, and vulnerability remediation. Picture a scenario where an organization's threat intelligence feed identifies a malicious IP address. Instead of relying on human intervention, an automated system updates the firewall rules to block the IP in real time. Similarly, machine learning (ML) tools filter through false positives in alerts, enabling security teams to focus on genuine threats. This seamless integration of automation not only reduces workloads but also ensures consistent and timely responses across the security landscape.

Vulnerability management

This is the proactive effort to identify, classify, and address weaknesses in systems and applications before attackers can exploit them. It's a dynamic process, requiring vigilance as new vulnerabilities emerge daily. Consider an enterprise running weekly vulnerability scans on its infrastructure. When a high-severity flaw is discovered in a widely used application, the organization prioritizes patching the affected systems immediately. This approach, combined with regular updates and a comprehensive inventory of software and dependencies, keeps attackers at bay and ensures that known vulnerabilities don't become active threats.

Incident detection and response

The speed and effectiveness of an organization's response to security incidents often determine the extent of the damage. Incident detection and response revolves around identifying security breaches, assessing their impact, and taking prompt action to isolate and remediate the threat. Imagine a ransomware attack that begins encrypting files on a corporate network. Using a Security Orchestration, Automation, and Response (SOAR) platform, the security team can quickly execute a predefined playbook. This might include isolating the affected systems, halting data exfiltration, and initiating backup restoration processes. By automating these responses, organizations reduce downtime and limit the fallout of security incidents, ensuring business continuity.

These pillars enable organizations to adopt a *proactive*, *automated*, and *continuous* approach to security, ensuring that systems remain secure even as threats evolve.

If you would like to learn more about this topic, I recommend checking out BMC's SecOps Security & Compliance Guide (*https://oreil.ly/HE-OR*) and Fortinet's SecOps overview (*https://oreil.ly/vCoXi*).

Thinking deeply about the SecOps pillars of practice, you can understand where the deficiencies for security occur:

Reactive nature of SecOps

In many organizations, SecOps functions as a reactive force, responding to incidents only after they have occurred. This approach, while necessary for managing crises, often leaves systems vulnerable during critical windows when threats are emerging but not yet addressed. Consider the Colonial Pipeline ransomware attack in 2021. Faced with an unexpected and sophisticated ransomware intrusion, the organization was unprepared to mitigate the attack proactively. Instead, operations were shut down entirely, leading to significant disruption in the energy supply chain and highlighting the costly limitations of a purely reactive approach. This incident underscores the need for SecOps to adopt proactive measures, such as real-time threat detection and prevention, to stay ahead of attackers.

Overwhelming volume of alerts

The sheer volume of security alerts generated by modern IT environments can overwhelm SecOps teams, a phenomenon often referred to as *alert fatigue*. When analysts are inundated with alerts, many of which are false positives, it becomes nearly impossible to distinguish critical incidents from noise. A stark example of this occurred during the 2013 Target breach. Despite multiple alerts warning of suspicious activity, the signals were lost in the overwhelming noise of the company's alerting system. As a result, attackers were able to exploit the system and steal millions of credit card records. This demonstrates how excessive alerts without effective prioritization can undermine security efforts and emphasizes the importance of AI-driven tools to filter and prioritize alerts effectively.

Slow incident response times

Timely response to security incidents is critical, yet many SecOps teams struggle with delays caused by resource limitations, coordination challenges, or incidents occurring outside regular working hours. These delays provide attackers with more time to inflict damage. The Equifax breach in 2017 is a prime example. Despite the vulnerability being identified and a patch made available, the delay in applying the patch allowed attackers to exfiltrate the personal data of 147 million people over a period of months. Effective SecOps requires automation, well-defined response playbooks, and cross-team collaboration to reduce response times and mitigate damage swiftly.

Siloed security practices

SecOps often operates in isolation from other departments, leading to a fragmented approach to security. Without collaboration with development or operations teams, vulnerabilities can remain unaddressed during critical phases of the software lifecycle. The Uber data breach in 2016 highlights the consequences of siloed practices. Poor internal security coordination allowed hackers to exploit vulnerabilities and access sensitive data, illustrating how a lack of integration between teams can leave organizations exposed. Breaking down these silos through shared workflows and integrated security practices is essential for holistic protection.

Inability to keep up with modern threats

The rapidly evolving nature of advanced persistent threats (APTs) and other sophisticated attacks often outpaces traditional SecOps capabilities. Manual processes and outdated tools struggle to detect or mitigate complex, multistage attack vectors. The SolarWinds supply chain attack exemplifies this challenge. Despite having robust SecOps defenses, many organizations were unable to detect for months the sophisticated backdoor planted in the Orion software. This underscores the need for modernized SecOps practices that incorporate automation, AI-driven detection, and real-time threat intelligence to stay ahead of increasingly complex threats.

Challenges with multicloud and hybrid environments

As organizations adopt multicloud and hybrid infrastructures, maintaining consistent security practices becomes a significant challenge. Disparate environments often lead to fragmented monitoring and inconsistent policies, creating blind spots that attackers can exploit. The Capital One breach in 2019 exposed this vulnerability when a misconfigured firewall in the company's cloud environment allowed an attacker to access sensitive data. This incident demonstrates the critical importance of unified security strategies and automation tools that can enforce consistent policies across diverse platforms.

Inconsistent application of patches and updates

Timely patch management is a cornerstone of security, yet many SecOps teams face difficulties applying patches across distributed and complex environments. Delays in patching leave organizations vulnerable to exploits that are already well-known to attackers. The WannaCry ransomware attack in 2017 starkly illustrates this issue. The malware exploited a Microsoft vulnerability that had been patched months earlier, but organizations that failed to apply the update suffered widespread disruptions. Ensuring that patch management processes are automated and prioritized based on risk can prevent such incidents and reduce the window of exposure.

Overreliance on manual processes

In many SecOps teams, manual processes dominate incident detection, investigation, and response. These processes are labor-intensive, prone to human error, and ill-suited for large-scale or fast-moving attacks. The NotPetya malware attack in 2017 exposed the limitations of such approaches. As the malware spread rapidly, overwhelmed SecOps teams struggled to contain it in time, leading to significant damage. Automating routine tasks and incorporating ML for threat detection can free up SecOps analysts to focus on complex decision making and strategic responses, improving both efficiency and resilience.

As I hope I have shown, SecOps plays a critical role in maintaining security in production environments, but its limitations in reacting to threats, dealing with alert fatigue, and keeping pace with modern threats have exposed organizations to significant risks. High-profile incidents such as those experienced by Colonial Pipeline, Equifax, and SolarWinds illustrate the need for SecOps teams to adopt more proactive, automated, and integrated approaches to security.

The Need for an Integrated Continuous Security Approach

Both DevSecOps and SecOps have made significant strides in improving software security, yet each approach operates with inherent limitations that leave organizations vulnerable to modern, sophisticated threats. DevSecOps focuses on embedding security earlier in the development cycle, while SecOps handles security in live production environments. However, the siloed nature of these practices, their overreliance on automation, and their challenges in dealing with advanced threats, alert fatigue, and cloud complexities expose gaps in overall security management.

A new approach, which I call *Continuous Security*, illustrated in Figure 2-3, is needed to integrate and build on both DevSecOps and SecOps to provide seamless, end-to-end security across the software lifecycle.

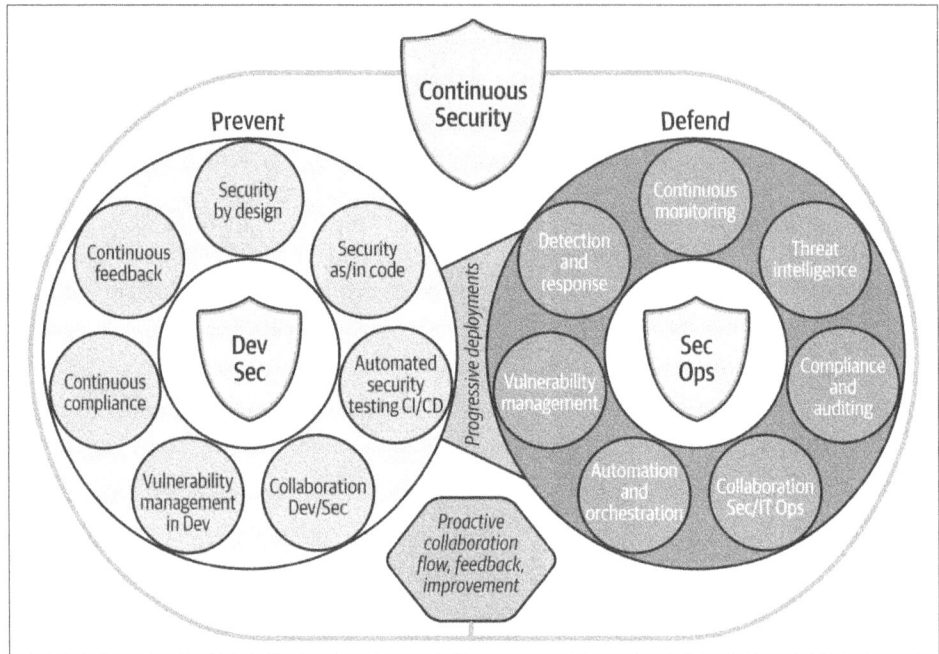

Figure 2-3. Continuous Security practices

Continuous Security: An Integrated Solution

Continuous Security seeks to unify the DevSecOps and SecOps models into a single, cohesive security framework that operates across both development and production environments. By addressing the limitations of each separate approach, Continuous Security offers several key benefits:

End-to-end security integration
Continuous Security ensures that security practices are embedded from code development through deployment and into ongoing operations. This avoids the gaps left by the handoff between development and operations, where vulnerabilities often arise due to a lack of communication and alignment.

Proactive threat detection
By combining the shift-left approach of DevSecOps with the real-time monitoring of SecOps, Continuous Security enables organizations to detect and mitigate threats early in the development process and continuously monitor for new

vulnerabilities in production. This reduces the chances of zero-day exploits or long-term, undetected threats.

Real-time, AI-driven automation

Continuous Security incorporates AI-driven security automation for both development and operations, allowing for the continuous adaptation to evolving threats. This overcomes the limitations of traditional static tools, offering dynamic threat detection, vulnerability management, and incident response.

Reduced alert fatigue and improved incident response

By unifying DevSecOps and SecOps, Continuous Security enables better contextual threat detection, reducing the false positives that lead to alert fatigue. AI can prioritize critical incidents, ensuring that security teams focus on real threats in both development and production environments.

Scalability and consistency across hybrid and multicloud environments

Continuous Security addresses the inconsistencies in policy enforcement and security monitoring that arise in hybrid and multicloud environments. With unified monitoring and automated compliance checks, Continuous Security ensures that vulnerabilities are detected and patched consistently, no matter where the system resides.

Mitigating Exploits with ML for Continuous Security

The evolution of cyber threats has demonstrated that neither DevSecOps automation tools nor traditional SecOps practices alone can address the complexity and speed of modern attacks. Sophisticated incidents such as the SolarWinds supply chain attack and the Colonial Pipeline ransomware breach reveal gaps in detection, response, and prevention strategies. These high-profile breaches highlight the urgent need for a more integrated, proactive, and intelligent security model. Continuous Security bridges this gap by combining DevSecOps principles with the real-time monitoring and operational awareness of SecOps. With AI-driven capabilities, Continuous Security ensures that vulnerabilities are detected, threats are neutralized, and systems remain resilient across the entire lifecycle.

By analyzing some of the cybersecurity incidents mentioned previously, we can explore how Continuous Security could have prevented or mitigated their impact. From supply chain attacks to widespread vulnerabilities, each of the following cases reveals critical lessons about the importance of automation, monitoring, and AI in creating a robust security posture. This approach is not just about reacting to threats but also about creating a resilient system that anticipates and adapts to them, reducing risk across both development and operational environments:

SolarWinds hack

The SolarWinds supply chain attack was a wake-up call for the cybersecurity industry, revealing the vulnerabilities inherent in trusted software distribution channels. Malicious code was injected into a SolarWinds software update, which was then deployed to thousands of customers, including major government agencies and corporations. DevSecOps automation tools failed to identify the malicious code during the development pipeline, and SecOps teams remained unaware of the anomaly for months, allowing attackers to exploit the compromised systems extensively. A Continuous Security approach, leveraging AI-driven monitoring and analysis, could have drastically altered the outcome. Continuous monitoring of the software development pipeline might have detected unusual activity, such as the insertion of unauthorized code. Similarly, real-time monitoring in production environments could have flagged unexpected behavior in systems using the compromised update. By shortening the window of exposure, Continuous Security would have limited the attack's impact and possibly prevented its widespread propagation.

Equifax data breach

The Equifax breach exposed the personal data of 147 million individuals, stemming from a failure to apply a widely publicized patch for a known vulnerability in Apache Struts. Despite being aware of the issue, the organization's inability to act swiftly left its systems exposed to attackers who exploited the vulnerability over several months. Continuous Security could have transformed Equifax's vulnerability management process. Automated scanning tools, integrated into both development and production environments, would have identified unpatched systems in real time. AI-driven patch prioritization could have ensured that critical vulnerabilities like this one were addressed promptly, preventing the breach altogether. Such a system emphasizes that patch management should never be a one-time activity and instead should be a continuous, automated process.

Colonial Pipeline ransomware attack

This attack disrupted fuel supplies across the United States, revealing critical gaps in proactive threat detection and incident response speed. The attackers exploited weaknesses in the pipeline's systems, and the SecOps team struggled to identify and isolate the threat in a timely manner, exacerbating the damage and leading to widespread disruption. A Continuous Security model would have mitigated the attack's impact by integrating early threat detection capabilities from DevSecOps with the real-time monitoring of SecOps. AI-powered tools could have identified early indicators of compromise, such as unusual system activity or unauthorized access attempts. When the attack was detected, automated incident response workflows could have isolated affected systems immediately, limiting the ransomware's reach and preserving operational integrity.

Log4Shell vulnerability

This exploited a flaw in the widely used Log4j logging library, enabling attackers to execute malicious code remotely. Many organizations faced challenges in identifying and patching the vulnerability across their sprawling development and production environments, leaving systems exposed for extended periods. Continuous Security offers a robust solution to vulnerabilities such as Log4Shell. Real-time automated scanning would have quickly identified instances of the vulnerable library across all environments, including hidden dependencies. AI-assisted remediation tools could have prioritized patching efforts, ensuring that critical systems were addressed first. By enabling rapid detection and remediation, Continuous Security minimizes the risk posed by such widespread vulnerabilities.

Uber data breach

Uber suffered a significant data breach due to poor internal security practices, including a misconfigured firewall and weak access controls. Attackers were able to access sensitive data, exposing the personal information of 57 million customers and drivers. The breach highlighted the dangers of inconsistent security practices across development and operational environments. A Continuous Security framework could have enforced consistent security policies across Uber's systems. AI-driven monitoring tools would have flagged misconfigurations, such as the improperly secured firewall, before attackers could exploit them. Additionally, automated enforcement of access control policies would have ensured that unauthorized users were unable to access sensitive systems. By eliminating such gaps, Continuous Security reduces the likelihood of breaches caused by human error or oversight.

These incidents illustrate the vulnerabilities inherent in traditional security practices and highlight the transformative potential of Continuous Security. By integrating AI-driven automation, continuous monitoring, and real-time response capabilities, organizations can build a security model that is proactive, adaptive, and resilient. The lessons from SolarWinds, Equifax, Colonial Pipeline, Log4Shell, and Uber demonstrate the critical need for a security approach that evolves alongside modern threats, ensuring robust defenses across every stage of the software and operations lifecycle.

One of the core advantages of predictive ML in Continuous Security is its ability to predict threats based on patterns, trends, and anomalies in data streams. In contrast to reactive security practices, which rely on incident response after a breach has occurred, ML algorithms can predict potential attacks by identifying anomalies that suggest malicious behavior. For example, ML models can be applied to analysis of user behavior, network traffic, and system performance metrics to detect subtle signs of an intrusion before it becomes a full-fledged attack. This proactive approach ensures that threats are addressed in real time, reducing the likelihood of zero-day vulnerabilities being exploited.

Predictive ML models learn from historical data and continuously adapt to new attack vectors, making it possible to detect previously unknown threats. This adaptability is especially crucial in combating AI-driven cyberattacks, which can evolve more quickly than manual intervention or static, rule-based systems. By integrating predictive ML into Continuous Security, organizations can stay ahead of emerging threats and apply preventive security measures, such as automatically patching vulnerabilities or blocking suspicious activity before it escalates.

AI-Augmented Tools for Continuous Monitoring and Response

AI-augmented tools leverage predictive ML to provide continuous monitoring across both development (DevSecOps) and operational (SecOps) environments. These tools are essential to the integrated aspect of Continuous Security because they allow organizations to monitor and secure systems across the entire software lifecycle, from code inception to deployment and ongoing production. The following are examples of AI-augmented tools used for Continuous Monitoring and Response:

Automated vulnerability detection
   Predictive ML applied together with software composition analysis (SCA) and SAST code scanning tools can scan code repositories and detect vulnerabilities or weaknesses early in the development process, reducing the risk of these issues making it to production. Tools powered by AI can identify security flaws, such as insecure coding practices or vulnerabilities in third-party libraries, much more quickly than traditional methods. By integrating these tools into DevSecOps pipelines, organizations ensure that security checks are continuous and automatic.

Real-time threat detection
   AI-augmented tools use ML algorithms to analyze observable system behavior (e.g., logs, alerts, and traces) in production environments, identifying suspicious patterns that may indicate a security breach. These tools are particularly effective at handling vast amounts of data generated in complex, multicloud or hybrid environments, where traditional SecOps teams may struggle to keep up with monitoring. Predictive ML models enable faster threat detection, helping SecOps teams respond to incidents in real time and minimize damage.

Adaptive incident response
   Predictive ML not only detects potential threats but also aids in automating responses to incidents. For instance, AI-driven tools can trigger automated workflows that isolate compromised systems, revoke access privileges, or deploy patches without human intervention. This capability is crucial in Continuous Security practices, where seamless integration between DevSecOps and SecOps is required to ensure that incidents are addressed promptly, whether they occur during development or in live production environments.

Enhanced security collaboration and unified operations

A major limitation of traditional security models is the siloed nature of DevSecOps and SecOps teams. Predictive ML, integrated into AI-augmented tools, enables more effective collaboration between these two domains by providing a unified security view that spans development and operations. For example, DevSecOps benefits from predictive ML by embedding security checks early in the development pipeline, ensuring that potential vulnerabilities are addressed proactively; SecOps benefits by leveraging real-time data analytics, powered by AI, to detect and respond to incidents as they occur in production environments.

By breaking down silos and providing continuous, AI-driven insights across both development and production environments, predictive ML supports the unified, end-to-end security posture required for Continuous Security. It allows organizations to close the gap between development and operations, ensuring that security is consistent, dynamic, and continuously improving.

Continuous learning and improvement

One of the standout capabilities of predictive ML in Continuous Security is its ability to continuously learn from new data. Unlike static, rule-based systems, which require manual updates, predictive ML models adapt to new threats automatically. As more data is collected, AI-augmented tools refine their algorithms to become more accurate in predicting and preventing attacks. This continuous learning ensures that security practices remain up-to-date in a rapidly evolving cyber threat landscape.

For example, a predictive ML model that has detected certain types of phishing attacks can evolve to identify more sophisticated variants as attackers modify their techniques. Similarly, AI-driven tools that monitor network traffic can continuously learn the baseline "normal" behavior of systems, making it easier to detect anomalies indicative of an insider threat or APT.

Recent examples of Intelligent Continuous Security in action

As cyber threats become increasingly sophisticated, traditional security measures often struggle to keep pace. Predictive ML has emerged as a cornerstone of Intelligent Continuous Security, offering the ability to identify and mitigate risks before they escalate. By analyzing vast amounts of data in real time, these tools uncover subtle patterns and deviations that might otherwise go unnoticed. In doing so, they enable security teams to shift from reactive to proactive defense strategies, minimizing vulnerabilities across both development and production environments.

Recent high-profile incidents such as the SolarWinds attack, the Log4Shell vulnerability, and the Capital One data breach demonstrate the critical need for predictive ML in addressing modern security challenges. These cases highlight how AI-augmented tools, when integrated into Continuous Security practices, can detect anomalies, automate responses, and adapt to evolving threats, creating a resilient and scalable defense system for organizations.

The SolarWinds attack revealed how vulnerable trusted software supply chains can be. Malicious actors inserted backdoors into a SolarWinds software update, compromising thousands of customers, including government agencies. Predictive ML tools could have played a pivotal role in detecting the unusual activity associated with this attack. By continuously monitoring the development pipeline, ML algorithms might have flagged anomalies such as the unauthorized code changes introduced during the build process. Additionally, continuous monitoring of deployment environments would have provided early warning signs of the malicious behavior exhibited by the compromised updates, potentially limiting the scope of the breach.

The Log4Shell vulnerability in the Log4j library exposed the challenges of identifying and remediating widespread security flaws across diverse environments. Predictive ML could have transformed the response to this critical issue. By continuously scanning codebases and dependencies in both development and production environments, AI-augmented tools would have detected the presence of the vulnerable library automatically. Moreover, these tools could have prioritized remediation efforts by assessing the risk levels of affected systems, ensuring that high-impact environments were patched first. This proactive approach would have significantly reduced the window of exposure and minimized the risks associated with delayed patching.

The Capital One data breach, which resulted from a misconfigured firewall in a cloud environment, underscores the importance of real-time anomaly detection and adaptive response capabilities. Predictive ML could have identified the misconfiguration much earlier by analyzing network traffic patterns and identifying deviations indicative of unauthorized access. For example, AI-powered tools could have flagged the unusual data exfiltration behavior as it occurred, enabling the security team to respond swiftly and prevent further exposure. By automating the detection of configuration errors and integrating with real-time monitoring, predictive ML helps organizations close gaps in their cloud security infrastructure.

Predictive ML is more than a tool. It is a transformative capability that redefines how organizations approach security in integrated development and operations environments. By enabling continuous monitoring, real-time threat detection, and adaptive responses, AI-augmented tools powered by predictive ML provide a proactive and scalable defense against evolving threats. These technologies empower security teams to identify risks sooner, respond more quickly, and adapt more effectively, ensuring a robust and resilient security posture.

As cyber threats grow in complexity and scale, the integration of predictive ML into Continuous Security practices has become essential. It allows organizations to maintain an always-on defense that evolves in tandem with the threat landscape, protecting critical systems and data across the entire software lifecycle. In an era where speed and precision are paramount, predictive ML ensures that security is not just reactive but anticipatory, safeguarding organizations against the challenges of tomorrow.

Generative AI and Its Vital Role in Intelligent Continuous Security

Generative AI technologies, driven by advances such as transformers powering large language models (LLMs) and diffusion models underlying modern generative systems, are revolutionizing Intelligent Continuous Security. Unlike traditional AI, which focuses on pattern detection and automation of predefined tasks, generative AI (GenAI) introduces transformative capabilities by generating new data, simulating potential attack vectors, and dynamically adapting security measures. Transformers enable the contextual analysis required for tasks such as identifying subtle security vulnerabilities or crafting automated response strategies, while diffusion models excel in creating highly realistic simulations such as synthetic attack scenarios for proactive defense testing. Together, these technologies empower the automation of complex, integrated security workflows across DevSecOps and SecOps, addressing the evolving challenges of today's threat landscape with unmatched adaptability and precision.

Here are some examples:

Dynamic threat simulation and scenario generation
GenAI is particularly effective at simulating attack scenarios and helping organizations anticipate potential threats in ways that traditional models cannot. By generating realistic threat simulations, such as potential exploits or attacks, GenAI helps security teams prepare for evolving and complex threats.

Automating penetration testing
GenAI models can automatically generate realistic penetration tests by simulating various attack vectors that might be used by real-world hackers. This allows organizations to test their defenses in a proactive and adaptive manner, identifying vulnerabilities that traditional testing methods may miss.

Simulating social engineering attacks
GenAI models can simulate phishing attacks, creating highly convincing emails or text messages that mimic real-world social engineering tactics. Security teams can then use these simulations to train employees and test their ability to recognize and respond to phishing attempts. GenAI allows organizations to test and improve their defenses continuously, ensuring that security teams are prepared for both known and emerging threats. Traditional AI models, while effective at detecting specific patterns, lack the ability to create realistic, evolving attack scenarios that mirror the sophistication of modern cybercriminals. In contrast, GenAI provides dynamic, automated simulations that enable end-to-end testing of an organization's security posture.

Automated workflow generation and complex integration
GenAI is also uniquely suited to automating complex security workflows across the integrated aspects of Continuous Security. In the Intelligent Continuous Security model, multiple security tasks—including vulnerability scanning, compliance checks, incident response, and patch management—must operate seamlessly across DevSecOps and SecOps environments. GenAI models can automate these processes by generating workflows that account for the complexity and interdependence of different security functions.

Automating incident response playbooks
GenAI can be used to automatically generate incident response playbooks that are tailored to the specific needs of an organization. These playbooks can evolve over time, adapting to new threats, technologies, and environments. By learning from past security incidents and simulating potential future attacks, GenAI models can dynamically generate and update response plans, reducing the time it takes to detect and mitigate security breaches.

Orchestrating security workflows
Integrated security practices require the automation of workflows that span development, operations, and security. GenAI models are particularly capable of generating cohesive workflows that connect various security tools and processes. For example, a GenAI-powered system can automatically trigger vulnerability scans, apply patches, and update compliance documentation as part of a Continuous Security loop, without human intervention. The ability of GenAI to understand and orchestrate the dependencies between different security tasks makes it a critical enabler for end-to-end security automation.

Dynamic policy generation and enforcement
Another area where GenAI excels is in policy generation. It can generate security policies based on contextual information about the organization's infrastructure, compliance requirements, and risk appetite. These policies can then be dynamically updated based on changes in the security landscape or the organization's operating environment. By automating policy generation, GenAI ensures that security policies are always up-to-date and aligned with the organization's goals.

Continuous monitoring and adaptive defense
GenAI supports continuous monitoring and adaptive defense strategies, which are essential for the integrated, always-on nature of Continuous Security. As security threats evolve, GenAI models can dynamically adjust security parameters and configurations to adapt to new risks in real time.

Adaptive configurations
GenAI models can generate adaptive security configurations for firewalls, intrusion detection systems, and access controls based on real-time data. By

continuously analyzing the organization's network traffic, user behavior, and system activity, GenAI can dynamically adjust security settings to preemptively block potential threats or mitigate ongoing attacks.

Real-time incident generation and analysis

One of the key advantages of GenAI in Continuous Security is its ability to generate detailed incident analysis in real time. After identifying a threat or vulnerability, GenAI can automatically generate detailed reports and remediation steps, providing security teams with actionable insights to close security gaps more quickly. This capability significantly reduces mean time to detect (MTTD) and mean time to repair (MTTR), both of which are critical for minimizing damage from cyber incidents.

Threat intelligence and knowledge synthesis

GenAI models excel at synthesizing large volumes of data, including threat intelligence from various sources, and generating actionable insights that security teams can use to improve their defenses. Traditional AI models are often limited by the quality and quantity of their training data, but GenAI can generate new intelligence by synthesizing information from threat feeds, past incidents, and even external data sources such as social media or dark web forums.

Automated threat intelligence reports

GenAI can automatically generate threat intelligence reports that synthesize information from multiple sources. These reports provide security teams with up-to-date insights on emerging threats, vulnerabilities, and attack tactics. Additionally, GenAI models can generate tailored intelligence for specific sectors or threat profiles, ensuring that security measures are relevant to the organization's unique risk landscape.

Predictive threat models

GenAI can create predictive threat models that help organizations anticipate future attack trends based on current and past data. These models not only predict which types of attacks are likely but also can generate potential exploit scenarios to prepare defenses in advance. By automating this intelligence synthesis, GenAI allows security teams to be more proactive and agile in their defense strategies.

In the face of increasingly sophisticated cyber threats, traditional security measures often struggle to keep up. High-profile incidents such as the SolarWinds attack, the Log4Shell vulnerability, and the Colonial Pipeline ransomware attack have exposed critical gaps in detection, response, and remediation processes. These exploits underscore the need for a new approach to security—one that is not only proactive but also adaptable and capable of learning in real time. This is where GenAI technologies come into play, offering transformative potential to enhance Continuous Security by automating complex workflows and enabling dynamic, real-time defenses.

GenAI goes beyond the static capabilities of traditional AI by creating new data, simulating attack scenarios, and generating adaptive responses to evolving threats. Its integration into Continuous Security practices equips organizations with tools to proactively identify vulnerabilities, simulate potential exploits, and orchestrate automated responses across development and operational environments. By reviewing some of the recent, high-profile exploits mentioned earlier, we can see how GenAI could have mitigated their impact and why it is poised to redefine the landscape of security operations.

The SolarWinds attack revealed the vulnerabilities inherent in trusted supply chains. Attackers inserted malicious code into SolarWinds software updates, which were then distributed to thousands of customers. If GenAI had been part of the security workflow, it could have simulated threat scenarios that flagged unusual activity in the development pipeline, such as the unauthorized insertion of backdoors. Furthermore, adaptive defense models powered by GenAI could have dynamically reconfigured monitoring systems to detect anomalous behavior once the malicious updates were distributed, significantly reducing the window of exposure.

The Log4Shell vulnerability showcased the challenges organizations face in identifying and patching widespread vulnerabilities across complex environments. With GenAI, automated workflows could have continuously scanned for instances of the vulnerable Log4j library, both in development and production. GenAI's ability to simulate potential exploits would have enabled organizations to prepare targeted mitigation strategies before attackers could exploit the flaw. By automating vulnerability detection and patching processes, GenAI could have turned a reactive scramble into a proactive defense.

The Colonial Pipeline ransomware attack disrupted fuel supplies across the East Coast of the United States, highlighting the need for rapid response capabilities. GenAI could have dynamically created incident response workflows that automated containment measures, such as isolating affected systems, before the ransomware could spread further. Additionally, GenAI-powered tools could have generated detailed, real-time remediation plans to restore operations swiftly, minimizing downtime and financial loss. These capabilities would have provided the agility and precision needed to handle such a fast-moving attack.

GenAI technologies are revolutionizing Continuous Security by automating some of the most complex aspects of integrated security workflows. From simulating potential threats to generating dynamic policies and adaptive defenses, GenAI ensures that security measures evolve in real time to keep pace with emerging threats. These tools provide organizations with a proactive advantage, enabling continuous monitoring, automated responses, and seamless integration across both development and operational environments.

In a world where cyber threats are growing more sophisticated every day, GenAI offers a critical edge. By empowering organizations to anticipate and counteract vulnerabilities and attacks before they escalate, GenAI transforms Continuous Security into a robust, always-on defense mechanism. As the examples of SolarWinds, Log4Shell, and Colonial Pipeline illustrate, the integration of GenAI into security workflows is no longer optional; it is a necessary step toward building resilient, end-to-end protection in an increasingly dynamic threat landscape.

Summary

This chapter emphasized the integration of DevSecOps and SecOps into a unified approach to tackle the limitations of traditional security models. By combining these practices, Intelligent Continuous Security offers a seamless, adaptive security framework that addresses the vulnerabilities in both development and operational environments. This integrated approach harnesses AI-driven tools for real-time threat detection, vulnerability management, and compliance, enabling organizations to detect and mitigate security risks more effectively and ensure consistent protection throughout the software lifecycle.

Looking ahead, Chapter 3 outlines the foundational principles of Intelligent Continuous Security, focusing on the essential pillars, practices, and capabilities needed to implement it. This foundation highlights how AI supports a proactive and end-to-end security model, setting the stage for organizations to evolve their security practices in line with modern cyber threats.

Foundations of Intelligent Continuous Security

This chapter establishes the principles, frameworks, and practices required to build an integrated, adaptive, and intelligent security model. By leveraging generative AI (GenAI), large language models (LLMs), machine learning (ML), and AI agents, Intelligent Continuous Security addresses the growing complexity of modern IT environments while providing enhanced protection against emerging cyber threats. Each of these AI technologies contributes uniquely, from automating threat detection to enhancing collaboration and learning.

The chapter explores critical components such as the core principles of Intelligent Continuous Security, the maturity levels that guide organizations through their transformation journey, and eight pillars of practice that form the operational backbone of this approach.

Each section emphasizes the interplay of people, processes, and technology, illustrating how AI empowers teams to embed security into every phase of the software lifecycle. Together, these concepts provide a comprehensive foundation for implementing Intelligent Continuous Security that adapts to an ever-changing threat landscape while maintaining agility and scalability.

Core Principles and Concepts

Intelligent Continuous Security is built upon a set of fundamental principles that guide its implementation and ensure its effectiveness. These principles serve as the backbone for creating a security framework that is adaptive, proactive, and seamlessly integrated across the software lifecycle. They address the limitations of traditional

DevSecOps and SecOps practices by leveraging AI-driven capabilities to deliver continuous and automated protection without disrupting agility or innovation.

Figure 3-1 illustrates the principles, which are explained in the rest of this section.

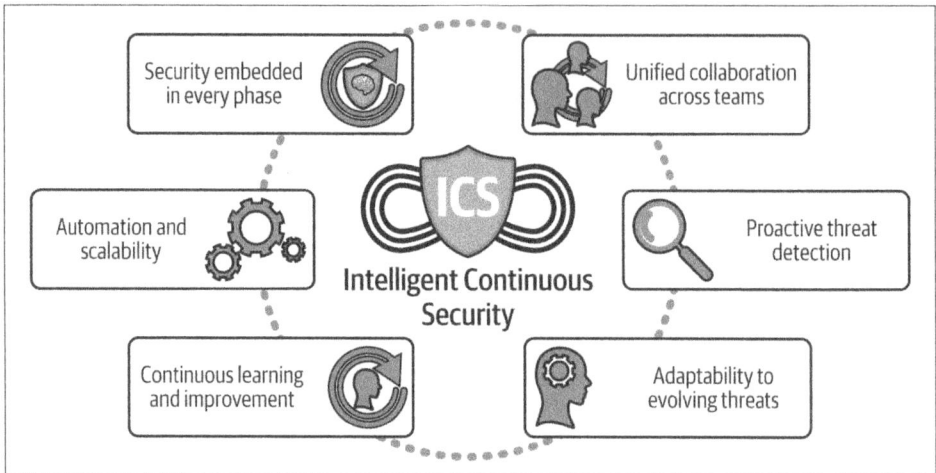

Figure 3-1. Intelligent Continuous Security principles

Security Embedded in Every Phase

One of the core principles is the integration of security into every phase of the software lifecycle, from requirements gathering and design to development, testing, and deployment. Unlike conventional approaches where security is a distinct phase, Intelligent Continuous Security ensures that security checks and safeguards are applied continuously. This integration minimizes the likelihood of vulnerabilities being introduced and propagates through the lifecycle. It also aligns with the shift-left philosophy by embedding security early, while maintaining continuous monitoring in post-deployment stages for comprehensive coverage.

The core principles guide the implementation of Intelligent Continuous Security and ensure its alignment with organizational goals. These principles include embedding security at every phase, leveraging AI to enhance the value stream, and fostering collaboration among teams.

Generative AI supports early security integration by generating threat models based on historical data, simulating potential vulnerabilities, and generating synthetic data for security testing during the design and delivery phases. This ensures that security is considered proactively across the lifecycle.

Proactive, AI-Driven Threat Mitigation

Intelligent Continuous Security relies on proactive, AI-driven threat detection and mitigation. Predictive analytics and ML models identify potential threats by analyzing patterns, behaviors, and anomalies in real time.

For example, supervised learning uses labeled datasets to train models for classification and anomaly detection. This includes techniques·such as decision trees, random forests, support vector machines (SVMs), and neural networks used together with data such as historical threat intelligence, known malware signatures, and labeled logs.

This capability enables organizations to address vulnerabilities and respond to threats before they escalate. By replacing reactive processes with predictive insights, security teams can focus on prevention rather than damage control, enhancing overall resilience.

ML enables real-time threat detection by analyzing behavioral patterns and identifying anomalies. GenAI can be used to create synthetic datasets to train these models, improving their ability to detect zero-day vulnerabilities and other forms of learning to anticipate novel and unknown threats.

Automation and Scalability

Automation is another cornerstone of this approach. Routine, repetitive security tasks, such as vulnerability scanning, compliance checks, and patch management, are automated using AI tools. Automation ensures consistency, reduces human error, and allows security operations to scale efficiently across complex, distributed systems. As organizations adopt microservices, multicloud architectures, and rapid release cycles, automation becomes essential to keep up with the speed and complexity of modern development environments.

AI agents play a vital role in automating routine tasks such as vulnerability scanning and patch management by continuously analyzing system configurations, detecting weaknesses, and triggering remediation workflows without human intervention. These agents can autonomously enforce security policies and respond to detected issues, ensuring scalability across distributed systems. For example, an AI-driven automated patching agent can monitor real-time threat intelligence feeds, correlate findings with internal vulnerability data, and autonomously deploy security patches based on predefined risk-based policies. These policies enforce security standards by ensuring that patches are applied only after compatibility checks, preventing downtime while maintaining compliance with industry regulations.

Unified Collaboration Across Teams

Intelligent Continuous Security fosters a culture of unified collaboration between development, operations, and security teams. By breaking down traditional silos, it promotes shared responsibility for security and ensures that all teams work toward common goals. This collaboration is supported by AI-powered tools that provide real-time insights, shared dashboards, and actionable recommendations to all stakeholders, encouraging transparency and accountability.

Natural language processing (NLP) can enhance collaboration by simplifying technical security insights into accessible language, enabling all teams to understand and act on shared goals. These models also assist in generating real-time reports tailored to different stakeholders.

Continuous Improvement and Adaptability

Adaptability and continuous improvement are fundamental principles. The dynamic nature of cybersecurity threats requires an approach that evolves alongside them. AI tools continuously learn from new data, incidents, and patterns to refine security models and strategies. Retraining or transfer learning is often more effective than online continuous learning because it allows models to incorporate high-quality, curated data and avoid compounding errors or drift that can occur with continuously updated models that lack proper validation. Organizations must also regularly evaluate and update their security policies, processes, and technologies to remain effective in the face of emerging risks.

ML continuously refines security practices by learning from new threat data and feedback. GenAI complements this by simulating attack scenarios for ongoing improvements to detection models. AI agents autonomously adapt security configurations to evolving threats, ensuring that defenses remain effective in dynamic environments. VUCA (Volatility, Uncertainty, Complexity, and Ambiguity) in relation to Intelligent Continuous Security (ICS) refers to the rapidly evolving threat landscape where AI-driven security solutions must continuously adapt to unpredictable cyber risks, sophisticated attack techniques, and dynamic regulatory requirements. These principles collectively ensure that Intelligent Continuous Security is not just a set of tools or processes but a comprehensive, integrated framework that adapts to the evolving threat landscape while maintaining the agility needed for modern software development.

What AI Can Do for Continuous Security

AI revolutionizes the way organizations implement Continuous Security by automating complex processes, improving threat detection, and enabling real-time responses. Traditional security methods often struggle to keep pace with the rapid evolution of cyber threats, the growing complexity of IT environments, and the demand for Continuous Integration and Continuous Delivery. AI, with its advanced analytical capabilities, provides the scalability, speed, and precision necessary to address these challenges, making it a cornerstone of Continuous Security.

Proactive Threat Detection and Prevention

One of the most significant contributions of AI to Continuous Security is its ability to detect and prevent threats proactively. Through ML and behavioral analysis, AI identifies patterns and anomalies that indicate potential vulnerabilities or malicious activities. Unlike traditional rule-based systems, AI models learn and adapt to evolving attack vectors, enabling the identification of zero-day vulnerabilities and advanced persistent threats (APTs) before they can cause harm. For example, AI-driven systems can monitor application behavior during development and flag unusual patterns that might indicate unsecured code or misconfigurations.

GenAI supports early security integration by generating threat models based on historical data and simulating potential vulnerabilities during design phases. This ensures that security is considered proactively across the lifecycle. For example, GenAI can create datasets that simulate rare attack patterns, enabling ML models to identify anomalies that might otherwise go unnoticed.

Security Workflow Automation

AI enhances the efficiency of Continuous Security by automating repetitive and time-consuming tasks, such as vulnerability scanning, compliance checks, and patch management. Automation ensures that these tasks are performed consistently and at scale, reducing the risk of human error. For instance, ML enhances AI-powered tools such as Checkmarx One by improving code analysis and vulnerability detection in Continuous Integration/Continuous Delivery (CI/CD) pipelines, enabling automated identification of security flaws, reducing false positives, and adapting to evolving threat patterns over time. This capability enables development teams to focus on delivering features without compromising security.

Real-Time Incident Response

In production environments, AI plays a critical role in real-time incident detection and response. By analyzing network traffic, system logs, and user behavior, AI can quickly identify anomalies and trigger automated responses to mitigate threats. For example, AI can isolate compromised endpoints, block malicious IP addresses, or patch vulnerabilities without waiting for human intervention. This rapid response capability minimizes the impact of security incidents and ensures business continuity.

Enhanced Threat Intelligence

AI significantly enhances threat intelligence by aggregating and analyzing data from diverse sources, including global threat feeds, internal logs, and external reports. Using NLP and advanced analytics, AI synthesizes this information to provide actionable insights. These insights enable security teams to anticipate emerging threats and prioritize defenses based on the organization's specific risk profile. AI-driven threat intelligence systems can also recommend tailored security measures, ensuring that defenses remain effective against the latest attack strategies.

Continuous Monitoring Support

Continuous Security relies heavily on monitoring applications, networks, and systems for potential vulnerabilities or breaches. AI enables this monitoring to be both comprehensive and dynamic. By leveraging predictive analytics, AI can forecast potential threats based on historical data and evolving patterns. This capability allows organizations to address vulnerabilities before they are exploited. Additionally, AI reduces alert fatigue by filtering false positives, false negatives, and unexploitable vulnerabilities, and by prioritizing genuine threats, ensuring that security teams focus on the most critical issues.

Adaptive Learning and Improvement

AI-powered systems continuously learn and evolve, ensuring that security measures stay up-to-date in the face of rapidly changing threats. ML models refine their detection capabilities by analyzing new data, incidents, and feedback from previous responses. This adaptive learning creates a virtuous cycle of improvement, where AI becomes more effective over time at identifying and mitigating risks. This capability is particularly valuable in addressing sophisticated attacks that evolve to bypass static defenses.

Collaboration Across Teams

AI enables collaboration between development, operations, and security teams by providing shared tools, dashboards, and insights. These tools ensure that all teams have real-time visibility into the security posture and can work together to address vulnerabilities. For example, AI-powered systems can generate reports that highlight risks in development pipelines while simultaneously recommending operational defenses, aligning the goals of DevSecOps and SecOps. An excellent example of an AI-powered system that facilitates collaboration across teams is Cycode, particularly when integrated with other DevSecOps tools. Cycode supports shared dashboards for real-time insights, AI-driven risk assessment, collaborative features, and actionable recommendations and automation.

Conclusion

AI transforms Continuous Security by enabling proactive, automated, and adaptive approaches to threat detection, mitigation, and monitoring. Its ability to analyze vast amounts of data in real time, learn from evolving threats, and automate security tasks ensures that organizations maintain robust defenses without compromising agility. As cyber threats become more sophisticated, AI's role in Continuous Security will only grow, making it an indispensable tool for modern enterprises.

Limitations and Pitfalls for AI and Continuous Security

While AI greatly enhances Continuous Security by automating processes, detecting threats, and improving scalability, it is not without limitations and potential pitfalls. These challenges can impact the effectiveness of AI-driven security systems if not addressed properly. Understanding these limitations and implementing mitigation strategies is crucial for maintaining a robust Continuous Security framework.

Data Quality and Bias

AI models rely heavily on high-quality data for training and operation. Poor-quality data, missing information, or biased datasets can lead to incorrect predictions or missed threats. For instance, if a dataset used to train an AI model lacks examples of certain attack patterns, the model may fail to detect those threats in real time.

Ideas for mitigation:

- Regularly update datasets with diverse, representative samples of threats from internal logs and external threat intelligence feeds.
- Implement data validation processes to ensure data accuracy and completeness before training AI models.
- Use techniques such as adversarial training to expose AI models to a wide range of attack scenarios and improve their generalization capabilities.

Overreliance on Automation

While automation is a strength of AI-driven security, overreliance on it can lead to complacency among security teams. Automated systems may miss nuanced threats that require human judgment, especially in complex or novel attack scenarios. Additionally, attackers may use AI to identify and exploit patterns in automated defenses.

Ideas for mitigation:

- Maintain a balance between automation and human oversight by combining AI tools with skilled security analysts who can handle edge cases and sophisticated attacks.
- Periodically review and refine automated processes to identify blind spots or gaps in coverage.
- Encourage collaboration between AI systems and human operators by providing tools that enhance analysts' decision making with AI-generated insights.

False Positives and Alert Fatigue

AI systems often generate large volumes of alerts, some of which may be false positives. This can lead to alert fatigue, where security teams become overwhelmed and may miss critical threats amid the noise.

Ideas for mitigation:

- Use AI models designed to prioritize and contextualize alerts based on severity thresholds, event types, and relevance, reducing the number of false positives.
- Implement tiered alerting systems that escalate only critical issues to human analysts.
- Continuously fine-tune AI algorithms with feedback from analysts to improve accuracy over time.

Cost and Resource Requirements

Deploying and maintaining AI-driven security systems can be resource intensive. High-performance hardware, skilled personnel, and ongoing maintenance are necessary to ensure that these systems operate effectively. Smaller organizations may find these requirements prohibitive.

Ideas for mitigation:

- Adopt cloud-based AI solutions or managed security services to reduce up-front infrastructure costs.
- Prioritize the implementation of AI tools in high-risk areas of the security workflow to maximize return on investment (ROI).
- Invest in training for existing staff to upskill them in AI and security operations, reducing the need for external expertise.

Lack of Transparency in AI Decisions

AI systems, especially those using deep learning, often operate as *black boxes*, making it difficult to understand how they arrive at specific decisions. This lack of transparency can create challenges in justifying actions to stakeholders or regulatory bodies.

Ideas for mitigation:

- Use explainable AI (XAI) models that provide clear reasoning for their decisions.
- Supplement AI-driven decisions with human judgment to provide additional layers of accountability.
- Document and audit AI-driven processes to ensure that they align with organizational and regulatory requirements.

> An excellent example of an XAI model is SHAP (SHapley Additive exPlanations). SHAP is a unified approach to explain the output of ML models by assigning each feature an importance value for a specific prediction. It is grounded in game theory and provides clear and consistent explanations for decisions, which makes it highly applicable for addressing transparency challenges in AI systems.

Vulnerability to Adversarial Attacks

Attackers can exploit weaknesses in AI models by feeding them adversarial data designed to mislead the system. For example, subtle alterations in input data may cause an AI system to misclassify or ignore a threat.

Ideas for mitigation:

- Implement adversarial training to expose AI models to potential attack scenarios and improve their resilience.
- Regularly test AI systems with simulated adversarial inputs to identify and address vulnerabilities.
- Use ensemble learning techniques to combine multiple AI models, making it harder for attackers to exploit a single model.

Ethical and Privacy Concerns

AI systems that monitor network traffic, user behavior, and system activity may inadvertently collect sensitive or personal data, raising ethical and privacy concerns. Mishandling this data can lead to legal and reputational risks.

Ideas for mitigation:

- Ensure that AI systems are configured to anonymize or aggregate data to protect user privacy.
- Establish clear policies for data handling, and regularly audit compliance with privacy regulations such as the General Data Protection Regulation (GDPR) or Health Insurance Portability and Accountability Act (HIPAA).
- Use AI ethically by aligning its deployment with organizational values and public expectations.
- When deploying LLMs, ensure compliance with data privacy laws such as GDPR, and avoid exposing sensitive data during model training or inference.

Conclusion

AI offers transformative capabilities for Continuous Security but comes with its own set of challenges. Organizations must address these limitations through proactive strategies, balancing AI automation with human expertise, ensuring data quality, and maintaining transparency and ethical standards. By acknowledging and mitigating these pitfalls, Intelligent Continuous Security can remain a reliable and adaptable framework for defending against evolving cyber threats.

Maturity Levels of Intelligent Continuous Security

This section introduces the maturity levels of Intelligent Continuous Security, providing a structured framework to assess and advance an organization's adoption of AI-driven security practices. These maturity levels are modeled on the principles of Capability Maturity Model Integration (CMMI), which defines progressive stages of development for improving processes and practices. In this context, the maturity levels describe the evolution of Intelligent Continuous Security across five distinct stages, with each level characterized by the typical state of people, processes, and technology factors.

This approach allows organizations to evaluate their current capabilities and identify gaps that need to be addressed to achieve higher levels of maturity. The five levels offer a roadmap for transitioning from initial, ad hoc implementations to fully optimized, adaptive security frameworks. By understanding the interplay between human expertise, automated processes, and advanced AI technologies at each stage, organizations can strategically plan their journey toward a resilient, proactive, and scalable security posture.

Continuous Security Maturity Level Concepts

The maturity levels for Intelligent Continuous Security, inspired by the CMMI framework, provide a structured way to evaluate an organization's security practices and guide its progress toward advanced, integrated, and adaptive security.

These levels, illustrated in Figure 3-2, categorize the state of people, processes, and technology at various stages of maturity, helping organizations identify gaps and set clear goals for improvement.

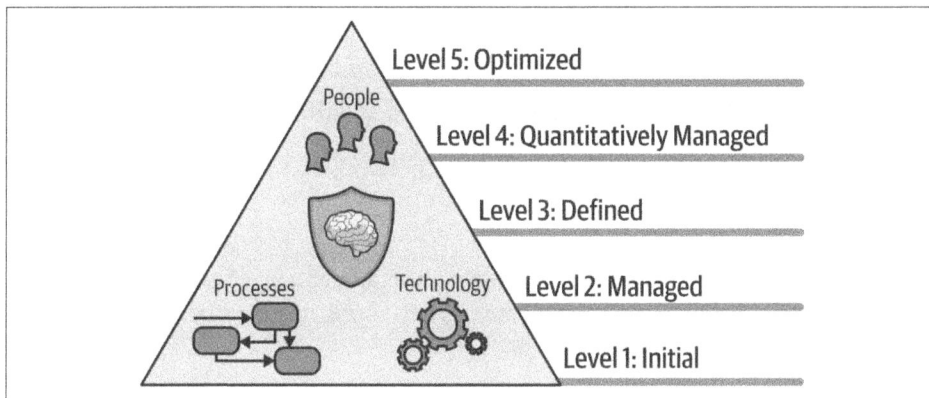

Figure 3-2. Intelligent Continuous Security maturity levels

Level 1: Initial (Ad Hoc and Unpredictable)

At this level, security practices are informal, reactive, and inconsistent:

People
Individuals handle security in an ad hoc manner, often without formal training or clear responsibilities. Security relies on individual expertise rather than structured teamwork.

Processes
Processes are undefined or exist as temporary fixes. Security measures are applied inconsistently, typically after incidents occur.

Technology
Minimal or no automation exists. Security tools are used sporadically, with little integration into workflows.

Level 2: Managed (Defined at a Project Level)

Security practices become more organized but are still applied independently within specific projects or teams:

People
> Roles and responsibilities for security are assigned within individual teams or projects, though collaboration across teams remains limited.

Processes
> Basic processes are documented, and some repeatability exists within individual projects. However, these processes are not standardized across the organization.

Technology
> Security tools are introduced, often manually operated, and used inconsistently across teams. Automation remains limited.

Level 3: Defined (Standardized Across the Organization)

A consistent, organization-wide approach to security emerges, with standard practices and policies:

People
> Cross-functional collaboration between development, operations, and security teams is established. Team members receive training in secure practices.

Processes
> Security processes are well-documented, standardized, and consistently applied across the organization. Compliance with policies becomes a priority.

Technology
> Basic automation is implemented, and tools are integrated into workflows, particularly in CI/CD pipelines. However, AI-driven capabilities are limited or experimental.

Level 4: Quantitatively Managed (Measured and Optimized)

Organizations begin using metrics and data-driven insights to improve security practices proactively:

People
> Teams operate with clear accountability and collaborate effectively using shared dashboards and reports. A security-first mindset is prevalent across the organization.

Processes
> Processes are monitored, measured, and optimized based on performance metrics. Continuous improvement cycles are established to refine security practices.

Technology
Automation is widely implemented with AI tools used for threat detection, vulnerability management, and compliance. Security workflows are integrated into all stages of development and operations.

Level 5: Optimized (Adaptive and Continuous Improvement)

At this level, security is fully integrated, adaptive, and continuously improving through AI-driven insights and automation:

People
Teams function cohesively, with security deeply embedded in the organization's culture. Individuals actively use intelligent tools to predict, prevent, and mitigate threats.

Processes
Processes are highly flexible and adaptive, continuously evolving based on new data, emerging threats, and feedback loops. They align seamlessly with business objectives.

Technology
Advanced AI capabilities enable proactive threat mitigation, real-time compliance, and automated responses. Systems are self-healing, and predictive analytics drive continuous improvements.

These five maturity levels provide a roadmap for organizations to evaluate their current state and plan their journey toward achieving Intelligent Continuous Security. Progression through these levels reflects increasing sophistication in people, processes, and technology, ultimately resulting in a robust, adaptive, and scalable security framework.

Intelligent Continuous Security Concepts

Intelligent Continuous Security concepts build upon the maturity levels framework by incorporating the role of AI at each stage of development. AI enhances security practices progressively, from basic automation and reactive tools at the lower levels to predictive, adaptive systems at the highest level. The integration of AI evolves alongside the organization's maturity in people, processes, and technology, enabling organizations to scale their security capabilities effectively and proactively.

Level 1: Initial (Ad Hoc and Unpredictable)

At this level, AI plays a minimal or experimental role in security, as practices are largely reactive and unstructured:

People

Security tasks are performed manually by individuals with limited knowledge of AI capabilities. Any use of AI is ad hoc and dependent on specific team members experimenting with available tools.

Processes

Processes are undefined, and AI is not embedded into workflows. Tools, if used, are isolated and lack integration with broader systems.

Technology

AI tools,such as simple anomaly detection systems, may be tested but are not fully operational. Any insights provided by AI are underutilized due to a lack of processes to act on them.

AI role

AI is primarily exploratory, used occasionally to augment manual efforts, such as running isolated scans for known vulnerabilities. AI tools, such as simple ML-based anomaly detectors, are used sporadically and without integration. AI agents may be tested in isolated cases but lack broader application.

Level 2: Managed (Defined at a Project Level)

AI begins to play a supporting role in specific projects, helping to improve consistency and reduce manual effort within teams:

People

Team members start to gain awareness of AI tools and their potential benefits. Security responsibilities are assigned within projects, and some personnel are trained in AI-driven technologies.

Processes

Basic security processes are defined at the project level, and AI tools are used to support repeatable tasks such as scanning for vulnerabilities or analyzing logs.

Technology

AI tools are selectively adopted for specific projects, often in the form of pre-packaged solutions for static code analysis or malware detection. Integration with other tools is limited.

AI role

AI augments manual efforts by automating routine tasks, such as generating alerts for common threats or identifying known patterns of malicious activity. GenAI is introduced for specific cases, such as vulnerability scanning within isolated projects. Teams begin to adopt LLMs for summarizing threat reports and improving awareness.

Level 3: Defined (Standardized Across the Organization)

AI becomes a core component of standardized security processes across the organization, providing consistent and reliable outputs:

People
> Teams across the organization are trained to use AI tools effectively, fostering collaboration between developers, security personnel, and operations teams. Security roles include specialists in AI-driven analysis.

Processes
> Security processes are standardized, and AI tools are integrated into CI/CD pipelines to perform consistent, automated checks during development and deployment. Policies ensure that AI tools are applied uniformly across projects.

Technology
> AI is embedded into workflows, offering advanced capabilities such as automated compliance checks and basic threat intelligence analysis. Tools integrate with existing systems for smoother operations.

AI role
> AI takes on a proactive role, continuously analyzing data and providing actionable insights, such as identifying misconfigurations in infrastructure or vulnerabilities in dependencies. AI is integrated into standardized workflows. LLMs generate shared insights, while ML models automate security testing in CI/CD pipelines.

Level 4: Quantitatively Managed (Measured and Optimized)

At this level, AI is deeply integrated into processes and tools, providing data-driven insights to improve security practices proactively:

People
> Teams use AI tools to generate and interpret security metrics, helping them measure performance and optimize processes. Roles such as AI security analyst emerge, focused on leveraging AI for continuous improvement.

Processes
> Security processes are continuously monitored and refined using metrics generated by AI systems. Feedback loops ensure that AI models are retrained with updated data to improve accuracy and effectiveness.

Technology
> AI-driven tools automate most security tasks, including vulnerability scanning, compliance validation, and incident prioritization. Systems begin to incorporate ML to detect previously unknown threats.

AI role

AI enables real-time monitoring, predictive threat detection, and prioritization of incidents, reducing alert fatigue and helping teams focus on critical vulnerabilities. AI agents take on active roles in managing risks and automating compliance tasks. ML models predict emerging threats, and GenAI simulates attack scenarios to enhance proactive defenses.

Level 5: Optimized (Adaptive and Continuous Improvement)

AI reaches its full potential, driving adaptive, autonomous, and self-healing security systems:

People

Teams are highly skilled in using and interpreting AI-driven insights. AI collaborates seamlessly with human decision making, allowing security personnel to focus on strategic initiatives.

Processes

Processes are fully adaptive, evolving, and continuously based on AI-driven insights and feedback loops. AI takes over routine decision making while humans intervene for complex scenarios.

Technology

Advanced AI capabilities include predictive analytics, automated threat remediation, and self-healing systems that respond to incidents without human intervention. Technology becomes scalable and robust, supporting even the most complex environments.

AI role

AI acts as the backbone of the security framework, automating nearly all routine tasks, predicting and mitigating risks before they materialize, and adapting processes based on real-time intelligence and past performance. At this level, AI technologies are fully embedded. ML and GenAI continuously improve processes, while AI agents autonomously monitor, respond to, and mitigate threats.

AI enhances Continuous Security by progressively taking on more sophisticated roles as an organization matures. From augmenting manual efforts at the lower levels to driving autonomous and adaptive security systems at the highest level, AI transforms how organizations address cybersecurity challenges. This framework provides a roadmap for leveraging AI effectively, ensuring that organizations continuously improve their security posture as they advance through the maturity levels.

Intelligent Continuous Security Pillars of Practice

This section outlines the eight Intelligent Continuous Security pillars of practice, which form a unifying framework that evolves with the organization's maturity and technological advancements. The eight pillars of practice are aligned with maturity levels and organizational needs. This model not only ensures robust defenses against emerging threats but also fosters a culture of shared responsibility and continuous improvement, making it an indispensable strategy for modern cybersecurity challenges. The model is illustrated in Figure 3-3.

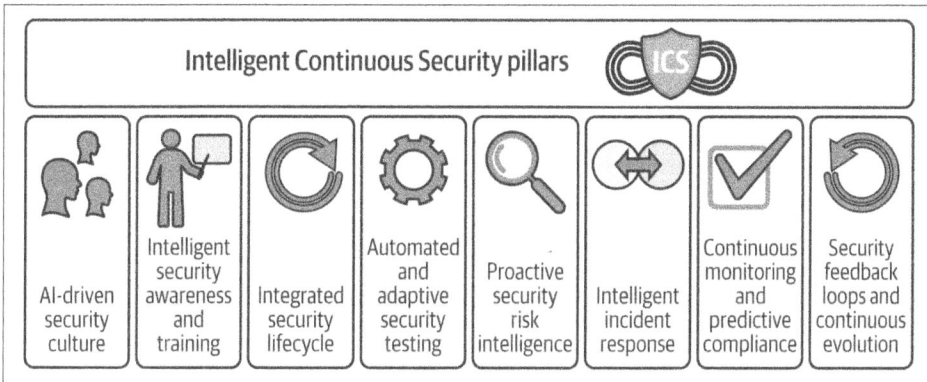

Figure 3-3. Intelligent Continuous Security pillars

AI-Driven Continuous Security Culture

A robust Continuous Security culture ensures that security is a shared responsibility across development, security, and operations teams, integrating it into daily practices and organizational values:

People
> AI assists in fostering collaboration by identifying patterns of miscommunication or workflow inefficiencies and suggesting improvements. AI-driven tools, such as shared dashboards, enable all teams to view and act on real-time security data, aligning efforts.

Processes
> AI streamlines processes by automating routine tasks such as status reporting and flagging security gaps early in the development lifecycle, making security awareness part of every workflow.

Technology

> Intelligent collaboration tools, such as real-time alerting and predictive analytics, help bridge gaps between teams, ensuring that security is a continuous, integrated process. LLMs facilitate collaboration by translating security objectives into accessible terms, while AI agents automate alerts to keep teams aligned.

Intelligent Continuous Security Awareness and Training

Awareness and training empower employees to identify and mitigate security risks proactively, fostering a security-conscious workforce:

People

> AI-driven training platforms deliver personalized and adaptive learning experiences, ensuring that team members receive role-specific education on secure coding, API security, network security, and emerging threats.

Processes

> AI analyzes training outcomes to identify knowledge gaps and recommends targeted follow-up sessions. Simulated phishing attacks and gamified learning exercises can be AI generated to enhance engagement.

Technology

> AI models continuously update training content based on the latest threat intelligence, ensuring that employees stay informed about evolving risks. GenAI delivers adaptive training modules tailored to individual needs, ensuring that employees stay informed about the latest threats.

Integrated Security Lifecycle

Integrating security into every phase of the software lifecycle ensures that vulnerabilities are addressed proactively:

People

> AI supports collaboration by providing role-based insights into security tasks, enabling team members to contribute effectively at each lifecycle stage.

Processes

> AI automates integration of security tools into CI/CD pipelines, ensuring that every code commit and deployment undergoes real-time security checks without slowing down workflows.

Technology

> AI enhances static and dynamic analysis tools, providing actionable recommendations for addressing security gaps during development and testing phases. ML automates code reviews and vulnerability scans, while AI agents monitor configurations and enforce security policies during deployments.

Automated and Adaptive Security Testing

Automation is essential for maintaining vigilance across fast-paced development cycles:

People
> AI simplifies security testing by offering user-friendly interfaces for automated tools, making them accessible to nonsecurity specialists such as developers.

Processes
> AI continuously scans for vulnerabilities in code and dependencies, dynamically adjusting test cases based on changing threat landscapes.

Technology
> AI-powered tools, such as fuzzing engines and automated vulnerability scanners, provide deep, scalable testing capabilities across diverse environments. AI-powered tools provide real-time feedback on vulnerabilities. GenAI enhances testing by simulating diverse attack vectors.

Proactive Security Risk Intelligence

Proactive security risk management identifies and mitigates vulnerabilities before they can be exploited:

People
> AI assists security teams in prioritizing risks by providing detailed analyses of potential impacts and recommended actions.

Processes
> AI enhances threat modeling by simulating attack scenarios and suggesting mitigations for high-risk areas.

Technology
> AI-powered risk assessment tools analyze patterns from historical data and real-time inputs to predict potential vulnerabilities and suggest proactive measures. ML models predict risks based on historical data, and GenAI assists in visualizing potential threat impacts.

Intelligent Incident Response

Quick and effective responses minimize the impact of security incidents:

People
> AI provides security teams with real-time data and insights, enabling faster decision making during incidents.

Processes

AI automates initial incident triage, categorizing threats and triggering predefined response workflows to minimize delays.

Technology

AI-driven Security Orchestration, Automation, and Response (SOAR) systems
isolate threats, deploy patches, and notify stakeholders automatically during incidents. AI agents autonomously execute predefined incident response workflows,
minimizing delays and human intervention.

Continuous Security Monitoring and Predictive Compliance

Ongoing monitoring and compliance ensure sustained protection and adherence to
regulations:

People

AI provides compliance teams with actionable dashboards that simplify auditing
and reporting tasks.

Processes

AI continuously monitors network traffic, system logs, and user behaviors, flagging anomalies and ensuring compliance with industry standards.

Technology

AI-driven monitoring tools aggregate data from various sources, detect deviations, and generate audit-ready compliance reports in real time. LLMs summa-
rize compliance requirements and generate audit-ready reports, while AI agents
ensure continuous adherence to standards.

Security Feedback Loops and Continuous Evolution

Feedback mechanisms drive iterative improvements to security practices:

People

AI helps identify recurring issues and provides recommendations for team training or process enhancements to prevent similar incidents.

Processes

AI collects and analyzes post-incident data, identifying trends and suggesting
areas for improvement in workflows or tools.

Technology

AI systems use historical data to refine detection algorithms and enhance overall
security measures, ensuring adaptive learning and continuous improvement.
GenAI synthesizes lessons learned from incidents into actionable recommendations, while ML models refine detection algorithms based on feedback.

These pillars, enhanced by AI capabilities, ensure that Continuous Security evolves to meet the demands of modern cyber threats, enabling proactive, automated, and scalable security practices across the organization.

Summary

This chapter provided a comprehensive framework for understanding the key elements required to establish and scale a robust Continuous Security model. By grounding the discussion in core principles, maturity levels, and pillars of practice, the chapter outlined how organizations can transition from traditional security models to a proactive, AI-powered approach. The chapter emphasized the integration of people, processes, and technology, with AI playing a transformative role in automating workflows, enhancing threat detection, and enabling continuous improvement.

One of the primary insights from this chapter is the progression through maturity levels based on the concepts of CMMI. These levels—from Initial to Optimized—serve as a roadmap for organizations to evaluate their current practices and plan strategic advancements. Each level is defined by the state of people, processes, and technology, with AI capabilities evolving from basic automation to fully autonomous, adaptive systems. The chapter also introduced the eight pillars of practice, which address critical areas such as fostering a security-first culture, integrating security across the software lifecycle, and leveraging AI to enhance monitoring, testing, and risk management.

Key takeaways from this chapter include the importance of embedding security as a continuous process rather than a one-time activity, the role of AI in overcoming the limitations of traditional security approaches, and the need for collaboration across teams to achieve seamless integration. By aligning security practices with business objectives and adopting AI-driven solutions, organizations can create an adaptive and resilient security framework. This foundation prepares organizations to face the challenges of modern cybersecurity threats while maintaining agility and innovation in their development and operational practices.

This foundation of Intelligent Continuous Security serves as a stepping stone for implementing advanced strategies discussed in the chapters that follow, enabling organizations to thrive in a rapidly evolving cyber threat landscape.

CHAPTER 4

Empowering Teams

This chapter explores the roles, responsibilities, and team structures required to implement your Intelligent Continuous Security framework effectively. By emphasizing collaboration, alignment, and adaptability, the chapter explains the interplay between stakeholders and the strategies needed to optimize performance.

As illustrated in Figure 4-1, a wide range of stakeholders requires a well-orchestrated network of teams, including executive leadership, security teams, IT operations, developers, and compliance officers. Each team contributes unique expertise, underscoring the importance of clear delineation of responsibilities and shared objectives. The chapter also examines the challenges organizations face when roles and teams are misaligned, highlighting the necessity of fostering a collaborative culture and leveraging intelligent tools to enhance communication and decision making.

Team topology is a recurring theme, illustrating how different organizational structures can influence success or failure. Proven topologies, such as integrated security teams and centralized Centers of Excellence (CoEs), offer valuable lessons in collaboration and efficiency. Conversely, flawed structures, such as isolated silos or overloaded teams, serve as cautionary tales. By addressing challenges and adapting to evolving needs, organizations can build resilient, agile frameworks that support their Continuous Security goals.

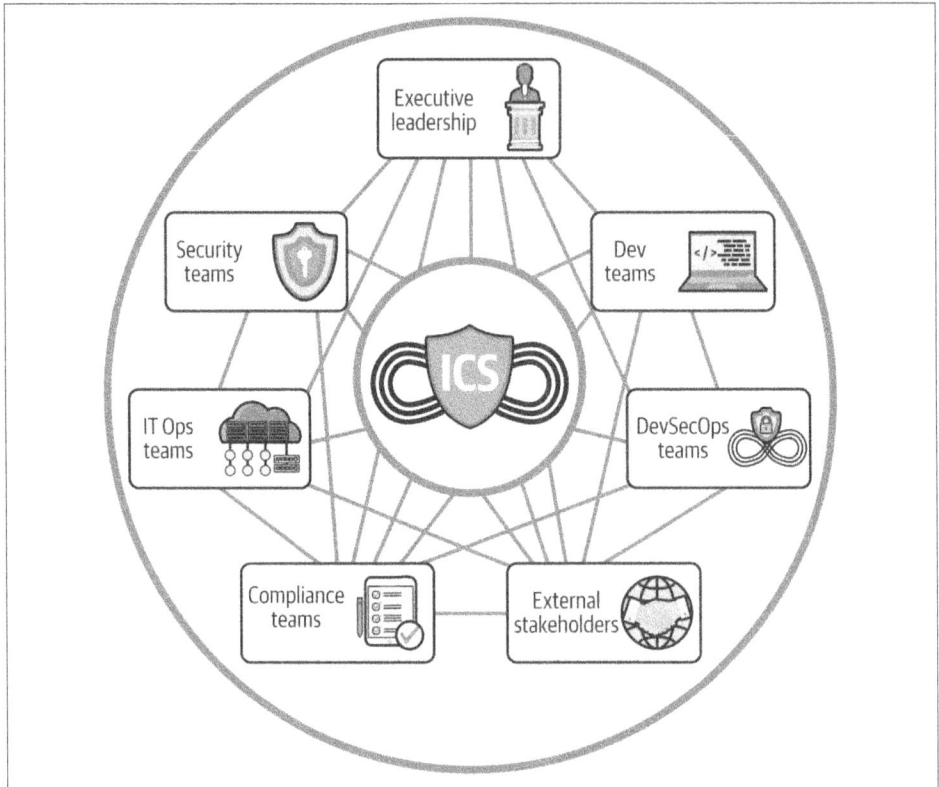

Figure 4-1. Empowering teams for Intelligent Continuous Security

Roles and Responsibilities

Each role shown in Figure 4-2 contributes unique expertise and responsibilities, with internal and external stakeholders collaborating to ensure seamless implementation and robust defense.

Within the organization, executive leadership provides strategic direction and oversight. The chief information officer (CIO) aligns IT strategies with broader business objectives, advocating for investments in AI-driven security tools and ensuring their alignment with long-term goals. The chief technology officer (CTO) evaluates the technological feasibility of these initiatives, ensuring seamless integration into existing infrastructure. Meanwhile, the chief information security officer (CISO) drives the development and execution of a robust security strategy. By focusing on risk management and regulatory compliance, the CISO bridges the gap between internal policies and external regulatory expectations, engaging with compliance teams and legal counsel to adapt security practices to emerging threats.

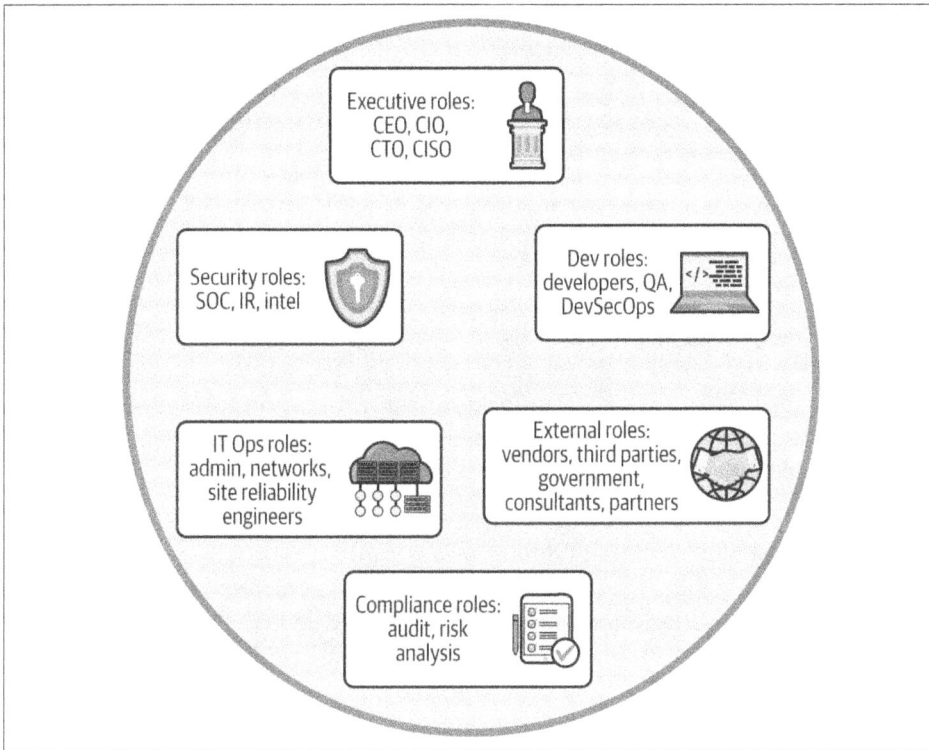

Figure 4-2. Roles and responsibilities

Security teams form the operational backbone of Intelligent Continuous Security. Security Operations Center (SOC) analysts continuously monitor the digital environment, responding to real-time threats with the support of AI tools. Some highly suitable tools include the following:

- Security information and event management (SIEM) platforms such as Splunk, IBM QRadar, and Microsoft Sentinel, which aggregate and analyze logs for real-time threat detection

- Endpoint detection and response/extended detection and response (EDR/XDR) solutions such as CrowdStrike Falcon, SentinelOne, and Palo Alto Cortex XDR, which automate endpoint threat detection and response

- Security Orchestration, Automation, and Response (SOAR) platforms such as Cortex XSOAR, Splunk SOAR, and Swimlane, which automate security workflows and incident response

- User and Entity Behavior Analytics (UEBA) tools such as Exabeam, Securonix, and Vectra AI, which detect behavioral anomalies using machine learning (ML)

Incident response teams take the lead during breaches, coordinating with legal teams, external forensic experts, and security vendors to contain and mitigate damage. Supporting these functions, threat intelligence analysts leverage AI-driven insights to predict and preempt risks, working closely with industry partners and third-party intelligence providers to stay ahead of sophisticated attacks.

Development and DevOps teams architect and integrate security into every stage of the software lifecycle. Developers and architects use AI-assisted tools during the design phase and to identify vulnerabilities during coding, ensuring that security is embedded from the outset. Quality assurance (QA) and test engineers validate these measures, maintaining high standards of application security before deployment. DevOps engineers oversee the integration of security tools into Continuous Integration/Continuous Delivery (CI/CD) pipelines, ensuring continuous oversight and a balance between speed and security. These teams work collaboratively with SOC analysts to align deployment monitoring with security protocols.

IT operations teams ensure that the infrastructure supporting Intelligent Continuous Security is robust and effective. IT administrators and site reliability engineers (SREs) manage the deployment and maintenance of security systems, interacting with external vendors to resolve technical issues and implement updates. Network engineers focus on securing digital frameworks using AI insights, working loosely with SOC teams to address vulnerabilities and maintain proactive defense mechanisms.

Compliance and risk teams safeguard the organization's adherence to regulatory frameworks. These teams collaborate with the CISO to ensure that security practices meet legal requirements, prepare for audits, and respond to inquiries from external regulators. Their efforts minimize risks while preserving the organization's reputation for security excellence.

End users play a vital role in reinforcing security measures. By following updated protocols, participating in training, and reporting anomalies, employees contribute to the organization's security culture. Their active engagement helps bridge potential gaps between operational and strategic security efforts.

Externally, vendors and third-party providers supply the tools and services essential for implementing AI-driven security solutions. Regulatory bodies and compliance organizations oversee adherence to cybersecurity standards, ensuring that the organization meets its legal obligations. Customers demand reliable and secure services, driving the continuous evolution of security practices. Industry partners and advisory consultants share insights, providing expertise to enhance threat intelligence and best practices. Technology providers, including AI platform vendors and cloud service providers (CSPs), enable the secure deployment and operation of advanced tools. Open source communities contribute innovative approaches to the development of Intelligent Continuous Security systems.

By aligning the efforts of these stakeholders, organizations create a dynamic, adaptive, and resilient security ecosystem capable of addressing the complexities of modern cybersecurity challenges. Through collaboration and clear delineation of responsibilities, this ecosystem safeguards organizational assets, data, and reputation in an ever-changing threat landscape.

AI Center of Excellence

Integrating AI roles, responsibilities, and skills into an organization requires thoughtful planning to ensure alignment with strategic goals and operational efficiency. As illustrated in Figure 4-3, an Intelligent Continuous Security CoE for AI can serve as a centralized hub, providing the expertise, tools, and governance necessary to maximize the value of Intelligent Continuous Security while promoting cross-functional collaboration.

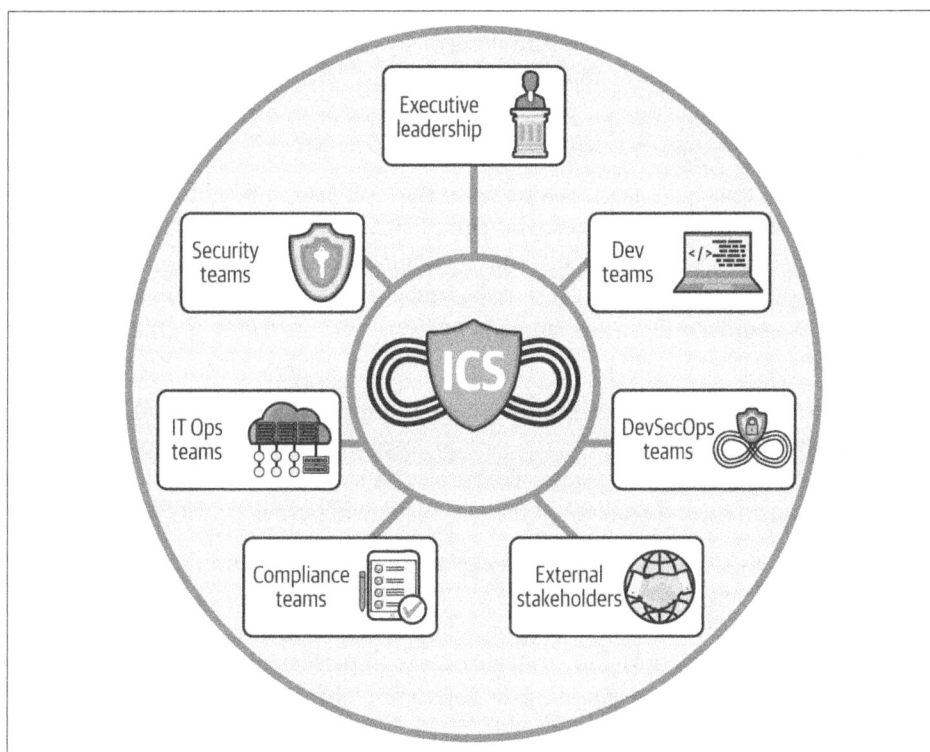

Figure 4-3. Intelligent Continuous Security Center of Excellence

The CoE becomes the organization's focal point for all AI-related activities, acting as a repository of knowledge and best practices. It houses a team of AI specialists, data scientists, and cybersecurity professionals who collaborate with one another and with other stakeholders to design, implement, optimize, sustain, and evolve AI-driven solutions. By centralizing expertise, the CoE ensures that the organization takes a unified approach to deploying AI technologies, avoiding duplication of effort and enabling consistent integration into security processes, development value streams, and IT operations.

A critical function of the CoE is to provide a standardized set of tools, frameworks, and methodologies for AI adoption. This ensures that all teams, from security and DevOps to compliance and IT, work with interoperable systems and adhere to common practices. The CoE not only facilitates the deployment of these tools but also trains teams to use them effectively, creating a seamless bridge between AI innovation and its practical application across the organization.

Collaboration is a cornerstone of the CoE's purpose. Acting as a central mediator, the CoE encourages cross-functional alignment, bringing together teams that traditionally operate in silos. For instance, the CoE works with security teams to develop AI tools for threat detection, while simultaneously collaborating with development teams to integrate these tools into CI/CD pipelines. This holistic approach ensures that AI becomes an embedded aspect of every relevant workflow rather than a standalone initiative.

Governance and oversight are also integral to the CoE's responsibilities. By establishing clear policies, ethical guidelines, and compliance standards, the CoE ensures that AI technologies are used responsibly and in alignment with regulatory requirements. This governance function mitigates risks associated with AI, such as biases in algorithms or vulnerabilities in implementation, and provides a framework for accountability.

The CoE also drives continuous improvement and innovation. It evaluates emerging AI technologies, pilots new applications, and integrates successful innovations into the organization's security ecosystem. This proactive stance ensures that the organization remains adaptive and resilient in the face of evolving cybersecurity threats.

The creation of a CoE for AI embeds AI expertise into the organizational structure in a way that enhances the capabilities of existing teams while fostering a culture of standardization and innovation. It positions the organization to harness AI's full potential, ensuring that tools and strategies are high performance, scalable, sustainable, and aligned with long-term security objectives. Through centralized leadership, the CoE acts as both a catalyst and a steward for Intelligent Continuous Security, bridging the gap between technological potential and practical implementation.

Collaboration Strategies

Collaboration is the cornerstone of success in Intelligent Continuous Security, as shown in Figure 4-4. The complexity of modern cybersecurity threats requires seamless interaction among diverse roles and expertise within an organization. When teams collaborate effectively, they can leverage collective knowledge, streamline workflows, and respond swiftly to threats. Conversely, when collaboration is poor, silos emerge, leading to misaligned priorities, inefficient operations, and increased costs and risks to cyberattacks.

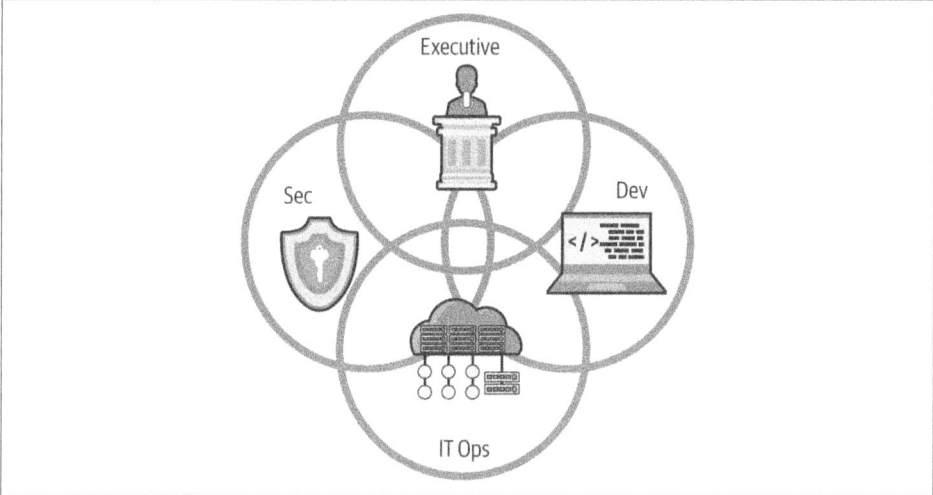

Figure 4-4. Collaboration strategies

A lack of collaboration often manifests in critical failures. For example, when security teams and developers fail to communicate, vulnerabilities may remain in code until exploitation occurs, disrupting operations and tarnishing reputations. Similarly, if compliance teams are excluded from discussions about AI implementations, organizations risk falling afoul of regulatory standards, resulting in legal penalties or breaches of customer trust. These scenarios underscore the necessity of fostering a culture of collaboration where all stakeholders work toward shared goals.

In this framework, executive leadership must serve as the guiding force, aligning all roles to the organization's overarching objectives. The CIO ensures that IT strategies, including AI initiatives, align with business goals, while the CTO works closely with developers, IT teams, and vendors to integrate AI tools into infrastructure seamlessly. The CISO bridges gaps between internal teams and external regulators, ensuring that security policies are both actionable and compliant.

Security teams rely on collaboration to function effectively. SOC analysts must communicate findings from real-time threat monitoring to incident response teams, enabling coordinated action during breaches. Threat intelligence analysts share their insights with SOC teams and development teams to proactively address vulnerabilities. These interactions require a constant flow of information and alignment on priorities, which can be facilitated through centralized tools and shared dashboards.

The interaction of development and DevOps teams with security and IT operations is equally critical. Developers must collaborate with QA and test engineers to validate the effectiveness of AI-assisted security tools, while DevOps engineers work with SOC teams to integrate continuous monitoring into CI/CD pipelines. IT administrators ensure that these pipelines are supported by robust infrastructure, maintaining open lines of communication with network engineers to address vulnerabilities proactively.

Compliance and risk teams depend on input from all other roles to fulfill their responsibilities effectively. They work with the CISO and legal counsel to align security measures with regulatory requirements, while also engaging with developers and IT operations to prepare for audits and ensure adherence to compliance frameworks.

Externally, vendors and technology providers play a collaborative role by supplying tools and expertise to enhance Intelligent Continuous Security. These providers work closely with internal teams to customize solutions, address technical challenges, and provide training. Additionally, regulatory bodies and compliance organizations interact with internal compliance teams to ensure alignment with industry standards, while industry partners and advisory consultants contribute insights to improve security practices.

To achieve success in Intelligent Continuous Security, the organization must foster an environment where these collaborative efforts are not merely encouraged but deeply embedded into daily operations. The implementation of shared platforms, regular cross-functional meetings, and centralized oversight through an AI CoE ensures that all stakeholders remain aligned. Through effective collaboration, organizations can transform the complexities of cybersecurity into a unified, adaptive defense system.

Team Topologies for Intelligent Continuous Security

Effective team topologies are critical for successfully implementing Intelligent Continuous Security (ICS), as they determine how security integrates into development, operations, and compliance workflows. This section explores optimal team structures that foster collaboration, automation, and Continuous Security enforcement, while also highlighting common anti-patterns that create silos, slow response times, and increase security risks.

Team Topologies That Work

For Intelligent Continuous Security to succeed, organizations must adopt effective team topologies that facilitate collaboration, adaptability, and alignment with strategic goals. A *team topology* defines how groups of people performing their functions in specific roles are structured, work together, and share responsibilities to achieve their objectives. Different topologies work best at various stages of organizational maturity, and understanding their strengths and limitations is critical to optimizing performance. This section discusses five team topologies that have proven effective in different organizational contexts.

Each of these topologies offers unique advantages and challenges, and their effectiveness depends on the organization's specific goals, culture, and maturity level. As organizations progress toward higher performance in Intelligent Continuous Security, they may need to evolve their team structures to address new complexities and opportunities. By choosing the right topology for the right stage of development, organizations can create a resilient and adaptive security framework that meets the demands of an ever-changing threat landscape.

The integrated security team

The integrated security team topology, illustrated in Figure 4-5, combines security, development, and operations teams into a single, cross-functional unit. In this structure, SOC analysts, developers, IT administrators, and QA engineers work side by side, leveraging shared tools and workflows.

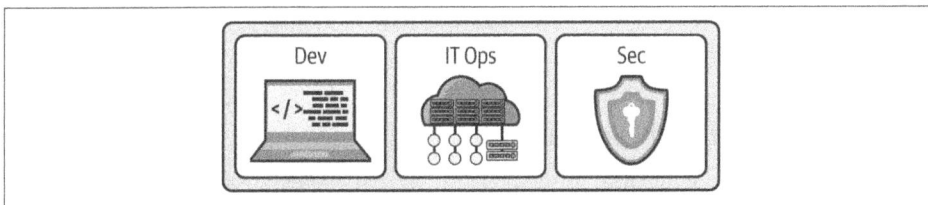

Figure 4-5. Integrated security team

This topology is advantageous because it eliminates silos and ensures that security considerations are embedded at every stage of development and operations. By fostering close collaboration, it accelerates cross-functional decision making and improves incident response times. However, it requires significant cultural alignment and training to ensure that each team member understands the discipline of every other member of the team. It is most effective in organizations with a strong emphasis on collaboration and a mature DevOps culture.

The CoE model

The CoE model, illustrated in Figure 4-6, establishes a centralized hub for AI expertise, tools, and governance. The CoE team includes AI specialists, data scientists, cybersecurity experts, and compliance officers who provide resources and guidance to other teams across the organization.

This topology centralizes knowledge and ensures consistency in AI implementation. It is particularly effective in large organizations with multiple business units that need standardized tools and practices. While the CoE model fosters innovation and strategic alignment, it may create dependencies that affect decision making if not managed carefully. As organizations mature, decentralizing some CoE functions to individual teams can help address this challenge.

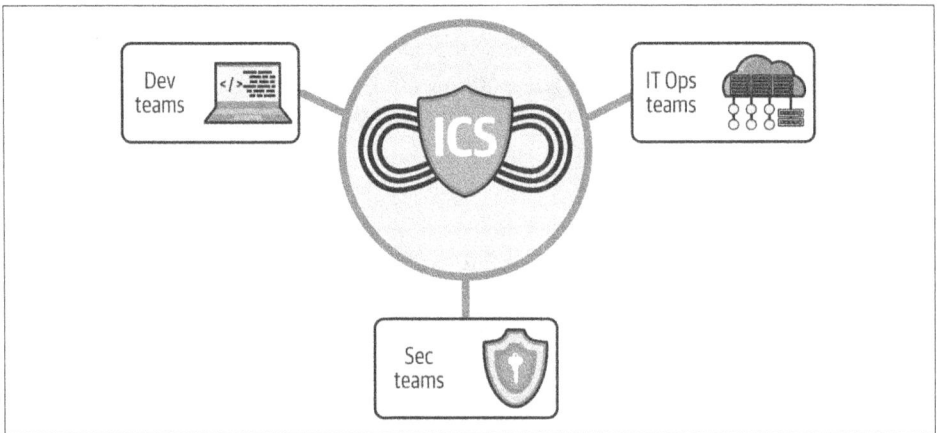

Figure 4-6. ICS Center of Excellence team structure

Embedded AI security expertise in teams

In this topology, shown in Figure 4-7, AI security specialists and cybersecurity experts are embedded within development, operations, and compliance teams. These specialists bring AI tools and knowledge directly into the workflows of their respective teams, enabling real-time problem-solving and integration.

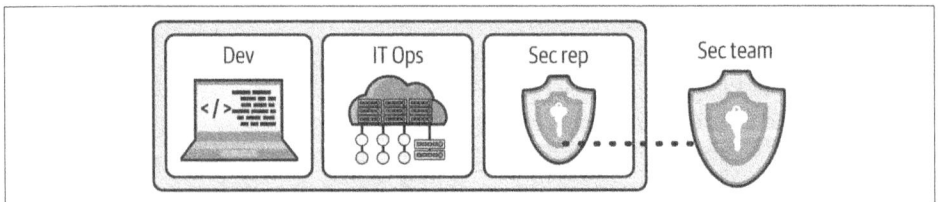

Figure 4-7. Embedded AI security team

The embedded model works well for organizations that require agility and rapid adaptation to emerging threats. It ensures that AI expertise is closely aligned with specific team goals, fostering autonomy and speed. However, it requires careful coordination to avoid duplication of effort or fragmentation of AI knowledge.

The platform team for security and AI

A platform team topology, shown in Figure 4-8, focuses on building and maintaining a centralized platform that provides AI-driven security tools and services to other teams. This platform may include threat detection systems, vulnerability management tools, and compliance dashboards.

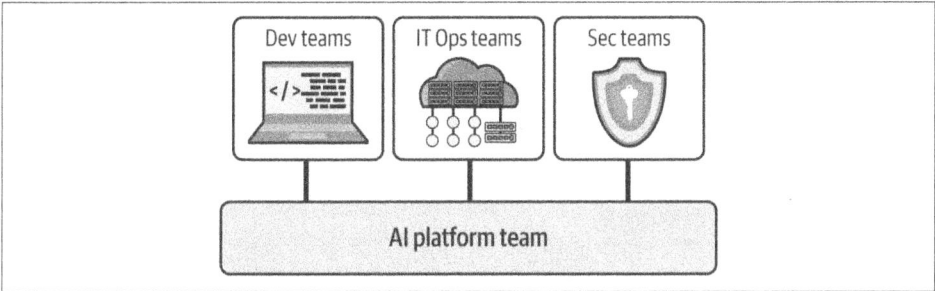

Figure 4-8. AI platform team

The platform team allows development, security, and operations teams to focus on their core responsibilities while leveraging standardized AI tools. It promotes scalability and efficiency by centralizing infrastructure management. The challenge with this topology lies in maintaining close alignment with user teams to ensure that the platform meets their needs and evolves with changing requirements.

The hybrid topology for transitional organizations

A hybrid topology can be effective for organizations transitioning to higher levels of maturity in Intelligent Continuous Security. This approach combines elements of the CoE model, embedded expertise, and platform teams, adapting the structure to specific use cases and maturity levels. An example is shown in Figure 4-9.

The hybrid topology allows organizations to experiment with different structures while leveraging the strengths of each. For example, a centralized CoE may oversee governance and innovation, while embedded experts address immediate team needs. This flexibility supports gradual organizational change but requires strong leadership to avoid confusion or misalignment.

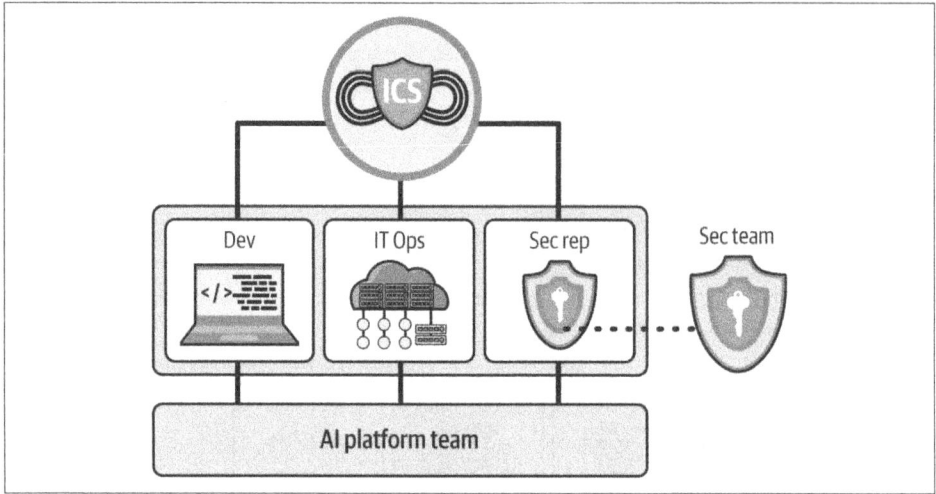

Figure 4-9. Hybrid team

Team Topologies to Avoid

While effective team topologies enable the success of Intelligent Continuous Security, certain organizational structures have consistently demonstrated an inability to achieve or sustain this goal. These failed topologies often arise from common misconceptions or temporary convenience, but their inherent flaws lead to inefficiencies, misalignment, and increased security risks. Recognizing and addressing these flawed structures is critical to building a robust security framework.

By identifying and addressing these flawed topologies, organizations can avoid the pitfalls that have derailed others. Acknowledging that no single structure is universally optimal, organizations should strive to adopt flexible, collaborative, and integrated approaches that evolve with their security needs and organizational maturity. Transitioning from these ineffective models to more adaptive topologies ensures a stronger, more resilient framework for Intelligent Continuous Security.

The isolated security silo

The isolated security silo topology, illustrated in Figure 4-10, keeps security teams separate from other functions, such as development and IT operations. This structure is often chosen by organizations that view security as a standalone responsibility rather than an integrated discipline. While it may allow security teams to specialize, it creates significant communication barriers, leading to delays in addressing vulnerabilities and a lack of alignment with development and operational workflows.

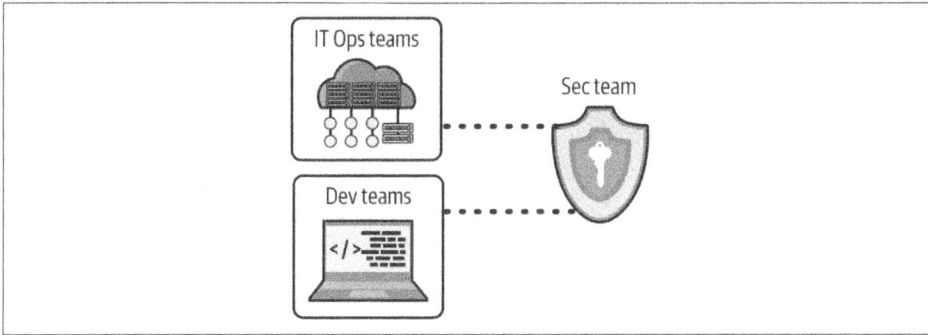

Figure 4-10. Isolated security team

This topology fails because it isolates security expertise, preventing it from being embedded into the development lifecycle. The consequences include inefficient hand-offs, lack of knowledge transfer, delayed detection of issues, last-minute fixes that disrupt delivery timelines, and poor response coordination during incidents.

The one-person security team

Some organizations rely on a single individual or a very small team to manage all aspects of Intelligent Continuous Security, as shown in Figure 4-11. This approach is often born out of resource constraints or a belief that AI tools can fully automate security processes. While this structure may seem cost-effective initially, it quickly becomes a bottleneck.

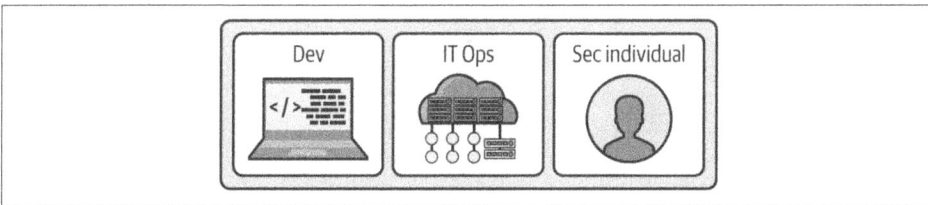

Figure 4-11. One-person security team

The one-person team is prone to failure due to the overwhelming workload placed on a single individual, leading to missed threats, burnout, and insufficient expertise to manage a dynamic security environment. Furthermore, this model lacks the collaborative input needed to integrate security into all facets of the organization.

The overloaded platform team

In this topology, shown in Figure 4-12, a centralized platform team is tasked with not only maintaining AI-driven security tools but also implementing and governing all security practices across the organization. Organizations adopt this structure to centralize responsibilities, expecting it to improve efficiency. However, this model often overburdens the platform team, leaving them unable to adequately address the diverse and specialized needs of different teams.

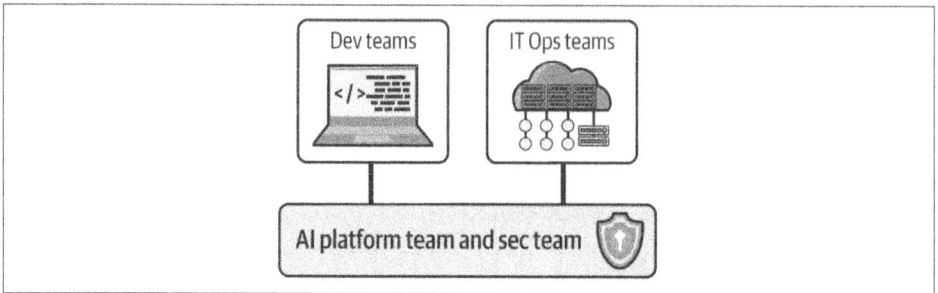

Figure 4-12. Overloaded platform team

The overloaded platform team struggles to meet the demands of a rapidly evolving threat landscape. User teams may experience delays in accessing necessary tools and updates, leading to frustration and the proliferation of shadow IT practices. Over time, the lack of responsiveness undermines both security and trust within the organization.

The isolated AI CoE

An AI CoE can be highly effective when it is integrated into the organization's value streams. However, as shown in Figure 4-13, when the CoE operates in isolation, disconnected from the day-to-day realities of security teams, development teams, and compliance efforts, it becomes a bottleneck rather than an enabler.

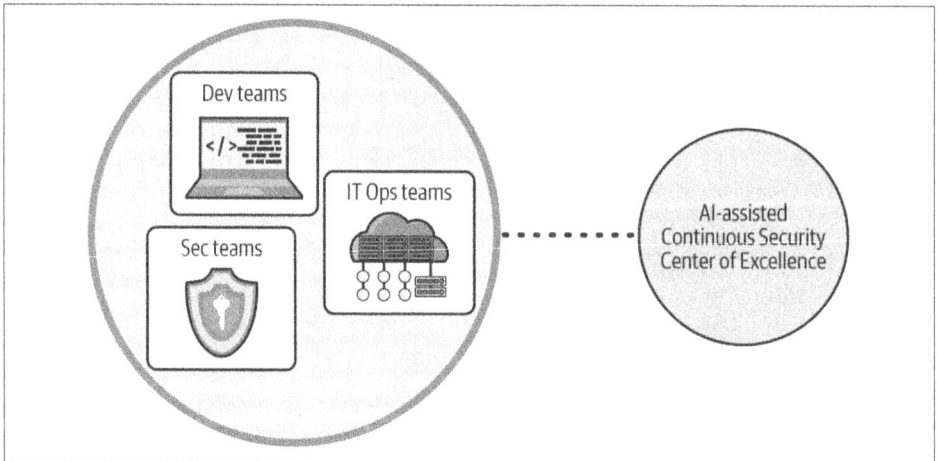

Figure 4-13. Isolated Center of Excellence

The isolated CoE fails because it lacks direct interaction with teams that apply AI-driven tools. The resulting gap between innovation and implementation leads to tools and practices that are misaligned with operational needs. This structure often results in underutilized AI investments and fragmented security strategies.

The inflexible hierarchical structure

Traditional hierarchical structures that enforce strict top-down decision making, as shown in Figure 4-14, often hinder the agility required for Intelligent Continuous Security. These structures are typically found in organizations with rigid chains of command, where decisions and initiatives are delayed by bureaucratic processes.

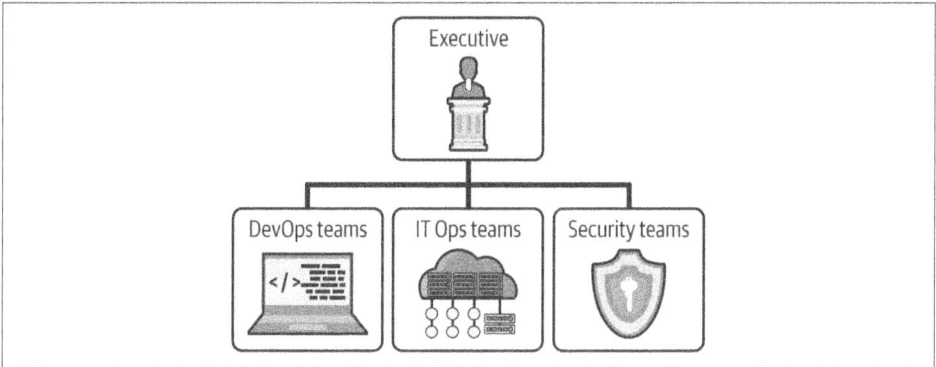

Figure 4-14. Inflexible hierarchical structure

This topology fails because it does not adapt to the fast-paced nature of cybersecurity threats. Security issues that require immediate cross-functional collaboration are bogged down in approval processes, leaving the organization vulnerable. Additionally, the lack of autonomy for teams stifles innovation and responsiveness, which are critical elements for effective AI implementation.

Overcoming Team Challenges

Achieving success with Intelligent Continuous Security requires recognizing and addressing the challenges that can arise within different team topologies. Whether an organization is employing a proven structure or transitioning away from a flawed one, understanding potential pitfalls and how to address them is essential for maintaining efficiency, alignment, and adaptability.

Addressing challenges in proven topologies

For the integrated security team, the biggest challenge is often cultural misalignment. When team members from diverse backgrounds—such as security, development, and operations—fail to adopt a shared mindset, misunderstandings and inefficiencies arise. To prevent this, organizations must invest in cross-training, joint team-building exercises, and shared performance metrics. If misalignment occurs, leadership should facilitate structured workshops to rebuild trust and realign team goals.

In the CoE model, dependency on the central team can create bottlenecks, especially as the organization scales. This can slow innovation and reduce responsiveness. To mitigate this, CoEs should focus on decentralizing some responsibilities by empowering individual teams with tools, templates, and training. When bottlenecks emerge, organizations should evaluate which functions can be delegated to specific teams while the CoE focuses on governance and innovation.

As time goes on, the CoE topology can evolve to a C4E (Center for Enablement) model. In ICS, a C4E acts as a strategic enabler rather than a bottleneck, ensuring that security practices are embedded into DevOps workflows without slowing down development and operations. Instead of a centralized security team enforcing rigid controls, a C4E provides reusable security automation frameworks, AI-driven compliance enforcement, and self-service security tools to empower product teams to integrate Continuous Security autonomously. C4E enhances ICS by offering Security as a Self-Service capability, which provides developers and engineers with preapproved security guardrails, automated compliance checks, and AI-driven vulnerability management.

Embedded AI expertise in teams can lead to fragmentation if AI specialists operate in isolation within their assigned teams. This diminishes the broader alignment of AI practices across the organization. Regularly scheduled knowledge-sharing sessions and CoE oversight can prevent this issue. If fragmentation occurs, creating cross-team AI guilds or working groups can reestablish cohesion and alignment.

For the platform team for security and AI, misalignment between the platform's capabilities and user team needs can result in underutilized resources. Regular feedback loops, including user surveys and advisory panels, help ensure that the platform evolves alongside team requirements. When misalignment is detected, conducting rapid feedback sessions and reprioritizing platform updates can address the gap.

The hybrid topology for transitional organizations can suffer from confusion if roles and responsibilities are not clearly defined. To counteract this, organizations should map out responsibilities at the start of the transition and provide ongoing updates as the structure evolves. If confusion arises, leadership must step in quickly to clarify roles, using documented workflows and realigned goals to eliminate ambiguity.

Transitioning from ineffective to proven topologies

Organizations using the isolated security silo must break down communication barriers and embed security into workflows. Transitioning to the integrated security team or embedded AI expertise in teams can address these issues. This requires creating shared tools and metrics, as well as embedding security specialists into development and operations teams to ensure continuous collaboration.

For the one-person security team, expanding the team is the first step toward transitioning to a sustainable model, such as the platform team for security and AI or the CoE model. Organizations should prioritize hiring or contracting additional expertise and leverage automated AI tools to reduce the burden on individual team members.

Organizations facing challenges with the overloaded platform team should adopt a hybrid approach by decentralizing noncritical functions to embedded teams while maintaining governance through the platform. Transitioning to a combination of embedded AI expertise in teams and the CoE model ensures scalability and responsiveness without overburdening the central team.

To address the shortcomings of the isolated AI CoE, organizations must integrate the CoE into day-to-day workflows. A transition to the platform team for security and AI or a hybrid model can align the CoE with operational teams, ensuring that innovation and implementation are synchronized.

Finally, for organizations trapped in the inflexible hierarchical structure, flattening the hierarchy and adopting the hybrid topology for transitional organizations enables faster decision making and better collaboration. Empowering teams with autonomy and integrating cross-functional workflows reduces delays and improves agility.

By proactively addressing these challenges and transitioning away from ineffective topologies, organizations can foster a dynamic and resilient framework for Intelligent Continuous Security. These strategies ensure that the organization remains agile, collaborative, and prepared to navigate the complexities of the modern cybersecurity landscape.

Summary

This chapter emphasized the importance of aligning team roles, skills, and structures to achieve success with Intelligent Continuous Security. By exploring both effective and ineffective team topologies, the chapter provided valuable insights into what does and does not work. The transition from flawed structures to proven models is essential for fostering a culture of collaboration and resilience in the face of evolving cybersecurity challenges.

One of the key takeaways is the necessity of flexibility and adaptability in team design. Organizations must recognize that no single topology is universally optimal; instead, team structures should evolve with the organization's maturity and changing needs. Proven topologies, such as integrated security teams and CoEs, highlight the benefits of cross-functional collaboration and centralized expertise. At the same time, the pitfalls of isolated silos and overloaded teams serve as cautionary examples of what to avoid.

Ultimately, the success of Intelligent Continuous Security depends on more than just tools and technology. It requires cohesive teams, clear communication, and a commitment to continuous improvement. By leveraging the strategies and lessons outlined in this chapter, organizations can build a robust, adaptive security framework that protects assets, fosters innovation, and supports long-term goals in an increasingly complex digital landscape.

CHAPTER 5

Generative AI and Machine Learning for ICS

The cybersecurity landscape has shifted dramatically in recent years. Traditional, rule-based defenses that once sufficed now struggle to keep pace with the sheer speed and sophistication of modern threats. Attackers are evolving faster than ever, exploiting gaps in static systems and adapting to the defenses deployed against them. This accelerating threat environment demands an approach to security that is not only reactive but proactive and adaptive. It's here that AI and machine learning (ML) emerge as game-changers, offering capabilities that were unimaginable just a decade ago. Recent breaches such as Log4j and MOVEit exploited vulnerabilities in widely used software, allowing attackers to execute remote code and exfiltrate sensitive data before traditional defenses could react. AI-driven real-time anomaly detection and automated patch prioritization could have mitigated these risks by identifying unusual behavior patterns early and autonomously enforcing security patches before exploitation occurred.

This chapter explores how AI and ML are being leveraged to redefine the very foundation of Continuous Security. Far from being mere buzzwords, these technologies are driving a paradigm shift in how organizations detect, respond to, and prevent threats. Generative AI (GenAI) creates entirely new content, from synthetic datasets for threat simulations to real-time response playbooks tailored to specific incidents. Meanwhile, ML analyzes massive streams of data to uncover anomalies, predict attack vectors, and automate responses—all with unparalleled speed and precision.

But the journey to integrating AI into security is not without its challenges. Beyond technical hurdles, there are questions of ethics, sustainability, and alignment with organizational goals. How do you ensure that AI datasets and researchers do not inadvertently introduce bias into threat detection? How do you sustain these systems so that they remain effective as the threat landscape evolves? And, critically, how do you validate that these technologies truly deliver on their promise without becoming overly reliant on them?

As you move through this chapter, you'll delve into the practical applications of GenAI and ML in security, explore the best practices for their deployment, and confront the tough questions surrounding their use. This is not just about adopting the latest technology; it's about building a security framework that is resilient, intelligent, and ready for the challenges of tomorrow. In a world where threats never stand still, neither can our defenses. AI and ML are the tools that make Continuous Security not just a goal, but a reality.

In today's fast-paced digital landscape, businesses face an ever-evolving threat environment. Adversaries are constantly refining their methods, making traditional, static approaches to cybersecurity increasingly ineffective. As illustrated in Figure 5-1, the integration of GenAI and ML is transformative for organizations striving to achieve Intelligent Continuous Security. Let's explore these technologies and their roles in reshaping how we protect our systems and data.

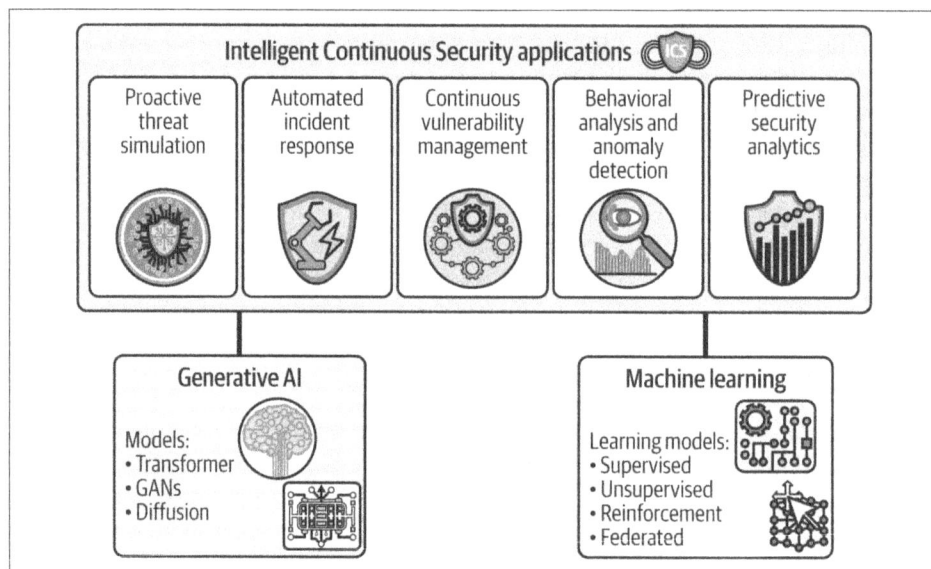

Figure 5-1. Integration of AI and ML for Intelligent Continuous Security

Generative AI for Continuous Security

GenAI represents a transformative approach within AI, emphasizing the creation of new content based on patterns learned from existing data. Unlike traditional AI models, which focus on classification or prediction, generative models are designed to *generate*—whether that's text, code, or even synthetic security datasets. This capability offers immense value in cybersecurity, where creating proactive measures is as critical as reactive defenses.

One powerful application of GenAI lies in the creation of synthetic datasets for training ML models. For instance, simulated attack scenarios or unusual network behaviors can prepare organizations to defend against novel threats. Beyond simulation, GenAI assists in automating repetitive tasks, such as drafting incident response playbooks, generating vulnerability reports, or creating detailed security documentation. By producing actionable outputs in real time, GenAI empowers security teams to stay ahead of attackers.

GenAI can also help with AI *privacy compliance*, which refers to GenAI's ability to automate and enforce data protection regulations by identifying, masking, and governing sensitive information in real time. AI-driven compliance tools can detect and redact personally identifiable information (PII), monitor data access, and ensure adherence to frameworks such as the General Data Protection Regulation (GDPR), California Consumer Privacy Act (CCPA), and Health Insurance Portability and Accountability Act (HIPAA), reducing human error and improving regulatory alignment at scale.

Generative adversarial networks (GANs) and diffusion models both generate synthetic data, but they do so in fundamentally different ways. GANs employ a competitive framework where a generator creates data and a discriminator evaluates its realism, making GANs highly effective for producing lifelike images, deep fakes, and security testing simulations (e.g., AI-generated phishing attacks or malware variants). In contrast, diffusion models generate data by starting with noise and iteratively refining it over multiple steps, making them particularly well suited for producing highly detailed, controllable synthetic data, such as anonymized training datasets for privacy-compliant AI applications.

Machine Learning for Continuous Security

ML underpins modern Continuous Security by enabling systems to identify patterns, make decisions, and adapt without explicit programming. Its power lies in its ability to detect anomalies, predict threats, and automate incident responses in dynamic threat landscapes. Unlike traditional security methods, which rely on predefined rules or signatures, ML thrives on its capacity to uncover unknown threats.

One of ML's core applications in Continuous Security is anomaly detection. By analyzing data from network logs, endpoint behaviors, and user activities, ML models establish baselines for normal operations. When deviations occur—such as unexpected access to sensitive files—these models rapidly identify and flag anomalies for further investigation. This capacity to detect the unknown provides a critical edge in combating emerging threats.

Several ML techniques drive these capabilities. *Supervised* learning, trained on labeled datasets, excels at identifying known malware or phishing attempts. In contrast, *unsupervised* learning processes unlabeled data to uncover unknown threats, such as insider risks, through clustering and anomaly detection. *Reinforcement* learning applications for security use cases are relatively novel but potentially could allow systems to adapt over time by interacting with their environment, optimizing performance in tasks such as intrusion detection by minimizing false positives. Additionally, *federated* learning, which is also relatively novel, has the potential to enable organizations to collaboratively train ML models across distributed systems, balancing insights with data privacy—a crucial factor in today's collaborative cybersecurity efforts.

Combining Generative AI and Machine Learning for Continuous Security

The convergence of GenAI's creative capabilities with ML's adaptability fuels innovative solutions for Continuous Security. Together, these technologies redefine how organizations approach threat simulation, incident response, and predictive analytics, among other areas.

One standout application is *proactive threat simulation*, where GenAI creates realistic attack scenarios for training security teams and ML models. By simulating new forms of ransomware, phishing campaigns, or zero-day exploits, organizations can evolve their defenses alongside emerging threats.

Automated incident response is another area of synergy. While ML algorithms in Security Orchestration, Automation, and Response (SOAR) platforms analyze threats and trigger automated responses, GenAI can dynamically generate incident response playbooks tailored to the specifics of the attack. This could help the organization minimize service disruption, or even prevent it.

In *continuous vulnerability management*, ML prioritizes vulnerabilities based on risk levels, while GenAI generates detailed remediation instructions or simulates the impact of exploits. This integration helps security teams allocate resources effectively.

Behavioral analysis and anomaly detection also benefit from the combination of these technologies. ML continuously monitors user and entity behaviors to identify deviations, while GenAI supplements alerts with actionable recommendations or detailed summaries for security teams.

Finally, *predictive security analytics* illustrates the forward-looking power of this integration. ML models identify trends in historical data, forecasting potential attack vectors or vulnerable systems. GenAI builds on this by simulating future attack scenarios, helping teams prepare mitigations in advance. This blend of predictive insights and generative foresight equips organizations with a proactive and dynamic approach to securing their environments.

GenAI and ML are not just tools; they are transformative forces in the evolving cybersecurity landscape. By integrating these technologies, organizations can build adaptive, resilient, and intelligent security frameworks capable of addressing today's threats while preparing for tomorrow's challenges.

AI and ML Technologies for Continuous Security

AI and ML are reshaping security practices across every phase of the product and service lifecycle, as shown in Figure 5-2.

By integrating these intelligent systems into practices, organizations can transition from reactive approaches to proactive, adaptive defenses. Let's take a deeper dive into how AI and ML bring value to each phase, weaving in practical, real-world scenarios to illustrate their impact.

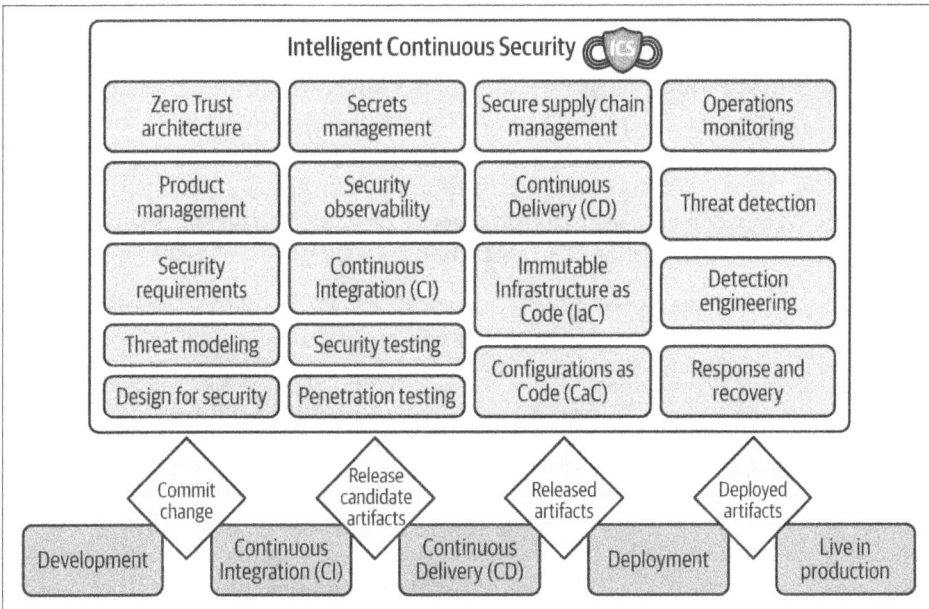

Figure 5-2. AI and ML technologies for Intelligent Continuous Security

Zero Trust architecture principles have become a cornerstone of modern security, with their "trust nothing, verify everything" philosophy. AI elevates these principles by dynamically assessing access requests based on behavior, context, and risk. For example, say a financial analyst logs in from their regular office computer daily. One day, an access attempt comes from an unfamiliar device in a different country. Instead of blindly granting access based on credentials alone, an AI system detects this as unusual behavior and immediately denies the request, requiring additional verification. By continuously analyzing patterns, AI doesn't just enforce Zero Trust; it adapts it to evolving risks.

Secrets management for things such as API keys and encryption credentials is often the Achilles' heel of security. Imagine a developer accidentally pushing an unencrypted API key to a public repository. Without AI, that mistake might go unnoticed until it's too late. Instead, an AI-powered scanning tool detects the exposure almost immediately, flags the incident, and even rotates the key automatically. This seamless intervention not only neutralizes the threat but also prevents human oversight from becoming a catastrophic breach.

Identity and access management (IAM) can feel like a delicate balancing act between security and usability. AI makes this easier by introducing adaptive authentication. Consider a system administrator logging in at odd hours from a new device. AI doesn't block them outright; instead, it intelligently escalates the security requirements, prompting for additional verification such as a biometric scan. When the administrator passes the challenge, access is granted seamlessly. This nuanced approach ensures security without unnecessarily frustrating users.

AI even supports product management by setting priorities for features and improvements. For example, say a healthcare app team uses an AI tool to analyze user feedback and identify recurring concerns about data privacy. The system flags this trend and suggests prioritizing end-to-end encryption in the next development cycle. By embedding AI into the decision-making process, product managers ensure that security becomes an integral part of user satisfaction and compliance efforts.

The security requirements phase is where security gets its first footing. AI can analyze past breaches and compliance standards to recommend robust requirements. Imagine a fintech startup working on a new payment app. AI scans historical data about financial sector breaches and suggests integrating multifactor authentication (MFA) and secure data encryption right from the start. These proactive recommendations ensure that security is not an afterthought but a foundational element of the project.

Threat modeling often feels like predicting the unpredictable. AI simplifies this by simulating likely attack paths and identifying weak points in the system design. For instance, a cloud service provider (CSP) designing a multitenant architecture uses an AI-driven tool to analyze its proposed network. The tool identifies risks such as lateral movement between tenants and recommends network segmentation to limit exposure. With AI's insights, the team fortifies its defenses before any vulnerabilities are introduced.

Design for security anticipates bad actors. AI validates architectural decisions by simulating how secure they would be under attack. Take a smart-home device manufacturer creating a new hub. AI simulates potential data breaches, flagging areas where sensitive user data might be exposed. The system recommends implementing end-to-end encryption and biometric authentication, strengthening API security. By incorporating AI early, the final design is robust and user trust is maintained.

During the Continuous Integration (CI) phase, security risks can be introduced with every code commit. AI integrates seamlessly into CI pipelines to prevent vulnerabilities from slipping through. Imagine a developer pushing code changes that inadvertently introduce an insecure input validation method, such as using simple string matching or regular expressions that are too lenient. Before the code merges, AI scans it, identifies the flaw, and even suggests a secure alternative. This real-time intervention keeps development moving while ensuring security.

Continuous Delivery (CD) thrives on speed, but every deployment carries potential risks. AI ensures that these risks are mitigated by analyzing deployment artifacts and configurations. Picture an organization deploying a Kubernetes cluster. An AI tool scans the configuration and detects an overly permissive role binding, which could allow unauthorized access. The deployment is paused and the AI recommends a more secure configuration, ensuring that production remains safe.

Automated security testing has always been crucial, but AI makes it smarter and faster. For example, a banking app undergoing final testing uses AI to simulate a range of attacks, from SQL injection to API abuse. The AI adapts its tests to the app's specific codebase, uncovering vulnerabilities that traditional tools might miss. By the time the app launches, it's resilient against even advanced threats.

Penetration testing is vital for uncovering vulnerabilities, but traditional methods can be slow and labor intensive. AI transforms this process into something more efficient and comprehensive. Imagine a global retailer preparing for its busiest shopping season. An AI-powered penetration testing tool simulates a ransomware attack, revealing gaps in the company's backup and recovery systems. These insights allow the IT team to shore up defenses before the busy season begins, ensuring uninterrupted operations even under potential threat.

Immutable Infrastructure as Code (IaC) ensures that systems are never modified after deployment, eliminating configuration drift. AI enhances this by validating IaC templates to ensure that they adhere to security best practices. For instance, an ecommerce platform deploying with IaC scripts for Terraform uses AI to analyze the configurations. The AI identifies an open port that could allow unauthorized access and flags it for correction. This proactive measure ensures that every deployed environment is secure, consistent, and compliant.

Managing Configurations as Code (CaC) brings consistency across environments, but even minor missteps can introduce vulnerabilities. AI tools continuously monitor and validate these configurations. Picture a telecommunications provider automating firewall rules through CaC. AI analyzes the rules and detects a misalignment that could allow unauthorized inbound traffic. Without disrupting operations, the AI corrects the configuration, maintaining security while ensuring compliance with industry regulations.

Progressive deployments, such as canary or blue-green strategies, allow for incremental rollouts. AI adds a critical layer of observability during these phases, monitoring for anomalies in real time. Consider a social media platform rolling out a new feature to a subset of users using a canary deployment strategy. AI detects unusual error rates and identifies potential security issues caused by the update. The system automatically halts the rollout and triggers a rollback, preventing a flawed release from affecting the broader user base.

Security observability provides deep insights into how systems behave, and AI takes this further by correlating logs, metrics, and traces to uncover hidden threats. Imagine a financial services company monitoring transactions for fraud. AI detects a subtle pattern of unusually small withdrawals spread across multiple accounts—behavior that traditional monitoring might overlook. By identifying and flagging these anomalies, AI enables the company to act quickly and prevent significant losses.

AI transforms operations monitoring into an intelligent, proactive process. Consider a cloud hosting provider experiencing a sudden CPU spike across several servers. Traditional dashboards might highlight the spike but leave the root cause unclear. AI not only identifies the spike but correlates it with unusual network activity, revealing that the servers are part of a cryptojacking attack. The system isolates the affected instances and deploys patched replacements automatically, minimizing downtime and disruption.

Incident response is often a race against time, and AI helps organizations stay ahead. Imagine a large enterprise hit by a phishing attack. AI quickly analyzes the scope of the breach, identifies compromised accounts, and disables them before they can be exploited further. Simultaneously, it generates a tailored incident response plan, enabling the security team to focus on recovery rather than triage. This streamlined response minimizes impact and ensures consistency across teams.

Threat detection requires equally sophisticated detection methods. AI excels by identifying patterns that human analysts might miss. For example, a government agency notices unusual communication between internal servers. AI flags the activity as lateral movement—a hallmark of advanced persistent threats (APTs). By intervening early, the agency prevents sensitive data from being exfiltrated, stopping the attack before it can cause irreparable harm.

Detection engineering focuses on crafting precise and actionable alerts, and AI makes these alerts smarter and more efficient. Imagine a SOC team drowning in false positives. AI refines the detection logic by analyzing historical data and tuning thresholds, reducing false positives by 70%. This allows analysts to focus on real threats, improving their productivity and the organization's overall security posture.

AI supports the entire response and recovery process, from containment to post-incident analysis. Picture a hospital system hit by ransomware. AI helps identify which systems are compromised, validates the integrity of backups, and guides the recovery process step-by-step. Once systems are restored, AI analyzes the attack to identify how the breach occurred and recommends measures to prevent similar incidents in the future. By learning from the attack, the organization emerges stronger and better prepared.

Continuous Security governance for compliance frameworks such as those from the National Institute of Standards and Technology (NIST) can use AI to automate continuous compliance processes. Imagine a manufacturing company undergoing an audit for ISO/IEC 27001 certification. AI continuously scans the company's configurations and processes against the standard, identifying gaps and generating detailed compliance reports. When regulations change, AI adapts, providing proactive updates to keep the organization ahead of the curve.

Secure Supply Chain Management: Safeguarding Dependencies

The software supply chain has become a significant target for attackers, as evidenced by high-profile incidents such as those against SolarWinds and Log4Shell. Secure supply chain management ensures that every dependency, from third-party libraries to vendor software, is verified, monitored, and protected. AI and ML bring a new level of vigilance and adaptability to this critical aspect of modern security.

In a traditional supply chain, ensuring the security of dependencies is often manual and fragmented, leaving gaps that attackers exploit. AI changes the game by continuously analyzing the software supply chain for vulnerabilities, misconfigurations, or malicious behavior. Imagine an organization relying on hundreds of open source libraries. Without AI, tracking vulnerabilities across this complex web of dependencies would be a monumental task. With AI, tools such as dependency scanners automatically flag outdated or vulnerable components, ensuring that they are addressed before entering production.

AI also excels at anomaly detection within supply chain processes. For example, if a software build process unexpectedly incorporates a modified dependency, AI can alert the team and halt the pipeline. In one instance, an enterprise software provider integrated an AI-powered supply chain monitoring tool that identified a compromised library added to its build process. By halting the deployment and recommending corrective actions, the AI prevented what could have been a devastating attack.

Beyond detection, AI supports remediation by providing actionable insights. For example, if a vulnerability is found in a commonly used library, AI tools can recommend alternative libraries, suggest secure configurations, or even generate patches. These capabilities significantly reduce the time and effort required to maintain a secure supply chain.

Collaboration is another critical component of secure supply chain management, and AI facilitates this by enabling federated learning across organizations. This approach allows companies to share insights about vulnerabilities without exposing sensitive data, fostering a collective defense against supply chain threats. For example, AI-powered threat intelligence platforms aggregate and anonymize data from multiple organizations to identify emerging risks across the software ecosystem.

Secure supply chain management is no longer optional—it's essential. By integrating AI and ML into this process, organizations can proactively manage their dependencies, mitigate risks, and ensure the integrity of their software from development to deployment. In an era where a single compromised component can affect thousands, AI empowers teams to protect their supply chains with speed and precision.

With AI and ML integrated into every phase of the product and service lifecycle, organizations can build a security posture that is dynamic, adaptive, and intelligent. From detecting hidden threats to automating compliance, the examples woven through this section show how AI transforms security into a seamless, proactive process. In an era of increasing complexity and sophistication, this approach is not just beneficial; it's essential for balancing prevention, detection, and correction security practices.

Evaluating and Selecting AI Technologies for AI-Assisted Continuous Security

Choosing the right AI technology for AI-assisted Continuous Security is one of the most consequential decisions an organization can make in its security strategy. The promise of AI lies in its ability to amplify defenses, automate complex tasks, and adapt to evolving threats. However, the risks of making a poor choice are equally significant. A poorly selected AI technology can lead to false positives that drown security teams in noise, false negatives that let real threats slip through, and integration issues that disrupt workflows rather than enhance them. Moreover, investing in an ill-suited or overly complex solution can waste time and resources while failing to address the security challenges the organization set out to solve.

Given these stakes, organizations must follow a systematic, stepwise process to evaluate and select the right AI solution. Careful evaluation ensures that the chosen technology aligns with business needs, integrates seamlessly with existing systems, and delivers measurable improvements in security outcomes.

The Importance of a Methodical Approach

When an organization decides to seek out AI technologies for a specific security application, the journey begins with clarity. Rushing to adopt the latest tool or vendor without a structured evaluation risks solving the wrong problem—or introducing new ones. Imagine a retail company facing challenges in detecting insider threats. If the company hastily deploys an AI-powered endpoint detection tool designed for external attacks, it may fail to address the real need while incurring additional complexity in managing unnecessary capabilities.

A methodical approach, illustrated in Figure 5-3, allows organizations to narrow their focus, establish clear objectives, and measure each potential solution against those objectives. It also ensures that stakeholders across security, operations, and IT align on what success looks like, which is critical for the long-term adoption and effectiveness of any chosen technology.

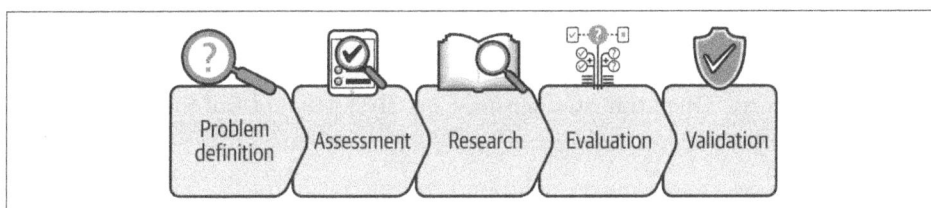

Figure 5-3. Evaluating and selecting AI and ML technologies for Continuous Security

A Stepwise Process for Evaluation and Selection

The process begins with defining the problem and understanding the environment in which the AI solution will operate. For example, consider an organization struggling with anomaly detection across its cloud infrastructure. The first step is to articulate the challenge; is the priority reducing false positives, improving detection speed, or addressing blind spots in hybrid cloud environments? Clearly identifying the problem ensures that the evaluation focuses on solutions capable of addressing those needs.

Next comes an assessment of the organization's current capabilities and gaps. If the existing security stack includes robust endpoint monitoring but lacks advanced network visibility, the evaluation should prioritize AI tools with strong network analytics capabilities. At this stage, organizations should also consider their readiness to implement and maintain an AI solution. A sophisticated tool requiring extensive customization may not suit a smaller organization with limited resources.

The next step involves surveying the available solutions. Vendor research should include a review of each tool's capabilities, scalability, and track record in environments similar to the organization's own. For example, a financial institution evaluating AI solutions for fraud detection might prioritize tools with proven success in detecting anomalies in large-scale transactional data. Engaging with peer reviews, analyst reports, and case studies provides valuable insights into how these tools perform in real-world scenarios.

Once a short list of potential solutions is established, organizations should arrange for demonstrations and hands-on trials. This step is critical for understanding not just the technical features but also the usability and compatibility of the solution. For instance, a manufacturing company evaluating an AI-powered intrusion detection system might run a trial simulating a known threat to observe how effectively the tool identifies the attack and how actionable its alerts are. Trials help validate vendor claims and uncover limitations that may not be apparent from product documentation alone.

With trial data in hand, organizations can move to detailed comparisons, measuring each solution against predefined criteria. These criteria should cover functional requirements, technical performance (accuracy, speed, and scalability), integration requirements (compatibility with existing systems and workflows), and operational considerations (ease of use and support). Stakeholder input is crucial here; what works for a Security Operations Center (SOC) analyst may not suit the IT operations team, and vice versa.

Due diligence doesn't stop once a solution is selected. Contract negotiations should include detailed service level agreements (SLAs) and clear expectations for support, updates, and future roadmap alignment. Organizations should also plan for a phased implementation, starting with a limited deployment to validate the solution in a controlled environment before scaling up. This approach minimizes disruption and provides a safety net for adjustments.

Validating the Choice

Selecting a solution is only the beginning. *Validation* ensures that the chosen AI technology delivers on its promises. During initial deployment, metrics should be established to measure success. If the solution is designed to enhance threat detection, key performance indicators (KPIs) might include a reduction in false positives, improved detection speed, and greater coverage of attack vectors. For example, a healthcare organization implementing an AI-driven anomaly detection tool might monitor how well the tool flags unusual data access patterns indicative of insider threats.

Regular reviews and feedback loops with stakeholders are equally important. These ensure that the tool adapts to the evolving needs of the organization and remains aligned with its security goals. If gaps or inefficiencies emerge, these reviews provide an opportunity to recalibrate or even reconsider the solution.

Finally, organizations should maintain an iterative mindset. AI technology evolves rapidly, and today's cutting-edge solution may require enhancements or replacements in the future. A validated choice is not just one that works today but one that positions the organization for success as threats and technologies *evolve*.

The process of evaluating and selecting AI technologies for AI-assisted Continuous Security is a journey that requires care, clarity, and collaboration. By defining the problem, assessing organizational needs, thoroughly vetting potential solutions, and validating performance post-deployment, organizations can ensure that their investment delivers meaningful, measurable security outcomes and improvements. Choosing wisely doesn't just protect against today's threats. It builds a foundation for resilience in the face of tomorrow's challenges.

Ethical Considerations in Evaluating AI Technologies for Security Applications

Ethical considerations are increasingly critical in evaluating and selecting AI technologies for security applications, as illustrated in Figure 5-4. These technologies hold immense power to enhance defenses, automate tasks, and adapt to evolving threats. However, their misuse—or even unintended consequences of their use—can raise significant ethical concerns, including privacy violations, discrimination, lack of transparency, and erosion of trust. Addressing these issues is not just a matter of corporate responsibility; it directly impacts the long-term success and acceptability of the chosen solutions.

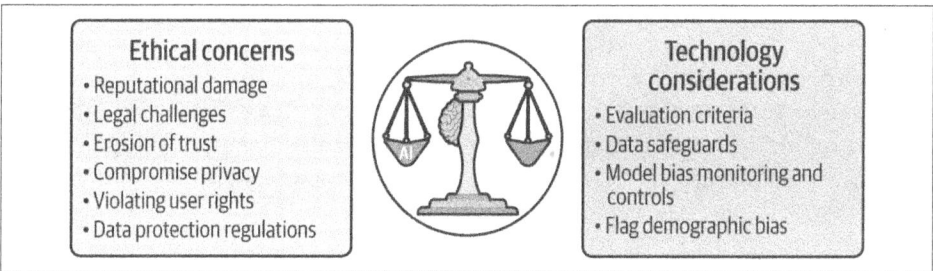

Ethical concerns	Technology considerations
• Reputational damage • Legal challenges • Erosion of trust • Compromise privacy • Violating user rights • Data protection regulations	• Evaluation criteria • Data safeguards • Model bias monitoring and controls • Flag demographic bias

Figure 5-4. Ethical considerations of AI technologies

The Stakes of Ethical Missteps

When AI technologies are deployed in security contexts, they often operate in sensitive environments, analyzing vast amounts of data, making decisions, and influencing workflows. Poor ethical practices in this domain can lead to profound consequences. Imagine an AI-powered threat detection tool that uses biased training data. Such a system could disproportionately flag specific groups or regions as risks, leading to reputational damage, legal challenges, and erosion of trust with stakeholders.

Another potential issue arises with privacy. AI technologies for anomaly detection or identity verification often require access to sensitive personal data. Without strict ethical guidelines, these tools could inadvertently collect or expose more data than necessary, violating user rights and data protection regulations such as GDPR or CCPA. For instance, a company implementing AI to monitor employee behavior might cross ethical boundaries by surveilling personal activities unrelated to work, leading to employee dissatisfaction and potential legal action.

Incorporating Ethical Considerations into the Evaluation Process

Ethical considerations should be a central part of the evaluation and selection process for AI technologies in security applications. This requires a multifaceted approach, beginning with clear definitions of acceptable practices and extending through ongoing governance after deployment.

The first step is to evaluate the data practices of the AI technology. Transparency about the types of data the system requires, how it processes that data, and what safeguards are in place to protect it is paramount. For example, an organization considering an AI-powered facial recognition tool for access control should scrutinize how the system stores and processes biometric data. Can it function with anonymized data, or does it unnecessarily store PII? Systems that prioritize privacy-preserving methods, such as differential privacy or federated learning, should be given preference.

Another critical aspect is the bias and fairness of the AI system. Bias in training data can lead to discriminatory outcomes, particularly in technologies used for threat detection or identity verification. During evaluation, organizations should ask vendors to provide detailed documentation about the datasets used to train their models. For example, an AI tool for fraud detection should demonstrate that its algorithms do not disproportionately flag transactions from certain demographic groups or geographic regions as suspicious. Independent audits and fairness testing tools can help identify and mitigate biases before deployment.

The transparency and explainability of the AI model are also vital. Black-box algorithms that provide little insight into how decisions are made can lead to mistrust and hinder effective response during incidents. Consider an AI tool that flags network anomalies as potential threats. If it cannot explain why a particular activity was flagged, security teams may struggle to act effectively, undermining both trust and operational value. Vendors offering models with built-in explainability, such as interpretable ML techniques, can provide a clear advantage in this regard.

Governance and Accountability: Balancing Security and Ethics

Ethics in Intelligent Continuous Security doesn't stop at the evaluation phase. It requires ongoing governance and accountability. Organizations should establish policies to ensure that AI systems are used responsibly and in alignment with ethical principles. These policies should include regular audits, stakeholder feedback loops, and mechanisms for handling disputes or unintended consequences.

For example, a multinational corporation using AI for insider threat detection might set up an ethics committee to oversee the tool's implementation and use. This committee could review cases where employees are flagged by the system, ensuring that decisions are fair, unbiased, and respect individual rights. Such governance structures not only reduce the likelihood of ethical missteps but also build trust among employees and other stakeholders.

It's important to recognize that ethical considerations and security goals are not inherently at odds. In fact, they are often complementary. A system that respects privacy and minimizes bias is more likely to be accepted by users, reducing resistance and ensuring smoother adoption. Ethical technologies also align better with regulatory requirements, reducing the risk of legal challenges or fines.

For instance, a hospital implementing AI to detect unauthorized access to patient records could choose a solution that anonymizes data wherever possible, aligning with both ethical principles and legal mandates such as HIPAA. By demonstrating a commitment to ethical practices, the hospital not only enhances security but also reinforces trust with patients and regulators.

In conclusion, ethical considerations are an integral part of evaluating and selecting AI technologies for security applications. Neglecting these factors can lead to significant operational, reputational, and legal risks. By prioritizing ethical principles—such as data privacy, fairness, transparency, and accountability—organizations can ensure that their AI technologies not only meet security objectives but also align with broader societal expectations. In an era where trust is a key differentiator, ethically grounded AI is not just the right choice; it's the smart choice.

Sustaining AI Technologies in Security Applications

Choosing the right AI technology for a security application is just the beginning. Sustaining that technology over time is equally critical to ensure that it remains effective, relevant, and aligned with organizational needs. As illustrated in Figure 5-5, AI systems are not static; they require ongoing care and feeding to maintain their accuracy, adapt to evolving threats, and integrate seamlessly with shifting organizational priorities. Without proper maintenance, even the most advanced AI solutions can degrade, becoming inefficient or even counterproductive.

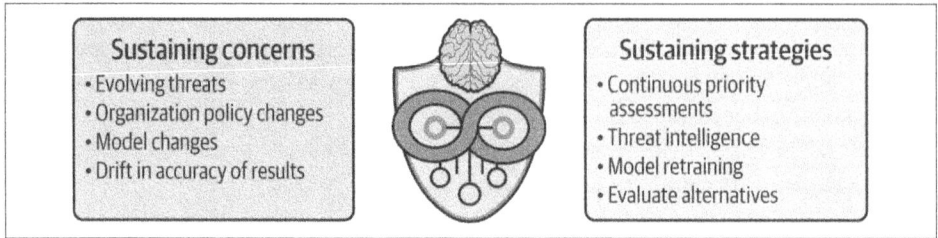

Sustaining concerns	Sustaining strategies
• Evolving threats	• Continuous priority assessments
• Organization policy changes	• Threat intelligence
• Model changes	• Model retraining
• Drift in accuracy of results	• Evaluate alternatives

Figure 5-5. Sustaining AI security solutions

Sustaining AI technologies involves multiple dimensions: keeping the underlying models up-to-date, managing data quality, adapting to changes in the threat landscape, and ensuring that the solution continues to align with organizational goals. For example, consider an AI-powered intrusion detection system. When first deployed, it performs exceptionally well at flagging unusual network activity. Over time, however, as attackers evolve their tactics or as the organization's network grows, the system's effectiveness may diminish unless its detection models and data inputs are regularly updated. Left unchecked, this stagnation could lead to a rise in missed threats or an overwhelming number of false positives.

One of the primary challenges in sustaining AI technologies is managing *model drift*, a phenomenon in which the AI's predictions become less accurate as the underlying data or environment shifts. In security applications, this drift is often caused by changes in user behavior, infrastructure upgrades, or new attack techniques. For instance, a behavioral anomaly detection system might be trained on data from a pre-pandemic workplace environment. As employees shift to hybrid or remote work, their behavior changes dramatically, causing the system to flag legitimate activity as suspicious or to miss real threats altogether. The solution to this challenge lies in continuous retraining of models using up-to-date data that reflects the current environment. Organizations should implement a robust pipeline for regularly feeding fresh, labeled data into their AI systems and periodically testing their accuracy against newly observed scenarios.

Another key aspect of sustaining AI technologies is ensuring *data quality*. AI models are only as good as the data they consume, and in security, that data can come from logs, telemetry, user activities, or external threat feeds. Over time, data pipelines may encounter issues such as incomplete logs, duplicate entries, or misaligned timestamps, all of which can degrade the AI's performance. Take, for example, an AI-driven security information and event management (SIEM) system that relies on log data from hundreds of devices. If a subset of those devices stops reporting due to misconfigured agents, the system's visibility is compromised. The solution involves establishing rigorous data monitoring processes and creating automated alerts to flag anomalies in data ingestion.

Sustaining AI also means addressing *evolving threats*. Attackers constantly refine their techniques, creating new patterns of behavior that may not align with an AI's original training data. For example, a fraud detection system might excel at identifying traditional phishing attacks but struggle to detect sophisticated voice phishing (*vishing*) schemes that combine social engineering with stolen data. To counter this, organizations must stay ahead of attackers by incorporating external threat intelligence into their AI models. Partnerships with vendors offering curated threat feeds or participation in industry-sharing groups can provide valuable data to augment and refine the AI's understanding of emerging risks.

A more subtle but equally important challenge lies in ensuring that AI technologies remain aligned with organizational needs. Security priorities can shift over time— what was once a critical capability may become less relevant as the organization evolves. For instance, an ecommerce company might initially prioritize fraud detection during checkout, only to later realize that insider threats in its supply chain present a greater risk. Regular reviews with stakeholders are crucial to reassess whether the AI solution still aligns with the organization's goals. These reviews should include performance metrics, feedback from end users, and discussions about emerging requirements.

Knowing when it's time to replace an AI technology with an alternative is equally critical. This decision often arises when the costs of maintaining the current system outweigh the benefits. Signs that it may be time for a change include persistent false positives or false negatives despite retraining, significant integration challenges with new systems, or the emergence of superior alternatives in the market. For example, consider an organization using an AI-powered threat detection system that fails to integrate with its newly adopted Zero Trust framework. If patchwork fixes prove too cumbersome or expensive, the organization might decide to replace the tool with a solution designed for native compatibility with Zero Trust architectures.

Replacement decisions should always be validated through a pilot phase, where the new solution is tested side-by-side with the existing one. During this phase, performance, scalability, and user experience are closely monitored to ensure that the replacement delivers tangible improvements. For instance, a healthcare provider transitioning from an outdated anomaly detection tool to an AI-driven endpoint protection platform might run both systems in parallel, using real-world data to compare accuracy and responsiveness.

As you have learned, sustaining AI technologies for security applications requires more than technical upkeep. It demands a dynamic approach that incorporates retraining, data quality management, threat adaptation, and alignment with evolving goals. Organizations that treat AI as a living system rather than a one-time deployment will reap the benefits of enhanced security, greater resilience, and long-term return on investment (ROI). By addressing challenges proactively and knowing when to pivot to newer technologies, security teams can ensure that their AI solutions remain a valuable asset in an ever-changing landscape.

Summary

The exploration of AI and ML in this chapter underscores their transformative potential in creating a robust, adaptive, and intelligent security posture. As cybersecurity challenges grow in complexity, the traditional approaches of static rules and reactive measures are no longer sufficient. Instead, the dynamic capabilities of AI and ML enable organizations to stay ahead of attackers, operating in real time to identify, predict, and neutralize threats. These technologies are not just tools. They are fundamental shifts in how we think about security.

One of the central takeaways from this chapter is the importance of integrating AI and ML at every stage of the security lifecycle. From proactive threat modeling and automated security testing to anomaly detection and response automation, these technologies provide layers of intelligence that enhance and streamline security processes. By leveraging AI, security teams can focus their efforts where they are most needed, rather than being overwhelmed by false positives or buried in routine tasks. The result is a more efficient, accurate, and effective defense system.

Another critical insight is the necessity of maintaining and adapting these systems over time. AI models are not static; they must evolve with the data they process and the threats they face. Organizations must commit to continuous retraining, monitoring for biases, and refining performance to ensure that these tools remain effective in the face of changing environments. This iterative approach ensures that the investment in AI delivers sustained value and resilience.

Finally, this chapter highlighted the ethical and strategic considerations that come with adopting AI for security. Transparency, fairness, and alignment with organizational goals are not optional; they are foundational to the successful deployment of these technologies. Organizations that embrace these principles will not only build stronger defenses but also foster trust among stakeholders, creating a security culture that is as forward-thinking as the technologies it employs.

The path to Intelligent Continuous Security is one of transformation, requiring thoughtful integration, ongoing stewardship, and a commitment to ethical practices. But as the examples and strategies discussed in this chapter illustrate, the rewards—improved agility, stronger defenses, and a proactive security posture—are well worth the effort. In the ever-evolving battle against cyber threats, AI and ML are not just enhancements; they are indispensable allies.

Understanding how Intelligent Continuous Security leverages AI technologies is only one aspect to achieving ICS. Successful adoption requires a structured, strategic approach. Chapter 6 introduces the Roadmap to Intelligent Continuous Security, a practical framework designed to guide organizations through a phased transformation from traditional security models to an AI-driven, continuously adaptive security posture. This roadmap will provide a clear, actionable path that aligns leadership vision, team dynamics, and technology integration, ensuring a smooth and effective ICS implementation. Chapter 6 equips organizations with the tools, templates, and best practices needed to operationalize ICS at scale while navigating common challenges.

Seven-Step
Transformation Blueprint for ICS

This chapter explains strategic and actionable transformation processes and tools that help organizations achieve well-engineered Intelligent Continuous Security (ICS) solutions. I call this process the *seven-step transformation blueprint*, referred to as the *blueprint* in this chapter. This blueprint was first described in my book *Engineering DevOps* (self-published using BookBaby, 2019). It has been proven successful in guiding transformations for many organizations. This chapter explains how the blueprint guides and assists organizations looking to transition from any ICS maturity level (as defined by the people, processes, and technology practices described in Chapter 3) to any higher ICS maturity level.

The blueprint emphasizes leadership vision, team alignment, current state analysis, solution design, and the integration of AI-assisted practices into real solutions that can be readily operationalized and expanded across multiple applications. The blueprint guides organizations in navigating common challenges and pitfalls as they work through their transformation steps.

Through real-world examples and a focus on continuous team alignment of people, processes, and technology practices, this chapter underscores the necessity of designing ICS solutions with observability, testability, scalability, and adaptability at their core.

No matter which ICS maturity level you start with, or whichever higher ICS maturity level you decide to transform to, following the guidance provided by the blueprint will improve your chances of achieving your goals and reduce your chances of running into pitfalls that are inherent with transformations that do not follow such a structured approach.

Seven Transformation Blueprint Steps

The seven-step transformation blueprint, illustrated in Figure 6-1, works as an infinite loop, ensuring a continuous cycle of improvement. Leveraging AI into each step facilitates turning data into actionable insights, automates repetitive tasks, and enables teams to focus on higher-level decisions as they work through the steps. Let's walk through each step with real-world examples and see how AI plays a critical role in making this transformation seamless.

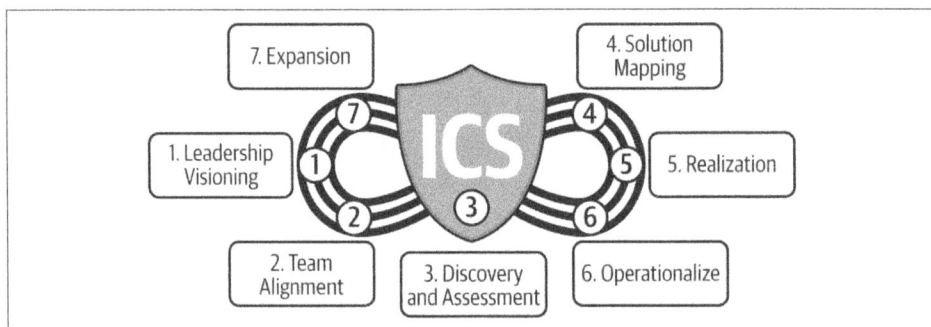

Figure 6-1. Seven-step transformation blueprint: the triple infinity symbol signifies that transformations require continuous alignment of people, processes, and technology practices

Step 1: Leadership Visioning

Transformation starts at the top. Leaders need to set a clear vision. Why? Because Continuous Security matters, and it needs to align with business goals. But here's where AI can help—leaders don't have to rely on intuition alone. AI tools can aggregate data from across the organization, highlighting vulnerabilities, compliance gaps, and risk trends. With this data, leadership can set measurable goals, such as reducing the time to detect threats by 30% or achieving uptime according to contracted service levels.

For example, after a major data breach, the leadership of a retail chain used AI-driven threat simulations to show their board the potential financial impact of another attack. This data made it easier to secure buy-in for the transformation because it wasn't just a hypothetical problem—it was backed by real, actionable insights.

Figure 6-2 illustrates the activities, tools, and deliverables for Step 1 of the blueprint.

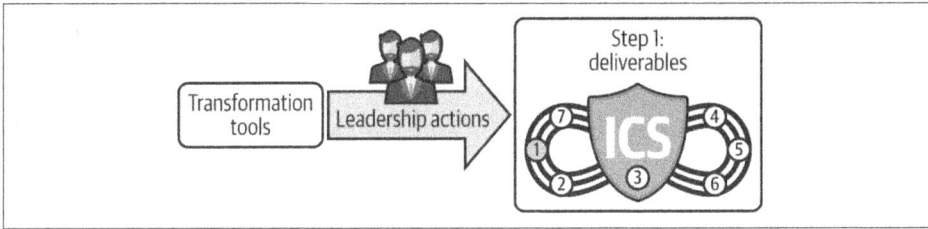

Figure 6-2. Step 1: Leadership Visioning

Step 1 activities

Successful ICS transformation begins with strong leadership. Organizations must identify transformation leaders who are not only committed to advancing security but also capable of setting the tone for change. These individuals will play a critical role in ensuring that security remains a top organizational priority, embedding it into the culture rather than treating it as a separate function. Without dedicated leadership, efforts to integrate ICS into existing workflows risk stagnation or misalignment with broader business objectives.

A well-defined strategy is equally essential. Establishing clear strategic goals provides direction and ensures that the transformation aligns with the company's long-term vision. These goals should not only address current security challenges but also anticipate future threats, creating a proactive rather than reactive security posture. A security transformation that is not tied to business objectives risks being seen as an operational burden rather than a strategic enabler.

To make meaningful progress, organizations must also be intentional about where they start. Selecting specific applications or systems as initial transformation targets allows for a focused deployment of resources. This targeted approach ensures that early initiatives serve as proof-of-concept (PoC) projects, demonstrating value before scaling to the broader enterprise. By iterating on early successes, organizations can refine their strategies, address unforeseen challenges, and build momentum for full-scale implementation.

Guiding this process requires structured documentation. Foundational materials, such as an ICS transformation scorecard and a strategic goals document, provide teams with a clear roadmap. These documents serve as living references, helping teams track progress, measure impact, and ensure that transformation efforts remain aligned with security and business priorities. Without these guiding artifacts, transformation efforts can drift, losing focus amid competing operational demands.

Step 1 deliverable outputs

A successful ICS transformation begins with strong leadership. Establishing a transformation leadership team ensures that security initiatives receive top-level commitment and alignment with the organization's broader business strategy. These leaders act as champions of change, driving the transformation forward, securing executive buy-in, and fostering collaboration across teams. Without their guidance, security efforts risk being deprioritized amid competing operational demands.

To make progress tangible, organizations must carefully select pilot applications for transformation. Rather than attempting a sweeping overhaul all at once, teams should start with targeted applications which will allow them to focus efforts where measurable, impactful results can be achieved. These pilots serve as PoC implementations, demonstrating the value of ICS practices while refining strategies for broader deployment.

Tracking progress requires more than anecdotal success stories. A structured ICS transformation scorecard provides a framework for measuring quantifiable benchmarks, ensuring that each phase of the transformation delivers meaningful improvements. By tracking security enhancements, automation maturity, and operational efficiencies, organizations can assess their progress against predefined metrics and make informed adjustments along the way.

Clear direction is essential, and a strategic goals document serves as the guiding blueprint for the transformation. This document outlines key objectives, details the tactical approaches needed to achieve them, and ensures alignment across stakeholders. With a well-articulated vision, teams can work cohesively, making security an integrated and continuous part of their workflows.

Finally, committed next steps solidify the transformation's momentum. Defining specific follow-up actions ensures that progress does not stall after initial successes. By outlining concrete initiatives for Step 2, organizations maintain forward motion, reinforcing security as an ongoing, evolving priority rather than a one-time initiative.

Tools to help with Step 1

To accomplish Step 1, tools are required, including an ICS maturity model, an application scorecard, document templates, project management tools, and an internal documentation site. These tools and the use of these tools are explained in the following subsections.

Using the ICS maturity model to set strategic goals. The ICS maturity model, described in Chapter 3, helps organization leaders determine a baseline maturity level and decide on their strategic goals for transformation to higher levels of ICS maturity.

When you're starting a conversation about how to roadmap a transformation to ICS maturity levels, the best place to begin is with the ICS maturity model. Why? Because it gives everyone involved a clear, shared understanding of where the organization is today and where it can realistically go. Instead of diving straight into tools or processes, the maturity model frames the discussion with context, making it easier to prioritize, plan, and gain buy-in. Let's dig into why this approach makes sense.

You can't map a journey without knowing where you're starting from, right? That's exactly what the ICS maturity model provides: a high-level baseline. Whether your organization is currently at ICS Maturity Level 1: Initial (Ad Hoc and Unpredictable) or is already experimenting with AI-driven tools in accordance with ICS Maturity Level 2: Managed (Defined at a Project Level), the model helps teams take an honest look at their current capabilities. This isn't about pointing fingers; it's about getting a clear picture of strengths, gaps, and opportunities.

Figure 6-3 illustrates how to use the ICS maturity model to quickly determine a baseline for each application in your organization. The first step is to match the current state of your people, processes, and technology practices from the descriptions in Chapter 3. Note that you may find that the current states of these practice areas are at different levels of maturity, as illustrated in Figure 6-3. The overall current ICS maturity level is 1 because that is the lowest of the three practice areas. Bear in mind that it is important to have all three practice areas at the same level at any point in time, because when they are deviating, your practices are out of balance.

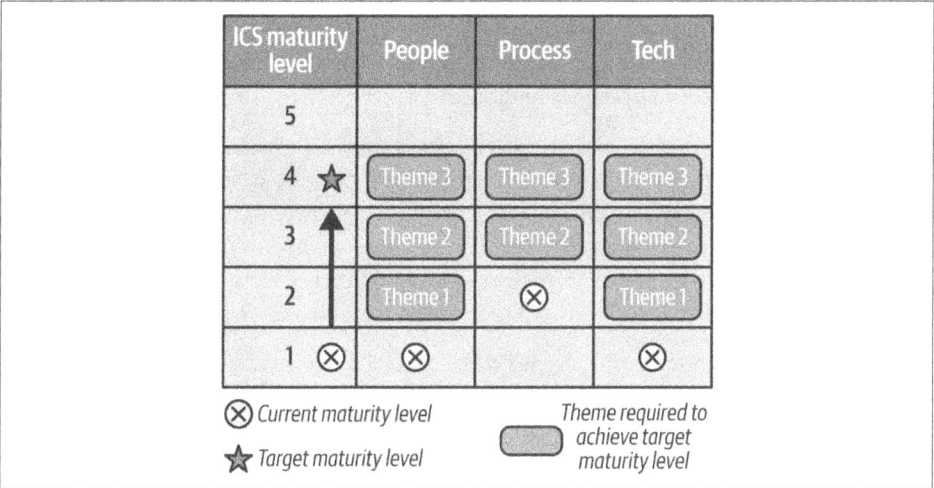

ICS maturity level	People	Process	Tech
5			
4 ☆	Theme 3	Theme 3	Theme 3
3	Theme 2	Theme 2	Theme 2
2	Theme 1	⊗	Theme 1
1 ⊗	⊗		⊗

⊗ Current maturity level
☆ Target maturity level
Theme required to achieve target maturity level

Figure 6-3. Using the Intelligent Continuous Security maturity model

Consider this example: leaders at a retail company might assume the company is ahead of the curve because it has automated vulnerability scanning, at least for some applications. But when they use the ICS maturity model, they realize they're stuck at

ICS Maturity Level 2, with little integration of security into their Continuous Integration/Continuous Delivery (CI/CD) pipeline or operations. That realization becomes the starting point for the transformation roadmap, with a goal to transform to ICS Maturity Level 3: Defined (Standardized Across the Organization).

The maturity model isn't just about what's wrong; it's also about what's possible. By breaking ICS maturity into clear levels, the model helps leadership and teams align on what success looks like. Maybe the first transformation goal is to reach ICS Maturity Level 3, where automated tools and collaboration start driving proactive outcomes. Or maybe the goal is to scale up to ICS Maturity Level 5: Optimized (Adaptive and Continuous Improvement), where autonomous AI systems handle threats in real time. The key is that the model sets realistic, actionable goals.

Here's how it played out for a healthcare provider: after a regulatory audit, leaders set their sights on ICS Maturity Level 3, where security checks would be fully integrated into their CI/CD pipelines. By focusing on that specific transformation goal, they avoided overwhelming their teams with lofty, overly ambitious goals.

Here's a trap many organizations fall into: they invest in advanced AI tools without the foundational practices to make those tools effective. The ICS maturity model prevents this by showing what's needed at each level—whether it's aligning teams, automating processes, or implementing predictive analytics. It helps organizations spend their resources wisely, building capabilities in the right order.

Leaders at a financial services firm learned this the hard way; they jumped into buying an AI-powered incident response tool, only to find that their manual processes and siloed teams couldn't support it. By stepping back and focusing on Level 2, they built the groundwork for success at higher levels.

Let's be honest: transformations often face resistance. Teams might worry that new processes will slow them down, or leadership might hesitate to invest without a clear return on investment (ROI). The ICS maturity model provides a narrative that cuts through the noise: "Here's where we are, here's where we need to go, and here's why it matters." It ties security maturity to real business outcomes such as faster incident response, reduced downtime, and stronger organization change management.

Leaders at an ecommerce company used the model to great effect; they showed how moving from Level 2 to Level 4: Quantitatively Managed (Measured and Optimized) could reduce meantime to detect (MTTD) by 40%, directly protecting revenue during peak shopping seasons. That clarity got everyone on board.

One of the best things about starting with the ICS maturity model is that it shows how AI grows with you. At Level 2, AI might just be helping with automated scans or basic log analysis. By Level 5, it's running the show, autonomously detecting, mitigating, and adapting to threats in real time. The model makes it clear that AI isn't a magic bullet but a progressive enabler that scales with maturity.

Think about a software as a service (SaaS) company just starting out; teams use AI for basic log analysis at Level 1 and slowly expand to anomaly detection and predictive modeling by Level 4. The maturity model gives them a clear path to follow, with AI's role evolving along the way.

Starting your ICS transformation with the maturity model isn't just logical, it's essential. It gives you a clear starting point, sets realistic goals, and ensures that everyone is aligned on the journey ahead. Plus, it ties AI into the narrative in a way that makes sense, showing how it adds value at every step. Without this foundation, your roadmap risks being directionless or overly ambitious. With it, you've got a compass to guide your transformation—and the confidence that you're heading in the right direction.

Using a scorecard to choose which applications to transform. An application transformation scorecard is a structured evaluation tool designed to assess applications based on key transformation factors. In the context of Intelligent Continuous Security transformation, the scorecard provides a quantitative and qualitative framework for prioritizing applications that are best suited for transformation efforts. By scoring applications across multiple dimensions, organizations can make informed decisions about which systems to focus on first, ensuring that resources are allocated where they will have the greatest impact.

At its core, the application scorecard is built around 10 key factors, each of which influences an application's readiness for transformation. Lead time is a crucial metric, capturing how long it takes to move an application from backlog to deployment. Applications with longer lead times tend to benefit most from automation and DevOps integration, as reducing cycle time directly enhances business agility. Leadership commitment is another determining factor; without strong sponsorship from key decision makers, transformation efforts risk being deprioritized or meeting resistance from stakeholders.

Beyond leadership, the culture of the application team plays a defining role in success. DevOps and ICS transformations thrive in environments where teams—spanning product owners, developers, quality engineers, operations, infrastructure, and security—are open to collaboration and change. If an application's culture is resistant to new ways of working, transformation efforts can stall before they gain momentum. Application architecture is another critical factor. Modern, modular, or service-oriented architectures are inherently more adaptable to automation and security improvements, whereas monolithic applications often require more substantial refactoring to realize similar benefits.

The size of the product team also influences transformation feasibility. Larger teams, typically those with at least 15 members spanning multiple disciplines, tend to justify more significant investments in automation, security tooling, and process improvements. Conversely, smaller teams supporting niche applications may not deliver enough ROI to warrant full-scale transformation. The duration of expected changes further informs prioritization; applications undergoing ongoing or long-term modifications are better candidates for embedding ICS and DevOps practices than stable applications with minimal change demands.

Impact and risk assessment helps balance business priorities. Applications that hold strategic value and visibility—but without extreme levels of operational risk—are ideal transformation candidates. High-impact applications that do not pose existential risk to the business allow organizations to experiment with security improvements and automation without introducing critical disruptions. Similarly, applications that experience frequent change requests are strong candidates for modernization, as automating repetitive processes and integrating Continuous Security can yield immediate efficiency gains.

Lastly, tooling compatibility and effort per release serve as practical indicators of transformation potential. If an application's existing toolchain does not require a complete overhaul to implement DevOps and ICS automation, it becomes a more feasible candidate for early transformation efforts. Likewise, applications where significant manual effort is required for builds, testing, and deployment stand to gain the most from security automation, reducing time and cost while enhancing overall resilience.

The application scorecard is not just a theoretical exercise. It provides a data-driven approach for decision making. By scoring applications across these 10 dimensions, organizations can establish clear priorities, focus on high-impact wins, and systematically integrate ICS and DevOps principles into their software development and operational workflows. In doing so, they ensure that transformation efforts are not just aspirational but are also grounded in measurable progress.

Using document templates. A well-structured ICS strategic goals document is essential for guiding application teams through the complexities of security transformation. Without a clear and consistent approach, security initiatives risk becoming fragmented, misaligned with business priorities, or failing to gain traction across teams. A well-defined strategic goals document provides both a roadmap and a reference point, ensuring that every application undergoing transformation follows a consistent framework while allowing for necessary adaptations based on specific use cases.

At the heart of this document is an introduction that articulates the strategic imperative behind the ICS transformation. Security threats are evolving rapidly, regulatory requirements are becoming more stringent, and software delivery expectations are continuously increasing. Organizations that fail to integrate Intelligent Continuous Security risk exposing themselves to operational disruptions, compliance failures, and reputational harm. The introduction establishes why the transformation is necessary and how it aligns with the company's broader business objectives, ensuring that security is treated as a core business enabler rather than an isolated operational function.

A mission statement provides a measurable objective, ensuring that transformation efforts have a defined starting point and a clear goal. This section outlines the organization's current ICS maturity level, identifying existing gaps in security automation, real-time monitoring, and proactive risk management. Equally important, it must define the target maturity level, setting expectations for what success looks like. Whether the objective is to integrate AI-driven threat detection, implement continuous compliance enforcement, or automate Policy as Code (PaC), having a well-articulated mission helps maintain focus on meaningful, long-term security improvements.

Security transformation is most successful when the business and staff benefits are clearly articulated. From a business standpoint, the document must highlight how reducing security incidents, minimizing compliance risks, and improving system reliability directly contribute to financial stability and operational resilience. For engineering and operations teams, the transformation reduces overhead by automating manual security processes, streamlining compliance workflows, and enabling faster, more secure software releases. Clearly defining these benefits ensures buy-in from leadership and frontline practitioners alike.

To ensure alignment across teams, the document should define the key technical elements required for the transformation. This section should outline essential security capabilities such as continuous threat detection, automated security scanning, secure software supply chains, and runtime security controls. Without explicit guidance, application teams may implement security measures inconsistently, introducing operational complexity and increasing risk. Alongside these technical elements, the document should also provide guidance on technology choices, helping teams select approved security tools, frameworks, and infrastructure components that align with enterprise architecture and compliance policies.

A transformation without a structured execution plan remains aspirational. The strategic goals document must include a timeline with major milestones, outlining phases such as initial security assessments, PoC implementations, scaled rollouts, and ongoing optimizations. By mapping out these phases, teams can plan their security enhancements in alignment with business priorities, ensuring that improvements do not disrupt critical operations.

Because security transformation is an ongoing process, the document should include a link to an internal documentation site, providing teams with access to detailed security frameworks, compliance guidelines, implementation best practices, and tooling instructions. Security is not static; regulatory requirements, threat landscapes, and best practices evolve. By linking to continuously updated documentation, organizations ensure that teams always have the latest guidance needed to navigate complex security and compliance challenges.

Finally, the document should conclude with a brief statement clarifying its intended use. This reinforces that the strategic goals document is not a rigid directive but a structured guide for executing ICS transformation within the organization's applications. By establishing a standardized approach while allowing flexibility for adaptation, the document becomes a powerful enabler of scalable, effective, and measurable security transformation across the enterprise.

Using project management tools.   Managing an ICS transformation requires more than technical execution. It also demands structured coordination, transparency, and alignment across multiple teams. Project management tools serve as the backbone of this effort, providing a centralized platform to document and track all activities involved in the transformation. From high-level strategic initiatives down to individual security enhancements, these tools ensure that work is prioritized, dependencies are managed, and progress is continuously visible. Without structured project tracking, security initiatives risk becoming fragmented, delayed, or deprioritized in favor of short-term development pressures.

At the highest level, project management tools help define *epics* and *themes*, which represent broad security transformation goals. An epic might focus on automating security testing across the CI/CD pipeline, while a theme could encompass proactive risk management and compliance enforcement. These high-level initiatives provide structure for breaking down complex security transformations into manageable components. Within each epic, multiple *user stories* are created—specific security improvements such as integrating dynamic application security testing (DAST) into CI/CD or deploying Infrastructure as Code (IaC) security scanning. Each user story, in turn, is further decomposed into *tasks*, ensuring that individual engineering and security teams have well-defined, actionable work items.

By tracking progress at each level—themes, epics, user stories, and tasks—organizations gain real-time visibility into the transformation's momentum. Project management tools allow teams to assign ownership, monitor bottlenecks, and ensure that security work is completed in alignment with delivery timelines. More importantly, they facilitate cross-team collaboration, allowing security engineers, developers, and operations teams to work in tandem without security becoming an afterthought. As ICS transformation efforts evolve, these tools provide an auditable history of changes, helping organizations measure security improvements over time and refine their approach based on real-world results.

Using an internal documentation site.   An internal documentation site is essential for supporting an ICS transformation, serving as a centralized knowledge repository that ensures consistency, accessibility, and efficiency across all teams involved. Security transformation is not just about deploying new tools. It requires teams to adopt new processes, align with enterprise security standards, and integrate best practices into their daily workflows. Without a structured, easily accessible resource, teams are forced to navigate security improvements in an ad hoc manner, leading to inconsistencies, redundant effort, and an increased risk of noncompliance. A well-maintained documentation site provides a single source of truth, eliminating confusion and accelerating the adoption of ICS principles.

At the core of this repository is the ICS transformation goals document, which defines the organization's security vision, maturity targets, and key objectives for embedding ICS into software delivery and operations. Beyond strategy, the site should include guidance papers covering specific transformation areas, such as best practices for integrating security into CI/CD pipelines, secure software supply chain implementation, and compliance automation frameworks. These documents provide actionable recommendations, helping application teams understand not just what needs to be done but also how to do it effectively. Additionally, the site should house technical implementation guides, including playbooks for automated security testing, IaC security validation, and AI-driven anomaly detection, ensuring that teams have detailed, step-by-step instructions for execution.

To drive continuous improvement, the documentation site should also capture results from previous transformations, offering insights into what has worked well, common pitfalls, and lessons learned. Case studies from early adopters within the organization can provide valuable reference points, helping newer teams avoid unnecessary missteps. Other useful resources include compliance mapping documents, linking ICS practices to industry regulations such as the General Data Protection Regulation (GDPR), Health Insurance Portability and Accountability Act (HIPAA), and National Institute of Standards and Technology (NIST) security frameworks, ensuring that teams remain aligned with legal and policy requirements. By maintaining an evolving, well-organized documentation site, organizations create an ecosystem where security transformation becomes repeatable, scalable, and embedded as an integral part of the software lifecycle.

Step 2: Team Alignment

Transforming to ICS requires more than a well-articulated strategy; it demands translation into actionable goals at the application level. Step 2, Team Alignment, bridges the gap between the broad ICS transformation vision defined in Step 1 and the practical realities of securing a specific application. This step, illustrated in Figure 6-4, ensures that the application transformation team—comprising developers, security engineers, operations specialists, and product owners—has a clear, shared understanding of how ICS principles apply to their domain. Without this alignment, the implementation risks becoming disjointed, leading to inefficiencies, misaligned priorities, and security measures that fail to integrate seamlessly into existing workflows.

Alignment is critical because application teams operate within unique contexts—each with its own architecture, risk profile, development cadence, and compliance requirements. By refining the broader ICS strategy into tailored objectives for a specific application, the transformation team creates clarity on key outcomes: What threats must be prioritized? Which automation investments will yield the highest security and operational benefits? How should security testing and monitoring be embedded into the development pipeline? Establishing this common understanding ensures that security enhancements align with business objectives rather than becoming isolated, bolted-on initiatives.

Without a structured alignment phase, teams may move into Step 3 without a clear direction, leading to redundant or misfocused efforts. Instead, a well-aligned application transformation team enters the discovery phase with defined priorities, allowing team members to assess existing security practices, identify gaps, and determine the most impactful ICS improvements. Alignment transforms ICS from an abstract goal into a roadmap for real, application-level security enhancements—laying the foundation for effective, measurable progress in the next steps.

Figure 6-4. Step 2: Team Alignment

The success of an ICS transformation hinges on selecting the right team to drive change at the application level. In Step 2, an application transformation team is assembled, responsible for guiding the application's journey through the remaining five steps of the transformation blueprint. This team should include key stakeholders across development, security, operations, infrastructure, and product management, ensuring that all perspectives are represented. Their role is to interpret and apply the ICS transformation strategy in a way that aligns with the unique requirements and constraints of the application. Without a dedicated team that understands both security and business priorities, the transformation risks being either too generic or misaligned with the realities of software delivery.

Once formed, the team begins by studying the ICS transformation strategic goals document developed in Step 1. This document encapsulates the overarching vision for ICS across the organization, detailing objectives such as shifting security left, automating compliance, enhancing threat intelligence integration, and establishing Continuous Security validation. While these high-level principles provide direction, they must be refined into actionable, application-specific goals. The transformation team analyzes the document through the lens of its application's architecture, existing security posture, development workflows, and risk profile, identifying which elements are most relevant and achievable.

Next, the team determines which portions of the strategic goals are critical for the application and how they should be prioritized. Some security objectives, such as Continuous Security testing and automated vulnerability remediation, may be universally applicable. Others, such as integrating AI-driven threat detection, may be more relevant for applications handling sensitive or high-volume transactions. The team balances ambition with feasibility, ensuring that the selected goals align with the application's development lifecycle, compliance requirements, and business value. This step also involves engaging with key stakeholders outside the core transformation team, such as executives, product managers, and governance teams, to validate priorities and secure buy-in.

With these decisions made, the transformation team creates an application-specific ICS transformation goals document. This document serves as a guiding reference for the remaining transformation steps, defining measurable objectives, expected security improvements, and key integration points within the application's delivery pipeline. It should include clear success criteria, such as reducing MTTD and mean time to repair (MTTR) vulnerabilities, ensuring that security checks are embedded in CI/CD workflows, or achieving compliance automation targets. By making these goals explicit, the team ensures that every subsequent decision, from tool selection to process optimization, supports the broader transformation effort.

The structured alignment provided in Step 2 ensures that the transformation does not stall due to misinterpretation or lack of direction. With a dedicated team in place and a well-defined set of application-specific ICS goals, the organization can confidently move into Step 3, where the team will assess the application's current security posture, identify gaps, and chart a course for implementation. This workflow ensures that ICS adoption is not an abstract initiative but a focused, application-driven transformation that delivers measurable security improvements.

Step 3: Discovery and Assessment

The success of an ICS transformation depends on precisely defining application-specific security requirements before designing and implementing solutions. Step 3, Discovery and Assessment, ensures that ICS transformation efforts are driven by concrete, application-centric needs rather than generalized security mandates. This step establishes a clear, prioritized set of security requirements that will directly inform the solution design phase in Step 4. By systematically examining the application's current state—its security practices, workflows, and operational constraints—organizations can avoid misalignment between transformation goals and practical implementation.

This phase begins by discovering the current state of the application's security posture, encompassing people, processes, and technologies. Security is a function not just of tooling but also of how teams interact, how decisions are made, and how security is integrated into daily workflows. The transformation team collects information on the application's architecture, its development and deployment pipeline, compliance obligations, and existing security controls. This comprehensive assessment ensures that no critical security risks or operational challenges are overlooked before moving forward with solution design.

As illustrated in Figure 6-5, Step 3 employs multiple discovery methods. Application discovery surveys provide structured input from key stakeholders, offering a broad view of security maturity. Pillars of practice gap assessments benchmark the application's security capabilities against ICS best practices, highlighting deficiencies and areas for improvement. A current-state value stream map visually represents the flow of work, helping to pinpoint inefficiencies, security bottlenecks, and areas where automation could enhance security. Additionally, interviews with engineers, security professionals, and operations staff bring valuable qualitative insights, revealing pain points, workarounds, and organizational constraints that impact security decision making.

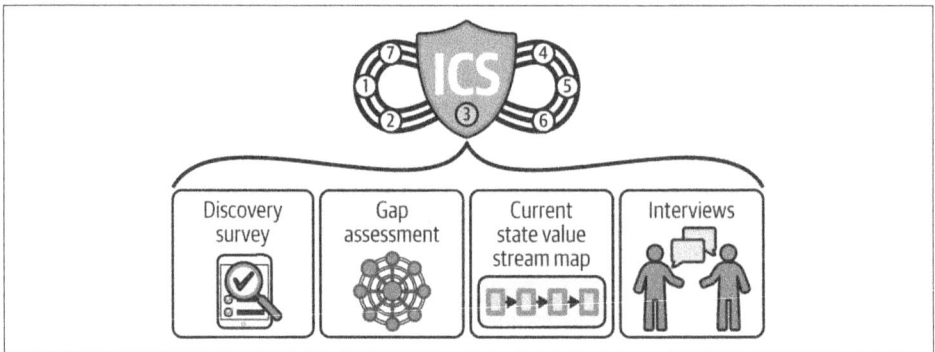

Figure 6-5. Step 3: Discovery and Assessment

Once data collection is complete, the transformation team analyzes the findings to synthesize a consolidated and prioritized set of solution requirements. These requirements define exactly what the ICS solution must address, such as automating security testing, improving incident detection and response, or integrating compliance checks into the CI/CD pipeline. Each requirement is linked directly to the application-specific goals established in Step 2, ensuring that the transformation remains tightly aligned with business and technical priorities. The goal is to produce actionable, well-defined security enhancements that can be realistically implemented in Step 4.

By the end of Step 3, the organization has not only defined the security improvements needed for the application but also established a baseline against which future progress can be measured. This baseline provides a reference point for evaluating the impact of security changes made in later steps. It also helps avoid transformation drift—where security initiatives lose focus over time—by ensuring that every change is anchored to the original, well-defined objectives.

The benefits of Step 3 extend beyond just setting direction for Step 4. By engaging key stakeholders early, organizations foster buy-in and alignment across teams, reducing friction during implementation. By grounding decisions in real-world data, they ensure that the ICS solution will be practical, effective, and tailored to the application's needs. Most importantly, by establishing a comprehensive security baseline, they create a measurable way to track progress, refine strategies, and demonstrate value as the ICS transformation unfolds.

Step 3 produces a structured set of deliverables that serve as the foundation for designing an ICS solution in Step 4. These deliverables provide a fact-based understanding of the application's security posture, ensuring that transformation efforts remain aligned with the application's specific needs rather than generic security mandates. By the end of Step 3, the organization will have a clear description of the application's current state, an assessment of ICS practice gaps relative to the eight ICS pillars of practice, a value stream map highlighting security inefficiencies, and a set of prioritized solution requirements. Each deliverable plays a critical role in shaping an effective and targeted ICS implementation.

The current-state description provides an objective, detailed account of the application's existing security practices across people, processes, and technology. It documents how security is integrated—or not—into development and operations workflows, which security tools are currently in use, and what governance or compliance controls are enforced. The description also outlines how security responsibilities are distributed across teams, whether security activities occur proactively or reactively, and to what extent security is automated versus manual. This baseline understanding prevents misalignment and ensures that all stakeholders share a common perspective before defining improvements.

The gap assessment of ICS practices evaluates the application's security posture relative to the eight ICS pillars of practice, as defined in Chapter 3. These pillars represent the core capabilities required for Intelligent Continuous Security, covering areas such as Continuous Security culture, Continuous Security awareness training, security integration in the lifecycle, automated security testing, proactive security risk management, rapid incident response, continuous monitoring and compliance, and security feedback and continuous improvement. By assessing gaps against the practices associated within each of these pillars, the transformation team can identify specific weaknesses within the application's security implementation. For example, an application might have strong security monitoring but lack effective automated security testing, leading to late-stage vulnerability detection. This targeted analysis ensures that security improvements are not just abstract recommendations but concrete, application-specific priorities.

The current-state value stream map visualizes the entire application delivery process, overlaid with security activities to highlight bottlenecks, inefficiencies, and blind spots. This map shows where security interventions currently occur, how security checks impact development speed, and where vulnerabilities might escape detection. By understanding security friction points—such as manual approval gates, redundant scanning steps, or lack of early-stage security validation—the transformation team can propose improvements that enhance security while streamlining development workflows. The value stream map is particularly useful for identifying opportunities to shift security left, embedding security earlier in the pipeline without slowing down innovation.

The prioritized solution requirements synthesize all discovery findings into a clear, actionable roadmap for security enhancements. These requirements define which security improvements are needed, why they matter, and how they align with the application's ICS goals from Step 2. Prioritization is key; while a full transformation may include dozens of potential security enhancements, not all have equal urgency or impact. The team ranks security initiatives based on risk reduction, implementation feasibility, and expected benefits, ensuring that Step 4 focuses on the highest-value improvements. Examples of prioritized requirements may include automating security testing in CI/CD, integrating AI-driven threat detection, enforcing PaC for compliance, or improving real-time security observability.

These deliverables ensure that the ICS transformation is built not on assumptions but on real, application-specific data. Rather than jumping straight into solution design, Step 3 ensures that ICS improvements are aligned with business and technical realities, reducing the risk of implementing solutions that are impractical, redundant, or misaligned with development workflows.

Additionally, these deliverables establish a measurable security baseline, which serves as a reference point for evaluating the impact of ICS changes over time. As new security capabilities are implemented in later steps, the organization can track improvements in vulnerability detection rates, security automation levels, compliance adherence, and incident response times. This data-driven approach ensures that security transformation efforts remain focused, iterative, and continuously optimized rather than being a one-time initiative.

By the end of Step 3, the transformation team is equipped with a precise understanding of the application's security needs and a structured plan for addressing them.

With this clarity, the organization is ready to proceed to Step 4, where security enhancements will be architected to seamlessly integrate into the application's development, deployment, and operational workflows.

Step 4: Solution Mapping

With a clear understanding of the application's security posture established in Step 3, the next step in the ICS transformation journey is Step 4, Solution Mapping, as illustrated in Figure 6-6. This step ensures that ICS improvements are not just conceptual, but are structured into an actionable, application-specific implementation plan. Step 4 transforms the prioritized solution requirements from the previous step into a well-defined roadmap, aligning technical improvements with business objectives. Without a structured design phase, security initiatives risk being disjointed, uncoordinated, or misaligned with the development and operations workflows.

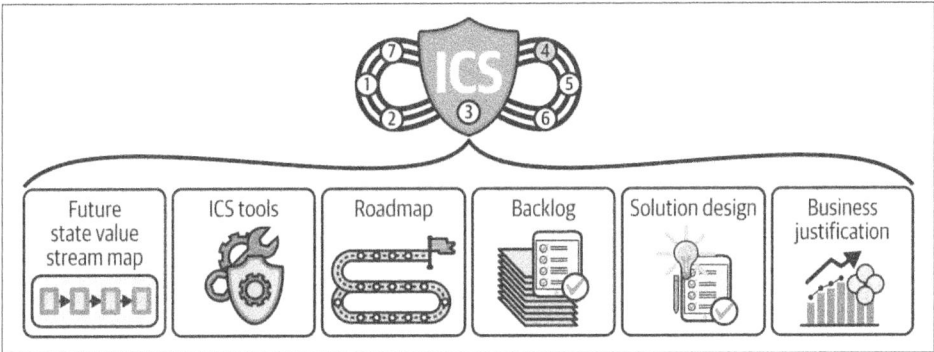

Figure 6-6. Step 4: Solution Mapping

The Solution Mapping phase begins with a detailed analysis of the solution requirements documented in Step 3. These requirements define what must be improved, why it matters, and how success will be measured. The transformation team evaluates dependencies, feasibility, and trade-offs to ensure that the proposed solutions are practical and achievable within the constraints of the application's architecture, team structure, and release cycles. This analysis prevents overengineering security solutions while ensuring that critical security gaps are effectively addressed.

To visualize the impact of ICS improvements, a future-state value stream map is created. This map extends the current-state value stream map developed in Step 3, illustrating how the application's security posture will evolve with the planned improvements. It highlights where security automation will be introduced, where bottlenecks will be removed, and how ICS practices will be embedded into DevOps workflows. The future-state map serves as a guiding reference, ensuring that security enhancements streamline—not disrupt—the software delivery process.

The transformation team then develops a solution roadmap, structuring the implementation into themes, epics, and user stories. This approach ensures that the ICS transformation is incrementally delivered rather than attempting an all-at-once overhaul. Themes represent high-level security capabilities (e.g., automated security testing, real-time threat detection), while epics break them into application-specific initiatives (e.g., integrating SAST/DAST tools into CI/CD, implementing security observability). User stories provide detailed tasks that teams will execute in upcoming sprints, ensuring that security improvements are actionable and aligned with Agile development cycles.

To secure leadership alignment and investment, an ROI case is developed alongside the solution roadmap. The ROI case outlines the business value of ICS improvements, quantifying benefits such as reduced security incidents, faster compliance validation, improved development velocity, and lower remediation costs. It ensures that decision makers understand why the proposed ICS solution matters, how it impacts business risk, and why it is worth prioritizing. A well-structured ROI case increases stakeholder commitment and accelerates funding approval for security initiatives.

The final output of Step 4 is a solution recommendation that synthesizes all findings into a clear, structured proposal. This recommendation provides the technical plan, implementation roadmap, expected benefits, and leadership buy-in strategy, ensuring that ICS transformation efforts move forward with confidence. The solution is now no longer an abstract concept but an engineered plan, designed to fit seamlessly into the application's development and operational workflows.

Step 4 ensures that security transformation is not left to improvisation or ad hoc decisions. Instead, it provides a structured, data-driven approach to designing ICS improvements that align security, engineering, and business objectives. By the end of this phase, the organization has a clear vision of what the ICS-enhanced application will look like, a prioritized execution plan, and leadership support to move forward into implementation in Step 5.

Step 4 also translates the findings from Step 3 into a structured plan for implementing ICS improvements. This step ensures that security transformation is not just a conceptual exercise; rather, it is a data-driven, actionable initiative with clear priorities, investment justification, and leadership alignment. The key deliverables of this phase establish the technical, operational, and strategic foundation for execution in Step 5.

A future-state value stream map is created to illustrate how security enhancements will be embedded into the development and operational workflows. This map extends the current-state value stream map from Step 3, demonstrating where security automation, risk-based controls, and compliance checkpoints will be integrated. By visualizing the expected improvements—such as reducing security review cycle times, automating vulnerability scanning, or implementing real-time threat detection—the transformation team ensures that ICS solutions will enhance security without adding friction to delivery.

A tools recommendation document is developed to specify the technologies required to implement the ICS solution. This includes security testing tools (SAST, DAST, software composition analysis [SCA]), compliance automation platforms, AI-driven threat detection systems, PaC frameworks, and observability solutions. The tool recommendations consider existing investments, interoperability with DevOps toolchains, and organizational security priorities, ensuring that the ICS implementation is both cost-effective and technically feasible.

The transformation team then roadmaps the ICS transformation, defining a structured timeline for security implementation. This roadmap outlines phased rollouts, dependencies, key milestones, and adoption strategies to ensure that security improvements are introduced in a manageable, incremental fashion. It provides clarity on when different capabilities will be introduced, how they will be tested, and how teams will adapt to new security processes. A well-structured roadmap prevents transformation fatigue by ensuring that security adoption is progressive and aligned with development cycles.

A backlog of themes, epics, and user stories is created to operationalize the ICS transformation. This backlog ensures that security improvements are not treated as abstract goals but are integrated into Agile planning and DevOps workflows. Themes represent broad security capabilities (e.g., "Automated Security Testing"), epics break them into specific initiatives (e.g., "Integrate SAST into CI/CD"), and user stories define the granular work required to implement each improvement (e.g., "As a developer, I want security checks to run on every pull request"). This backlog enables cross-team collaboration and ensures that security work is prioritized alongside feature development.

To secure funding and leadership commitment, an estimate of ROI is developed. This ROI model quantifies the benefits of ICS improvements, including reduced security incidents, faster compliance validation, lower remediation costs, and improved development velocity. It presents a clear financial case for investing in ICS by comparing the projected security enhancements with their cost savings and risk reduction impact.

A solution recommendation is produced, consolidating all findings into a concise, structured proposal. This document summarizes the future-state vision, roadmap, technology choices, backlog, and ROI estimate. It provides a clear execution strategy that can be reviewed and approved by both technical and business stakeholders. This recommendation ensures that ICS transformation moves forward with a well-defined scope, realistic expectations, and measurable outcomes.

Finally, leadership alignment is secured to ensure executive sponsorship and commitment. Security transformation efforts often fail when they lack top-down support and cross-functional collaboration. The leadership alignment process involves presenting the solution recommendation, validating strategic priorities, addressing concerns, and securing the necessary resources for execution. This step ensures that ICS transformation is not just a security initiative; rather, it is a business priority, with clear ownership, accountability, and executive backing.

By the end of Step 4, the organization has a fully designed ICS transformation plan—technically feasible, financially justified, and strategically aligned. These deliverables ensure that Step 5 can proceed with confidence, focusing on practical, high-impact security improvements that integrate seamlessly into application development and operations.

Step 5: Realization

Step 5, Realization, is all about making things real. You roll out the solutions, integrate them into your workflows, and start seeing them in action. AI plays a hands-on role here, automating tasks such as vulnerability scanning and compliance checks. It can even monitor the rollout process itself, flagging issues in real time so that they don't derail progress.

As illustrated in Figure 6-7, Step 5 focuses on execution. This phase is where the transformation shifts from planning to implementation, ensuring that security improvements are deployed, tested, and integrated into daily workflows. The goal is to bring the ICS solution to life through structured implementation of user stories, validating its effectiveness through PoC trials, and enabling teams through training and governance activation. By the end of this step, the organization has a working ICS implementation that is ready to be fully operationalized in Step 6.

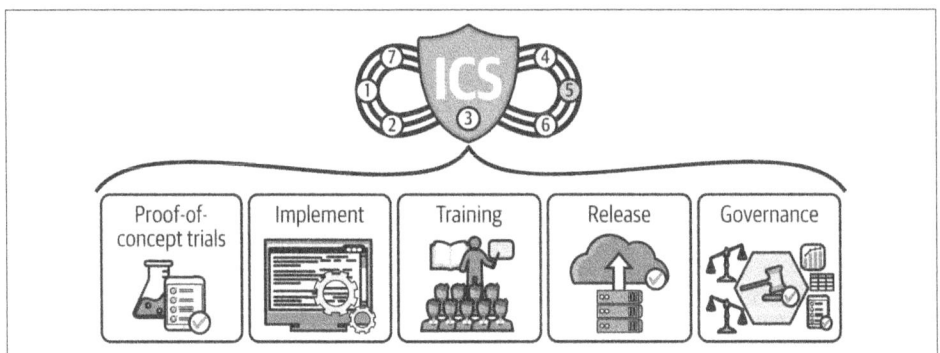

Figure 6-7. Step 5: Realization

Implementation begins with delivering user stories for each theme and epic defined in the solution roadmap. These user stories represent specific security capabilities—

such as integrating automated security testing into CI/CD pipelines, establishing runtime threat detection, or enforcing PaC for compliance automation. Each user story is implemented iteratively, allowing teams to validate progress in small increments. This approach ensures agility, reducing risks associated with large-scale security overhauls and enabling continuous feedback from stakeholders.

To ensure that ICS solutions are effective and practical, PoC trials are conducted to validate key implementations against real-world use cases. PoC trials allow teams to test solutions in controlled environments, ensuring that security enhancements deliver the intended benefits without negatively impacting development speed or operational efficiency. If issues arise, adjustments can be made before full-scale deployment. This iterative approach reduces friction and ensures that ICS capabilities integrate smoothly into existing development and operational workflows.

As ICS solutions are deployed, training is provided to development, security, and operations teams. Security transformation is as much about people and processes as it is about technology, and ensuring that teams understand how to use new security tools, interpret security metrics, and respond to threats is critical for long-term success. Training sessions focus on both technical enablement and cultural shifts, reinforcing security as a shared responsibility across engineering disciplines.

In parallel, governance practices are activated to ensure that new security processes are enforced consistently. This includes establishing compliance frameworks, security policies, monitoring protocols, and reporting mechanisms. Governance activation ensures that ICS practices do not degrade over time but instead become institutionalized as standard operating procedures. These governance measures provide visibility into security effectiveness, ensuring that teams remain accountable for maintaining a strong security posture.

Step 5 delivers a fully implemented ICS solution, ready to be operationalized at scale. By focusing on iterative deployment, validation through PoC trials, comprehensive training, and structured governance, this step ensures that ICS is not just deployed but also effectively adopted. Teams are equipped with the knowledge, tools, and frameworks needed to sustain and evolve their security practices, preventing ICS from becoming a one-time initiative.

With the solution successfully realized, the transformation moves into Step 6, which builds upon the foundation established in Step 5 by ensuring that ICS is maintained, continuously improved, and measured for effectiveness in a real-world production environment. The successful realization of Step 5 ensures that ICS enhancements are deployed and are fully embedded into daily operations, setting the stage for long-term security resilience.

Step 5 translates the planned ICS improvements into tangible security capabilities. This phase is where the transformation shifts from design to execution, ensuring that security solutions are implemented, tested, and deployed in a controlled yet iterative manner. By the end of Step 5, the ICS solution is no longer theoretical—it is validated, integrated, and ready for operationalization. The key deliverables of this step ensure that security measures are not only implemented but also proven effective, adopted by teams, and governed properly.

A critical first deliverable is the PoC trials. Before rolling out ICS improvements at scale, select solutions undergo real-world validation against actual application use cases. PoC trials test the effectiveness, scalability, and operational impact of security enhancements—such as automated vulnerability scanning, real-time threat detection, or compliance-as-code enforcement. These trials provide early feedback, allowing teams to refine security implementations before full deployment. If a solution fails to meet expectations, it can be adjusted, optimized, or replaced with an alternative before affecting production workflows.

Once PoC trials validate security enhancements, the next deliverable is the implementation of tasks associated with each user story. This includes executing the technical work required to integrate ICS capabilities into development pipelines, deployment processes, and runtime environments. Tasks may involve embedding security controls into CI/CD workflows, configuring infrastructure security policies, automating compliance validation, or deploying AI-driven security monitoring. Implementation is conducted iteratively, ensuring that security changes do not disrupt software delivery but instead enhance it.

With security implementations validated and refined, the next milestone is the release to production. This step involves deploying ICS solutions into live environments, ensuring that security improvements extend beyond staging and test environments. Security controls are applied to real-world software delivery, infrastructure, and operations workflows. This phase often includes gradual rollouts, feature flags, or canary releases to ensure stability and prevent disruptions to critical applications. Once in production, security enhancements are monitored for effectiveness, ensuring that they deliver the expected risk reduction and automation benefits.

To ensure adoption and proper usage of ICS improvements, training is a fundamental deliverable of Step 5. Security is only as effective as the teams implementing and using it. Training sessions equip developers, security engineers, and operations teams with the knowledge and hands-on experience needed to work effectively with new security tools and processes. This includes how to interpret security alerts, integrate security testing into their workflows, and follow newly established security best practices. By investing in training, organizations ensure that ICS improvements are not just deployed but also actively utilized to improve security outcomes.

In parallel, governance is initiated to formalize security policies, compliance enforcement, and Continuous Security monitoring. Governance ensures that ICS improvements become a sustainable part of the organization's security framework rather than a one-time initiative. This includes establishing security key performance indicators (KPIs), defining compliance standards, configuring monitoring dashboards, and setting up automated enforcement mechanisms. Governance activation ensures that security remains a measurable, enforceable, and continuously improved aspect of software delivery.

Step 5 delivers a fully implemented and validated ICS solution that is not only functional but also trusted by teams and governed by organizational policies. By focusing on real-world testing, structured implementation, gradual production deployment, training, and governance activation, Step 5 ensures that ICS is deeply embedded into software development and operational practices. These deliverables establish ICS as a repeatable, scalable, and automated security capability that evolves alongside application and infrastructure changes.

With the ICS solution realized, the next focus is Step 6, which ensures that ICS enhancements continue to evolve, adapt, and scale in production environments. Governance mechanisms are expanded, automation is fine-tuned, and security effectiveness is continuously measured. The success of Step 5 lays the foundation for long-term security resilience, ensuring that ICS is not a one-time transformation but an enduring capability.

Step 6: Operationalize

Once the solutions are live, the focus shifts to making them part of your daily operations. Step 6, Operationalize, ensures that security enhancements are scalable, reliable, and fully integrated into day-to-day operations. As illustrated in Figure 6-8, this step establishes the governance, monitoring, and support structures necessary to maintain and evolve ICS capabilities in a real-world production environment. Without this step, even well-designed security solutions risk stagnation or degradation over time.

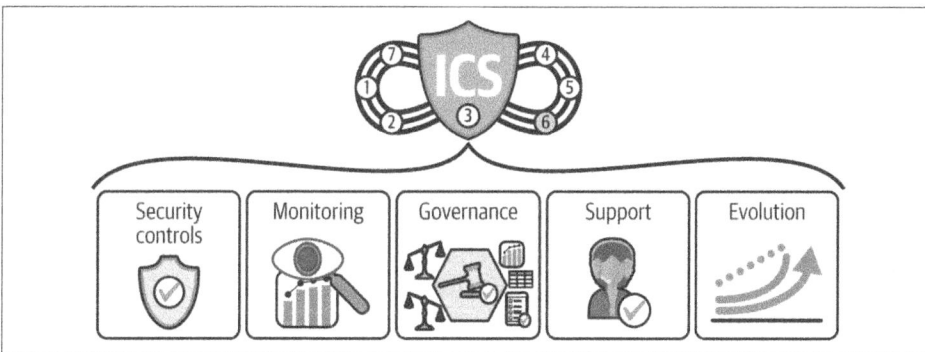

Figure 6-8. Step 6: Operationalize

Operationalization begins with monitoring and observability. ICS solutions must be continuously assessed for effectiveness, performance impact, and coverage gaps. Security telemetry is collected, analyzed, and correlated with operational data, ensuring that security controls function as expected without introducing unnecessary friction. Automated monitoring tools track threats, compliance adherence, and system health, while dashboards provide real-time visibility to security and operations teams. This ensures that ICS solutions are not only functioning but also delivering measurable value in reducing risk.

Governance structures are fully activated in this phase, ensuring that security improvements remain enforced, auditable, and adaptable. Policies established in Step 5 are now codified and continuously validated against real-world use. Compliance automation ensures that security controls align with internal policies and external regulatory frameworks. Governance also provides accountability mechanisms, ensuring that teams follow best practices and that deviations are quickly identified and remediated. By making security an operational discipline rather than a project milestone, organizations create a self-sustaining ICS framework.

To maintain resilience at scale, ICS solutions require dedicated support and ongoing expansion. Support teams ensure that security tooling remains up-to-date, properly configured, and continuously optimized for changing application needs. Feedback loops from developers, security engineers, and operations teams help refine security integrations and resolve friction points. Additionally, as application portfolios evolve, ICS solutions must be expanded to new teams, workflows, and architectures, ensuring consistent security coverage across all development and deployment environments.

ICS solutions are not static—they must evolve alongside the applications and infrastructure they protect. This phase includes a structured approach to continuous improvement, automation refinement, and innovation. AI-driven security enhancements, adaptive policy enforcement, and new threat intelligence capabilities can be integrated iteratively, ensuring that ICS practices remain effective against emerging attack vectors and evolving compliance requirements. By embedding security into an agile operational model, organizations maintain a proactive rather than reactive security posture.

Step 6 ensures that ICS is not just implemented but also institutionalized. By embedding security deep into DevOps workflows, activating governance and monitoring, expanding coverage, and enabling continuous evolution, this step guarantees long-term resilience and adaptability. With ICS fully operationalized, organizations achieve the ultimate goal of Intelligent Continuous Security, where security is not an afterthought but a seamless, automated, and continuously improving capability woven into the fabric of software delivery.

Step 6 ensures that ICS security improvements move beyond deployment and into sustainable, scalable, and continuously managed capabilities. This step formalizes the security solution's integration into daily operations, governance structures, and support models, ensuring that ICS practices remain effective at scale. By the end of this phase, security controls are enforced, monitored, and continuously refined, creating a resilient foundation for long-term security success.

The first key deliverable is controlled access, ensuring that only authorized users, services, and systems can interact with ICS-enabled security capabilities. Access controls must be precisely defined, continuously monitored, and dynamically adjusted based on risk and operational requirements. Role-based access control (RBAC), PaC frameworks, and just-in-time access mechanisms prevent privilege creep and unauthorized modifications. By enforcing controlled access, organizations ensure that ICS solutions remain secure, compliant, and auditable.

Monitoring is another critical deliverable, providing real-time visibility into security effectiveness, compliance adherence, and operational impact. Telemetry from security tools, application logs, and infrastructure observability platforms is aggregated to track threat detection rates, incident response times, and security automation efficiency. Monitoring is automated and proactive, triggering alerts when security controls fail, policies are violated, or anomalous activity is detected. This continuous feedback loop allows organizations to measure the impact of ICS security improvements and adjust as needed.

With ICS now embedded in daily workflows, governance structures are fully enforced. Security policies, compliance frameworks, and automated enforcement mechanisms are activated to ensure consistency, accountability, and regulatory alignment. Governance includes auditing security practices, measuring adherence to security service level agreements (SLAs), and defining escalation pathways for risk mitigation. It also provides the foundation for continuous improvement, ensuring that ICS solutions remain adaptable to evolving application architectures and threat landscapes.

A support model is established to maintain, troubleshoot, and refine ICS implementations. Support teams ensure that security solutions remain up-to-date, optimized for performance, and responsive to user feedback. Developers, security engineers, and operations teams collaborate to identify friction points, resolve misconfigurations, and continuously optimize security workflows. Support also plays a key role in expanding ICS adoption across new teams and applications, ensuring that security improvements are broadly adopted rather than siloed.

To prevent stagnation, ICS must undergo continuous evolution. This includes refining automation, integrating new security technologies, and adapting to changes in application delivery models, infrastructure, and compliance requirements. Evolution ensures that ICS remains proactive rather than reactive, enabling organizations to anticipate and counter emerging threats before they become vulnerabilities. AI-driven security analytics, adaptive threat modeling, and continuous compliance validation keep security capabilities ahead of attackers and aligned with business needs.

With ICS now fully operationalized, the final step in the blueprint is Step 7, Expansion. This step extends the ICS security model beyond a single application, scaling it across the enterprise. Lessons learned from early implementations inform standardized security practices, automation patterns, and governance frameworks, ensuring organization-wide security maturity. By building on the foundation established in Step 6, ICS becomes a core security competency, not just for individual teams, but for the entire enterprise.

Step 7: Expansion

You've rolled out Intelligent Continuous Security in one part of your organization. Now it's time to scale, as illustrated in Figure 6-9. With ICS fully operationalized in select applications, Step 7, Expansion, focuses on scaling security improvements across the organization. This step ensures that ICS is not confined to isolated teams or projects, but extends to other applications, pipeline variations, and deployment regions. Expansion transforms ICS from a single-application success story into a core engineering discipline, enabling security practices to scale efficiently without requiring teams to reinvent solutions for each new environment.

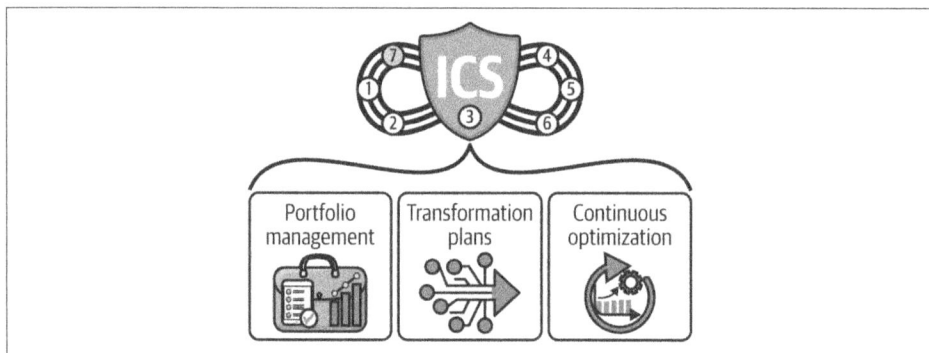

Figure 6-9. Step 7: Expansion

Expansion begins with proactively sharing recommended engineering practices. Organizations develop internal playbooks, reusable templates, and automation frameworks to simplify ICS adoption across diverse teams and architectures. By providing a structured approach, security best practices become repeatable and adaptable, accelerating transformation without introducing unnecessary complexity. Teams gain access to proven security integrations, standardized compliance enforcement, and scalable monitoring capabilities, ensuring a consistent, organization-wide security posture.

As ICS expands, variations in application pipelines, deployment models, and operational constraints must be accounted for. Not all applications share the same tech stack, regulatory requirements, or risk profile. ICS must be adaptable to different delivery models, ensuring that security automation is as effective in cloud native environments as it is in legacy systems. Security improvements must scale without disrupting developer velocity, ensuring that teams see ICS as an enabler rather than an obstacle. By refining solutions to fit diverse environments, organizations establish flexible yet enforceable security standards.

The expansion phase is not static; it is an iterative evolution cycle that drives continuous improvement. As ICS spreads across the organization, teams refine automation, optimize policies, and enhance security telemetry, leading to greater efficiency and resilience. Over time, these cycles of implementation, feedback, and iteration lead to security mastery. Organizations that successfully expand ICS at scale position themselves to seamlessly integrate next-generation security innovations, from AI-driven threat detection to autonomous security operations.

Once ICS reaches enterprise-wide adoption, security enters a state of continuous experimentation and learning. Rather than treating security as a one-time transformation initiative, organizations evolve into adaptive security cultures, where security innovations are rapidly tested, refined, and embedded into the software delivery lifecycle. This final step ensures that ICS remains resilient, forward-looking, and deeply ingrained in the organization's engineering DNA, securing applications not just for today's challenges, but for the future of digital transformation.

Step 7 delivers a structured approach for scaling ICS security improvements across the organization. This phase ensures that security is not confined to a single team or application, but becomes a strategic, repeatable, and continuously evolving practice. The key deliverables of this step provide governance, planning, and optimization frameworks to ensure that ICS is applied consistently, efficiently, and at scale.

A critical deliverable in this phase is portfolio management, which provides visibility into ICS adoption across all applications and business units. Organizations track which applications have fully implemented ICS, which are in progress, and which require further investment. Portfolio management ensures that security transformation efforts align with business priorities, compliance requirements, and risk exposure levels. By maintaining an organization-wide ICS adoption roadmap, security leaders can prioritize resources, measure impact, and drive accountability across all teams.

To enable structured expansion, organizations develop horizontal and vertical transformation plans. Horizontal expansion focuses on replicating ICS best practices across teams, application portfolios, and business units, ensuring that security automation is broadly adopted without duplication of effort. Vertical expansion refines ICS solutions for specific technology stacks, regulatory environments, and deployment models, ensuring that security frameworks remain effective across diverse architectures. Together, these transformation plans create scalable, adaptable security strategies that prevent fragmentation while allowing for customization where necessary.

As ICS becomes an enterprise-wide capability, organizations develop continuous optimization strategies to ensure that security practices remain effective, efficient, and future-proof. These strategies focus on enhancing automation, refining security policies, integrating emerging technologies, and evolving ICS with industry advancements. Continuous optimization ensures that ICS does not stagnate, but remains resilient and adaptable, proactively addressing new security challenges, evolving attack surfaces, and shifting regulatory landscapes.

With ICS fully embedded across the organization, security transformation moves into its final phase: sustaining and refining best practices over time. "Transformation Implementation Practices" explores the lessons learned from ICS implementations, highlighting what makes transformations successful and the common mistakes that organizations must avoid. By understanding these best practices and challenges, organizations can further refine their approach, ensuring that ICS remains an enduring, strategic advantage.

Transformation Implementation Practices

Figure 6-10 provides a practical framework, using AI-assisted tools and AI-generated templates, to guide the implementation of the seven-step transformation process. At the heart of this transformation is a *transformation consultant* who plays a pivotal role in orchestrating the inputs, outputs, and overall flow through the seven steps of the process. Let's break it down and dive into how this all works in practice.

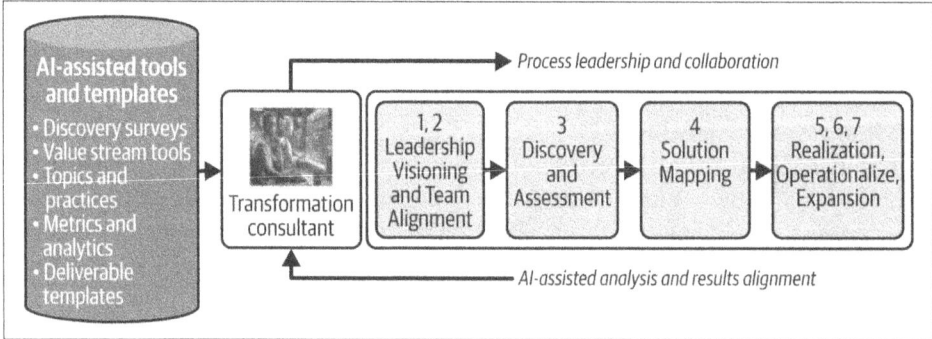

Figure 6-10. ICS transformation implementation practices

The Role of the Transformation Consultant

The ICS transformation consultant plays a critical role in ensuring the success of an organization's ICS transformation by providing expert guidance, strategic oversight, and hands-on support throughout the seven-step ICS transformation blueprint. With deep experience in digital transformations, security automation, and DevSecOps practices, the consultant works alongside transformation leaders and teams to navigate complexities, avoid common pitfalls, and align ICS initiatives with business, security, and operational goals. This role is essential because ICS transformation is not just a technology shift, but an organizational change effort requiring careful coordination across engineering, security, compliance, and leadership stakeholders. The consultant helps structure transformation activities, ensures that best practices are tailored to the organization's unique environment, and accelerates adoption by bringing a proven methodology, real-world insights, and industry benchmarks. Without this guidance, organizations risk misalignment, fragmented security adoption, and implementation roadblocks that can slow down progress, erode confidence, and undermine the long-term effectiveness of ICS initiatives.

A transformation consultant ensures that every phase of the process—visioning, assessment, solution mapping, realization, and beyond—runs smoothly, but they're not doing it solo. They rely on AI-assisted tools and AI-generated templates to streamline workflows, extract insights, and structure deliverables. Before kicking off each step of the transformation, the consultant ensures that these tools and templates are well-defined and available for use. Why? Because everything—the data you collect, the decisions you make, and the results you measure—needs to align with the overall goals. Think of it like building a house: the tools and templates have to match the design, or the entire structure falters.

As a real-world example, imagine a global bank initiating a security transformation after a regulatory audit flagged deficiencies. The consultant starts by defining templates for discovery surveys and compliance assessments, ensuring that every team provides input in a consistent format. This clarity reduces confusion and makes it easier to compare results across business units.

AI-Assisted Tools and AI-Generated Templates

Figure 6-10 emphasizes the importance of having a solid foundation of AI-assisted tools and AI-generated templates. These tools and templates aren't just for show; they're critical for collecting data, analyzing results, and structuring decisions. Let's break them down:

Discovery surveys

These are customized survey tools to gather baseline data about current ICS practices. Example: A healthcare provider might use surveys to uncover that 40% of its applications use outdated libraries, which pose compliance risks.

Value stream mapping tools

These map workflows identify bottlenecks or inefficiencies in the software security lifecycle. Example: A logistics company used value stream maps to pinpoint delays in its CI/CD pipeline caused by manual compliance checks. AI suggested automating these checks, cutting deployment times by 25%.

Metrics and analytics

These provide KPIs for tracking progress and identifying areas for improvement. Example: An ecommerce platform tracks and notices a steady improvement after implementing AI-driven anomaly detection.

Deliverable templates

These are templates that standardize outputs and inputs to the tools. Example: Templates include documents, risk reports, and roadmap plans, making them easier to communicate and act on with AI-assisted tools.

Topics and practices

All of the transformation topics and associated practices are codified in special templates for reference by the tools to bound the scope of workflows during transformation tasks. Example: A transformation team determines which of the many possible transformation topics and practices are important for transforming an application. Generative AI (GenAI) tools help with the selection and codification.

Consultant

The consultant ensures that these tools and templates are tailored to the organization's goals and standards, whether it's improving compliance, reducing vulnerabilities, or enabling rapid response to threats.

Phase-by-Phase Breakdown

Now let's connect the dots between the tools, templates, consultant, and transformation steps.

Leadership Visioning and Team Alignment (Steps 1 and 2)

This is where the transformation begins. Leadership defines the vision, and the consultant ensures that it's aligned with business priorities. Team alignment is critical; without it, security becomes a bottleneck rather than a business enabler. AI tools help here by translating vision into actionable insights.

Example: At a fintech company, the consultant used an AI-driven dashboard to show how existing vulnerabilities could lead to downtime, making the case for leadership buy-in. With AI translating technical risks into financial terms, teams quickly aligned around a shared goal.

Discovery and Assessment (Step 3)

The consultant rives this phase, using tools such as discovery surveys and AI-powered scans to assess current security practices. This step generates the raw data needed to design effective solutions.

Example: A retail company used AI-powered dependency scans to uncover a critical vulnerability in its customer-facing application. This discovery directly informed its risk prioritization during solution mapping.

Solution Mapping (Step 4)

The consultant collaborates with teams to design the future state, identifying tools and a transformation implementation roadmap consisting of epics, themes, user stories, and tasks needed to implement the ICS solution. AI plays a key role by modeling outcomes and visualizing how solutions will perform.

Example: In a manufacturing firm, the consultant used AI simulations to test various configurations of a security monitoring tool. This saved months of trial and error during implementation.

Realization, Operationalize, and Expansion (Steps 5, 6, and 7)

These steps bring the roadmap to life and scale the solution across the organization. The consultant orchestrates the solution roadmap activities, ensures that solutions are embedded in day-to-day operations, and continuously refines processes based on feedback. AI tools automate repetitive tasks such as vulnerability scanning and compliance reporting, making it easier to scale.

Example: A SaaS company deployed AI agents to monitor for compliance violations in real time. As the system expanded globally, the consultant ensured that regional teams were trained on how to interpret and act on AI's recommendations.

Why this framework works

The magic of this framework is its repeatability. By combining the consultant's orchestration skills with the power of AI-assisted tools, organizations create a transformation process that's scalable, measurable, and adaptable. Each phase builds on the last, creating a cycle of continuous improvement. Whether you're trying to strengthen compliance, reduce downtime, or adapt to emerging threats, this framework ensures that your transformation isn't just a one-off project, but a lasting competitive advantage.

Themes in the ICS Implementation Roadmap

This section discusses how you can think about a roadmap for implementing Intelligent Continuous Security. The ICS roadmap refers to the overall plan for implementing ICS. It is generated during Step 4 and used in Steps 5 through 7 to track implementation of the solution (Figure 6-11).

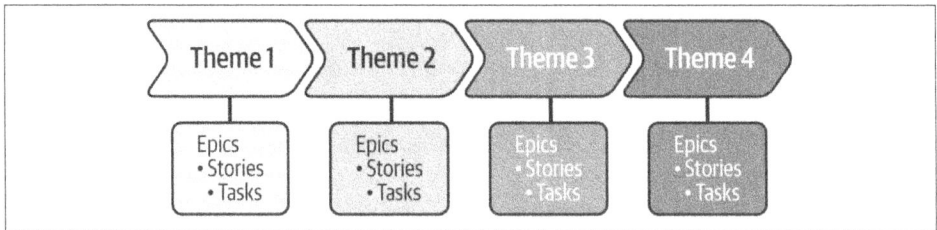

Figure 6-11. Transformation implementation roadmap

Each ICS transformation and every application will have its own customized implementation roadmap to suit the specific ICS transformation goals. The next few sections provide examples to illustrate the ICS implementation roadmap concept.

Theme 1 Example: AI-Enabled Security MVP

First things first, you need to start small, but smart. The goal here is to get an AI-enabled security platform up and running, even if it's just a minimum viable product (MVP). This phase focuses on automating basic security tasks such as vulnerability detection and compliance checks. You'll also set up environments where AI tools can simulate risks and detect potential issues before they hit production:

- Think about rolling out tools such as an AI-driven vulnerability scanner or a compliance tracker.
- Create templates for risk assessments and incident reporting so you have standardized outputs.
- And don't forget training. Teams need to know how to work with these tools. Even a half-day workshop can go a long way toward getting everyone aligned.

Here's a real-world take: a midsize SaaS company used this theme to deploy an AI-powered scanner in its CI pipelines. Within weeks, it was identifying vulnerabilities more quickly than ever, and by defining a few baseline metrics (such as detection rates), leaders could already see progress.

Theme 2 Example: Standardization and Scaling

Once your MVP is running, it's time to start scaling and standardizing. This theme is about bringing order to chaos. You'll integrate AI-driven security processes into your CI/CD pipelines and start expanding them to additional applications and environments. But scaling isn't just about CI/CD pipelines. It's also about people:

- Set up a Center of Excellence (CoE) to oversee security implementations and tool integration.
- Create *guilds* or specialized teams that share knowledge and focus on advanced AI capabilities.
- Don't forget reassessments. This phase is the perfect time to take stock of what's working and refine your processes.

For example, a financial services company used this theme to migrate all its applications to standardized pipelines with embedded AI tools. By the end, the company had trained its teams to identify risks collaboratively and saw a 30% reduction in deployment-related vulnerabilities.

Theme 3 Example: Coverage Expansion

This theme is all about expanding coverage—not just across more applications but also in the types of security practices you're running. AI really starts to shine here, with tools that can handle behavioral analysis, anomaly detection, and even adversarial testing:

- Start automating security enforcement during releases to catch issues at the last mile.
- Provide advanced training so that your teams can go deeper with tools that leverage GenAI and predictive analytics.
- Keep reassessing: what worked during scaling may need tweaking as coverage expands.

Here's an example: a logistics company expanded its ICS practices to include Internet of Things (IoT) devices in its supply chain. AI tools monitored device behavior, flagged anomalies, and prevented a potential breach in the company's tracking systems.

Theme 4 Example: Optimization and Continuous Improvement

The focus here is on autonomy and optimization. By now, your AI tools should be doing more of the heavy lifting, such as improving healing systems, real-time monitoring, and automated incident responses. Your role? Focus on refining processes and experimenting with new techniques:

- AI agents can autonomously fix vulnerabilities or adjust configurations without waiting for human intervention.

- Continuous monitoring tools provide predictive insights, so you're always ahead of emerging threats.

- And let's talk experimentation: try out new AI models and workflows to see what works best for your environment.

For instance, an ecommerce company reached this phase and implemented AI-driven self-healing systems that patched vulnerabilities in real time. Its MTTR dropped to almost zero, freeing up teams to focus on strategic initiatives instead of firefighting.

Why This Approach Works

By breaking the ICS journey into these four themes, you're not just adding AI tools and hoping for the best; you're building a system that can be sustained and that evolves with your organization. Each theme gives you clear priorities and measurable goals. Starting with an MVP ensures that you're focusing on the essentials, and scaling gradually allows teams to adapt without getting overwhelmed.

Continuous Security Macro-Flows (Epics)

When you're planning to implement each theme of the Intelligent Continuous Security roadmap, it helps to break things down into *macro-flow processes*—think of these as the big-picture steps or epics that guide your work. These processes provide a high-level structure while leaving room to adapt as you go. This section breaks down an example of how they play out for each theme provided in the preceding section.

Epics for Theme 1: AI-enabled security MVP

The goal here is to get a working foundation in place—an MVP for your ICS strategy. You're not aiming for perfection; you're aiming to prove the concept and establish a baseline for improvement:

Set up the environment
Create the infrastructure for AI-driven security workflows, including automated testing environments and simulation capabilities.

Deploy foundational tools
Roll out basic AI tools for tasks such as vulnerability scanning, compliance checks, and threat modeling.

Define standards
Build templates for deliverables such as risk assessments, reports, and metrics to ensure consistency across teams.

Train the team
Launch initial training sessions to familiarize teams with AI tools and their role in the ICS roadmap.

Measure and review
Establish baseline metrics and run retrospectives to identify what worked and what needs refinement.

Epics for Theme 2: Standardization and scaling

Now that you've got the basics in place, it's time to scale your practices across teams, applications, and pipelines. This theme is about creating consistency and expanding your reach:

Analyze the current state
Evaluate what's working in your MVP and where there are gaps in processes, tooling, or collaboration.

Standardize pipelines
Integrate AI-driven security into CI/CD pipelines, ensuring automation and consistency at every stage.

Expand application coverage
Migrate additional applications and systems into the ICS solution, focusing on high-risk areas first.

Establish governance
Set up a CoE to manage security implementations, oversee tool integration, and provide oversight.

Train and support
Build specialized guilds for knowledge sharing and advanced training, ensuring that teams are equipped to handle the expanded scope.

Reassess progress
Regularly review and adjust the framework to address new challenges or bottlenecks as you scale.

Epics for Theme 3: Coverage expansion

With your processes standardized, it's time to broaden your horizons. This theme is all about going deeper into security practices and extending AI's reach to more areas of the business:

Diversify security testing
Add advanced techniques such as behavioral analysis, adversarial testing, and anomaly detection to your toolkit.

Automate release pipelines
Extend AI-driven security enforcement into the release process, ensuring that vulnerabilities are caught and addressed prior to production.

Train for advanced use cases
Provide in-depth training on AI tools such as machine learning (ML) models, GenAI, and predictive analytics for your teams.

Scale across applications
Bring more applications, environments, and systems (including IoT and edge devices) under the ICS umbrella.

Continuously improve
Reassess your expanded coverage regularly to adapt to new threats, refine processes, and reduce false positives.

Epics for Theme 4: Optimization and continuous improvement

This is where ICS becomes a well-oiled machine. The focus is on optimization, autonomy, and continuous refinement to stay ahead of evolving threats:

Automate incident response
Use AI to create workflows that handle incident triage and resolution autonomously, minimizing human intervention.

Implement autonomous security
Deploy AI agents for self-healing systems that can detect vulnerabilities, apply patches, and reconfigure settings in real time.

Optimize monitoring
Use advanced analytics to continuously monitor systems for threats, trends, and systemic weaknesses.

Experiment with AI models
Test new AI models and techniques to improve accuracy and effectiveness, keeping your ICS framework on the cutting edge.

Refine governance
Regularly update policies, processes, and AI models to ensure alignment with business needs and compliance standards.

Iterate on metrics
Evolve your metrics to measure more sophisticated outcomes, such as mean time to prevent (MTTP) and predictive accuracy.

Why macro-flows (epics) matter

These macro-flow processes give you a clear sense of direction for each epic. They're flexible enough to adapt to your organization's needs while ensuring that you're moving forward in a structured, measurable way. By tackling ICS implementation one epic at a time, you avoid getting overwhelmed and create a foundation that's scalable, efficient, and resilient.

AI-Assisted Templates

When you're gearing up to implement Intelligent Continuous Security, it's tempting to dive straight into the work—starting *micro-flows* (or *stories*—more on those in "AI-Assisted Micro-Flows (Stories)" on page 140) and getting things moving. But here's the thing: without well-defined templates, those stories can quickly go off track. Think of templates as the foundation for your entire ICS transformation. They give you consistency, structure, and focus, ensuring that everything from discovery surveys to deliverable reports aligns with your goals. And when you bring AI into the mix, those templates become even more powerful, turning static documents into dynamic tools that actively guide your teams.

Starting with templates isn't just about being organized; it's about ensuring that everyone's rowing in the same direction. For example, a Discovery Survey template helps you collect baseline information about your current security posture, such as which processes are manual or where vulnerabilities are routinely missed. Without this clarity, how do you know where to begin? The same goes for value stream mapping tools, which let you create value stream maps of workflows in a template format and pinpoint bottlenecks, or Metrics templates, which define how you'll measure progress. These templates aren't just paperwork; they're the scaffolding for your ICS roadmap.

The process of creating these templates is as important as the templates themselves. You need buy-in from everyone involved, from security engineers to leadership, and the best way to secure that is through collaboration. Sit down with representatives from all your teams and work together to design templates that meet their needs. AI can give you a head start here. For example, an AI tool could analyze historical data to pre-fill a draft deliverable template for a compliance report, saving time and ensuring consistency. But don't stop there; test the templates in real-world scenarios, like a mock pipeline audit, to see where they shine and where they fall short. Refine them until they're not just good, but great.

Now, here's where it gets exciting: templates aren't static. With AI, they become living tools that adapt as your organization evolves. Imagine using Topics and Practices templates to guide your teams on best practices for integrating AI into their workflows. These templates can pull real-time recommendations from your existing systems, offering tailored guidance instead of generic advice. Or consider Metrics templates that automatically update dashboards with the latest KPIs, giving everyone a clear view of progress without hours of manual data entry. The result? Teams are empowered, workflows are streamlined, and your ICS stories practically write themselves.

Starting with templates also sets the tone for the entire transformation. It shows your teams that this isn't about throwing tools at a problem; it's about creating a well-thought-out system that works for everyone. And by involving people in the design process, you make the templates not just useful but genuinely accepted. They become part of the culture, not just another step in the process. So, before you start those micro-flows, take the time to get your templates right. You'll thank yourself later, when the pieces fall into place seamlessly and your ICS roadmap starts delivering results. Ready to explore what these templates could look like for your organization? Let's dive in!

AI-Assisted Micro-Flows (Stories)

Here are example stories for each theme in the ICS roadmap, tying them to the templates and processes outlined in the macro-flows. These stories provide a practical lens into how ICS implementation can be carried out in real-world scenarios.

Example stories for Theme 1: AI-enabled security MVP

The following are example stories that could be part of Theme 1:

Deploy an AI-driven vulnerability scanner.
Use a Discovery Survey template to identify high-priority systems and applications where vulnerabilities are common. Deploy an AI vulnerability scanner tool in these environments to automatically detect issues in codebases. Measure progress using a Metrics template, focusing on the number of vulnerabilities identified and resolved.

Set up a risk assessment framework.
Build and deploy a Risk Assessment template to standardize how risks are evaluated across teams. The story includes training teams on using the template and applying AI-powered tools to automate the assessment of risk levels.

Establish a compliance reporting process.
Use a Deliverables template to generate automated compliance reports with the help of AI tools. This story also includes setting up the infrastructure to pull compliance data from pipelines and ensuring that reports align with regulatory standards.

Run a team training workshop on AI tools.
Develop a training module for teaching topics and practices. Conduct a half-day workshop for cross-functional teams, introducing them to the MVP tools and AI capabilities. Include practical exercises on using the tools effectively.

Example stories for Theme 2: Standardization and scaling

The following are example stories that could be part of Theme 2:

Standardize CI/CD pipelines with embedded security.
Leverage the value stream mapping tools to analyze existing pipelines and identify security gaps. Integrate AI-driven security tools into these pipelines to automate vulnerability detection and compliance checks.

Set up a Security CoE.
Use the Topics and Practices template to define the roles and responsibilities of the CoE. The story involves recruiting team members, providing them with advanced training, and setting up governance processes for oversight.

Expand security coverage to additional applications.
Develop an Application Migration template to assess readiness and plan the integration of security tools into more applications. Use AI to identify high-risk applications and prioritize their migration into the ICS framework.

Conduct a mid-implementation reassessment.
Use the Metrics and Analytics template to analyze the effectiveness of current security practices. This story focuses on gathering data, running retrospectives, and identifying areas for improvement to refine the scaling process.

Example stories for Theme 3: Coverage expansion

The following are example stories that could be part of Theme 3:

Implement behavioral analysis for user activity.
Use the Topics and Practices template to define the scope of behavioral analysis. Deploy AI tools to monitor user activity for anomalies, integrating results into the Metrics template to track trends and potential risks.

Expand security to IoT and edge devices.
Build an Infrastructure Coverage template that outlines the specific security requirements for IoT and edge environments. AI tools are used to monitor device behavior and flag anomalies in real time.

Automate security enforcement in release pipelines.
Create a Release Automation template to define security policies and rules. Use AI to enforce these policies during the release process, catching vulnerabilities and compliance issues before deployment.

Train teams on GenAI for threat detection.

Develop a Training Module template focused on the use of GenAI for predictive and proactive threat detection. This story includes advanced hands-on training sessions and integration of new AI models into workflows.

Example stories for Theme 4: Optimization and continuous improvement

The following are example stories that could be part of Theme 4:

Deploy AI agents for self-healing systems.

Use the Topics and Practices template to guide the deployment of AI agents that detect vulnerabilities and automatically apply patches. This story includes testing and validating the agents in controlled environments.

Optimize continuous monitoring across all environments.

Use the Metrics and Analytics template to refine monitoring dashboards and integrate advanced predictive analytics. AI tools provide insights into trends, helping teams focus on systemic weaknesses.

Run experiments with new AI models.

Create an Experimentation template to document the goals, scope, and results of testing new AI models for anomaly detection and incident response. Use this template to iteratively refine your ICS capabilities.

Refine governance and update security policies.

Use the Deliverables template to document revised security policies and AI model updates. This story focuses on reviewing existing policies, incorporating lessons learned, and ensuring compliance with evolving standards.

How these stories drive success

Each story ties back to the templates, ensuring that the ICS implementation is both structured and aligned with broader organizational goals. By starting with these clear, actionable stories, teams can tackle ICS one step at a time while maintaining focus and consistency.

Common Pitfalls and Challenges: Sustaining ICS Solutions

Transforming to Intelligent Continuous Security isn't just about picking the right tools or setting up AI workflows. It's also about navigating a maze of potential pitfalls and challenges that can derail the journey. From cultural resistance to technical missteps, the path is rarely smooth. But the good news is that with the right strategies, these hurdles can become opportunities for growth. Let's dive into some common challenges and how to tackle them, with real-world examples to bring it all to life:

Lack of cross-team collaboration

One of the most common issues is that security, development, and operations teams don't collaborate effectively. Security might still be treated as a siloed function, seen as "their problem" rather than as a shared responsibility. This mindset often leads to delays, handoffs, and gaps in coverage, or outright failure to embed security into the lifecycle:

- *Fix:* Start by fostering a culture of shared accountability. Use tools such as Discovery Surveys and Value Stream Mapping templates to uncover where workflows break down and to encourage teams to align around shared goals. AI tools can help here too—think of an AI-driven dashboard that gives all teams visibility into security metrics, making collaboration easier.

- *Real-world example:* A financial services company struggled with fragmented communication between its security and development teams. By introducing regular security sprints and using a centralized AI-powered risk dashboard, the company built trust and cut vulnerability resolution times by 40%.

Overreliance on tools without a plan

It's tempting to think that deploying the latest AI-powered tool will magically solve your problems. But tools without a strategy often lead to wasted resources and frustrated teams. You end up automating chaos rather than improving processes:

- *Fix:* Always start with a roadmap. Templates such as Risk Assessments and Metrics and Analytics should guide how tools are deployed, ensuring that they solve actual problems. AI can also be used strategically, starting small— say, automating basic vulnerability scans—and scaling up as teams get comfortable.

- *Real-world example:* A SaaS company bought a suite of AI tools but saw little improvement because its workflows were poorly defined. Once it stepped back and used AI to map its security value streams, it pinpointed gaps and deployed tools where they made the most impact.

Resistance to change

People fear what they don't understand, and AI can feel like a black box to teams who are used to traditional methods. Resistance often stems from a lack of understanding about how AI works—or worse, fear that it will replace jobs:

- *Fix:* Education and inclusion are key. Run workshops to demystify AI, showing how it enhances—not replaces—team efforts. Use training modules to provide hands-on experience with AI tools, building confidence and trust. It's also essential to communicate early and often about the *why* behind the transformation.

- *Real-world example:* A healthcare provider faced pushback from its operations team when rolling out AI-driven monitoring tools. By running a half-day workshop where teams could test the tools and see how they reduced manual workloads, the company turned skeptics into champions.

Scaling too quickly

Trying to implement ICS across your entire organization at once can lead to burnout, technical debt, and systems that don't integrate well. It's the classic case of trying to boil the ocean:

- *Fix:* Focus on iterative and incremental implementation. Use the ICS roadmap themes: start with an MVP, standardize processes, expand coverage, and optimize over time. AI can support this by providing insights into which areas are ready to scale and which need more attention.

- *Real-world example:* A logistics company tried to roll out AI-driven anomaly detection across all its IoT devices in one go. It overwhelmed its teams and infrastructure. By scaling back to focus on high-priority devices first, it achieved measurable results that gave it the confidence to expand incrementally.

Poor metrics and measurement

If you don't measure the right things, you won't know whether your transformation is succeeding—or failing. Many organizations fall into the trap of tracking vanity metrics that look good on paper but don't drive real improvement:

- *Fix:* Use Metrics and Analytics templates to define meaningful KPIs that are balanced and tied to outcomes, such as MTTD, MTTR, or compliance rates. AI tools can provide real-time data and trend analysis to ensure that your metrics stay actionable.

- *Real-world example:* An ecommerce platform focused solely on the number of vulnerabilities detected, ignoring how long it took to resolve them. By shifting its metrics to MTTD and MTTR, the company reduced resolution times by 30% and saw a direct impact on uptime during peak shopping seasons.

Ignoring governance and compliance

AI and automation can create as many risks as they solve if not governed properly. Without oversight, you risk noncompliance with regulations or systems that drift from their intended purpose:

- *Fix:* Establish strong governance from the start. Use Deliverable templates to document compliance processes, guidelines, and policies. Regular reviews should be built into the roadmap, with AI tools providing continuous compliance monitoring and flagging potential issues before they escalate.

- *Real-world example:* A global bank implemented AI-driven compliance monitoring but didn't establish clear policies for reviewing flagged issues. This led to a false sense of security. Once leaders set up a CoE to oversee governance, they caught and resolved several high-risk gaps in their processes.

Here's why tackling these challenges matters: every transformation has hurdles, but the beauty of ICS is that it's designed to adapt. By addressing these pitfalls head-on—whether it's cultural resistance, tool overuse, or poor metrics—you set yourself up for success. AI is a powerful enabler, but it's not a shortcut. The real magic happens when people, processes, and technology come together with a clear strategy. Tackle one challenge at a time, and your ICS transformation won't just survive—it'll thrive.

Sustaining ICS is as much about what you build into the solution from the start as it is about how you maintain it over time. Many organizations fall into the trap of thinking that implementation is the finish line, when it's just the beginning. The truth is, ICS solutions need to be designed with sustainability in mind—baking in observability, testability, and adaptability to keep pace with evolving threats and organizational priorities. Let's break this down.

One of the key challenges is AI *model drift*, where the effectiveness of AI diminishes as threat landscapes evolve. You can't entirely avoid drifting, but you can design systems to catch it early. This is where observability comes into play. *Observability* isn't just about knowing something went wrong, it's about understanding why. For ICS, this means implementing *telemetry* for AI models: logging the decisions they make, the inputs they're processing, and the accuracy of their predictions over time. For example, a financial institution using AI for fraud detection built a dashboard that tracked false positives, detection rates, and unclassified anomalies in real time. This gave developers the insight to retrain their models every few months, ensuring that they stayed ahead of fraudsters.

Another critical consideration is *testability*. ICS systems must be testable at every layer—whether it's the AI models, automated workflows, or integrations between tools. Without testability, teams struggle to validate changes or updates, leading to potential regression. Imagine a logistics company that added a new AI-powered anomaly detection tool to its ICS framework. Without a robust testing strategy, developers accidentally introduced a configuration issue that caused false alerts to spike. The fix? Designing the ICS solution with automated testing pipelines from the start, including AI-specific tests to validate model behavior with synthetic datasets. This ensured that updates could be rolled out with confidence.

Then there's the issue of *tool sprawl*, which often emerges when new challenges lead to the addition of disconnected tools that do not interoperate well. To prevent this, ICS solutions should be designed with integration capabilities in mind. Think of it as building for the long game. Using an AI-driven orchestration layer can unify disparate systems, consolidating data streams and workflows. For instance, an ecommerce platform integrated its monitoring, vulnerability scanning, and compliance tools into a single dashboard. This wasn't just convenient; it gave the company a holistic view of its security posture and reduced the risk of something falling through the cracks.

Human factors also play a huge role in sustaining ICS. One common challenge is *complacency*: teams trusting AI too much and disengaging from active security management. This is where continuous feedback loops become essential. By designing ICS solutions that surface insights in ways that encourage collaboration, such as real-time dashboards or incident simulations, you keep humans in the loop. A healthcare provider solved this by embedding a regular threat readiness score into its ICS platform, based on team engagement with AI-generated alerts. Teams stayed engaged, and the organization avoided incidents that might have otherwise gone unnoticed.

Finally, adaptability to compliance changes needs to be baked in. Regulatory environments shift constantly, and ICS solutions should be able to pivot just as quickly. AI can help by monitoring changes in standards—say, a GDPR update—and highlighting areas that need reconfiguration. But the system must be built to act on those insights. One SaaS company addressed this by embedding compliance logic into its ICS workflows, so updates to regulations automatically triggered reassessments and configuration changes. This proactive approach saved the company from scrambling during audits.

Sustainability isn't something you tack on later; it's something you design for. Observability and testability ensure that you can detect and fix issues before they escalate. Integration capabilities prevent fragmentation as you scale. Feedback loops keep teams engaged, and adaptability ensures that your system evolves alongside new threats and regulations. By thinking ahead and building these elements into your ICS solution, you create a solution that survives and thrives.

Summary

This chapter outlined a dynamic framework designed to align people, processes, and technology in a way that transforms security from a reactive necessity into a proactive business enabler. A critical takeaway from this chapter is the importance of starting with a clear understanding of your organization's current maturity level using the ICS maturity model. This baseline not only highlights gaps but also sets realistic and measurable goals that drive meaningful progress.

Another core insight is the value of structuring the transformation journey into manageable themes, from building an AI-enabled security MVP to scaling, expanding, and optimizing practices. This phased approach allows organizations to grow their capabilities incrementally, ensuring that each stage builds on the success of the previous one. By embedding observability, testability, and adaptability into every phase, organizations can ensure that their ICS implementations remain effective and resilient, even as threats evolve and business needs change.

The roadmap emphasizes the importance of fostering collaboration and leveraging AI as an enabler rather than a replacement for human expertise. By utilizing AI-assisted tools and templates, organizations can standardize workflows, improve decision making, and achieve greater agility in their security practices. The chapter paved the way for exploring the Intelligent Continuous Security solutions, platforms, and tools that empower organizations to operationalize this roadmap effectively.

Chapter 7 dives deeper into the technologies and systems that make ICS a practical and powerful reality.

ICS Technologies

Intelligent Continuous Security (ICS) technologies are transforming how organizations approach cybersecurity. Traditional security models struggle to keep pace with the speed and complexity of modern software development and operations. Static policies, reactive threat detection, and fragmented security tools create blind spots that attackers exploit. ICS technologies solve these challenges by integrating AI-driven automation, real-time threat intelligence, and Continuous Security validation into every stage of the software lifecycle. However, simply adopting new security tools isn't enough. Organizations need a structured approach to governing, selecting, deploying, and evolving these technologies to maximize their effectiveness.

This chapter explores ICS technology frameworks, which provide the foundation for intelligent security automation, including AI-driven threat intelligence, vulnerability management, and a Zero Trust architecture. It also examines ICS technology governance, a structured approach to managing security tools and policies to ensure that they align with business objectives. Effective governance prevents security gaps and ensures compliance with regulatory requirements. The chapter then delves into ICS technology transformation tools that guide organizations through the definition, selection, onboarding, operation, and continuous improvement of ICS solutions. These tools help organizations make informed decisions, integrate security seamlessly, and measure the impact of their ICS investments.

ICS technologies must be more than a collection of disconnected tools. They need to work as part of a cohesive security strategy that evolves with the organization's needs. As security threats become more sophisticated, the ability to adapt, automate, and continuously improve security operations is essential. The following sections explore how ICS frameworks, governance models, and transformation tools can help organizations achieve real-time security, enhance automation, and proactively manage cyber risks.

ICS Technology Frameworks

An ICS technology framework is a structured set of technologies, tools, and practices designed to support the implementation and operation of ICS. It provides the foundation for automating, scaling, and enhancing security across the entire software lifecycle, from development to production, by integrating advanced technologies such as AI, machine learning (ML), and automation into security workflows.

An ICS technology framework isn't just another layer of security. It's a transformative approach that seamlessly integrates protection across every stage of the software lifecycle. From the moment code is written to its deployment and ongoing operations, ICS ensures end-to-end security coverage. It eliminates the traditional silos between DevSecOps, which secures development pipelines, and SecOps, which protects runtime environments, creating a unified, always-on security posture.

At the heart of an ICS framework is AI-driven automation, enabling security processes to evolve beyond static rule-based detection. ML together with recurring retraining continuously refines threat models, prioritizes risks, and enhances response mechanisms. Rather than reacting to security incidents after the fact, an ICS framework is inherently proactive and adaptive, identifying vulnerabilities before they can be exploited and dynamically adjusting defenses based on real-time AI insights and global threat intelligence.

Scalability is another defining characteristic. Whether implemented in a small team or across a multinational enterprise, an ICS framework remains flexible and extensible, integrating with existing security tools and workflows. This adaptability ensures that organizations don't have to rip and replace their current security stack, but instead can enhance their capabilities with AI-powered defenses. And because security threats never stop evolving, neither does an ICS framework. Continuous improvement mechanisms are built in, leveraging feedback loops from security incidents to refine detection models, response strategies, and risk prioritization over time. It's not just about keeping up with threats—it's about staying ahead of them.

The NIST Cybersecurity Framework (CSF) 2.0 provides a structured, widely recognized approach to managing cybersecurity risks, making it the ideal organizing structure for ICS technology frameworks. By aligning with the six core functions of Identify, Protect, Detect, Respond, Recover, and Govern, ICS frameworks ensure comprehensive security integration across the software lifecycle:

Identify

The Identify function establishes visibility into assets, risks, and vulnerabilities, forming the foundation for AI-driven risk assessment and policy enforcement.

Protect

Protect incorporates security controls, automated compliance checks, and real-time risk mitigation, embedding security into development pipelines and cloud native infrastructures.

Detect

Detect is where AI-powered monitoring, behavioral analytics, and anomaly detection come into play, enabling proactive threat identification before breaches occur.

Respond

When incidents happen, ICS frameworks leverage Respond capabilities for automated containment, orchestrated incident response, and adaptive remediation workflows.

Recover

Recover ensures resilience through AI-assisted self-healing mechanisms, automated patching, and post-incident analytics to improve future defenses.

Governance

The addition of Governance in CSF 2.0 is particularly critical for ICS, as it formalizes oversight of AI-assisted security practices, regulatory compliance, and continuous improvement cycles.

This structure allows ICS frameworks to go beyond traditional cybersecurity models, integrating AI-driven automation, real-time threat intelligence, and continuous adaptation to address evolving security challenges. By mapping ICS frameworks to CSF 2.0, organizations can ensure that they maintain a structured, scalable, and proactive security posture while aligning with industry best practices.

Figure 7-1 shows how 12 security technology frameworks align with the NIST CSF comprising Identify, Protect, Detect, Respond, and Recover.

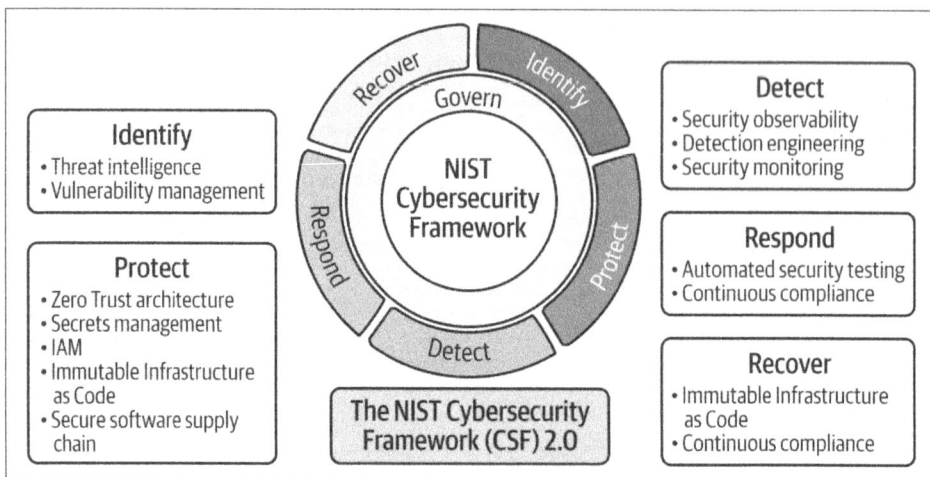

Figure 7-1. ICS technology frameworks related to the NIST CSF

Threat Intelligence

Threat intelligence serves as the security nervous system for ICS, ensuring that organizations don't just react to threats but anticipate them as well. By centralizing data from across the internet, dark web, and internal sources, threat intelligence platforms provide real-time insights into emerging attack patterns, indicators of compromise (IoCs), and adversary tactics. In an ICS framework, this intelligence is crucial for both DevSecOps and SecOps teams, ensuring that security decisions in development, runtime, and operations are based on the latest intelligence. Without a unified approach to threat intelligence, security teams are constantly playing catch-up, responding to breaches after damage is already done.

AI-driven threat intelligence transforms security from a passive, detective function into an active, predictive one. Traditional approaches rely on security analysts manually sifting through data, which is neither scalable nor effective against modern adversaries. AI steps in by correlating vast amounts of threat data, recognizing attack patterns, and prioritizing alerts based on real-world risk levels. This means ICS frameworks can integrate threat intelligence directly into Continuous Integration/Continuous Delivery (CI/CD) pipelines, ensuring that insecure code doesn't make it to production. For example, real-time threat intelligence feeds can update static and dynamic analysis tools, refining scanner parameters to detect emerging vulnerabilities more effectively. This intelligence can also drive targeted penetration tests, ensuring that newly discovered exploits are proactively tested against application code before release. Additionally, Policy as Code (PaC) mechanisms can enforce release gates, automatically blocking deployments if security scans or penetration tests identify high-risk vulnerabilities. By embedding threat intelligence into the delivery pipeline, organizations create an adaptive, intelligence-driven security posture that evolves with the threat landscape while maintaining development velocity.

SecOps teams can leverage AI-driven threat intelligence to enhance runtime security, enabling proactive threat detection and automated response. For example, ML models can analyze real-time telemetry from application logs, network traffic, and behavioral analytics, identifying anomalous patterns indicative of an impending attack. If AI detects unusual privilege escalation attempts or lateral movement, it can trigger automated containment actions, such as isolating affected workloads, enforcing just-in-time access restrictions, or dynamically updating firewall rules. By integrating AI-driven threat intelligence with runtime defenses, SecOps teams can preempt attacks before they escalate, reducing dwell time and minimizing operational impact without slowing down application performance.

Tools such as Recorded Future, ThreatConnect, and Anomali ThreatStream exemplify AI's role in modern threat intelligence. Recorded Future continuously analyzes open source and dark web threat data to predict risks before they materialize. ThreatConnect applies AI-driven correlation to organizational security logs, linking real-time incidents with known threats. Anomali ThreatStream automates threat intelligence ingestion, mapping IoCs to organizational environments, making sure defenses evolve as quickly as attackers do.

Take the SolarWinds Sunburst attack, one of the most sophisticated supply chain attacks in history. A well-integrated ICS framework with AI-driven threat intelligence could have detected the anomalous behavior in software updates far earlier. Instead of waiting for downstream victims to identify a breach, predictive analytics could have correlated telemetry data with threat intelligence feeds, flagging unusual patterns in the build pipeline. Organizations equipped with such proactive intelligence might have mitigated the impact, isolating affected systems before attackers could escalate their access.

Vulnerability Management

Vulnerability management is the backbone of proactive security in an ICS framework, bridging the gap between DevSecOps and SecOps. It ensures that security isn't a one-time checkbox exercise but a continuous process from code inception to deployment and runtime. Traditionally, DevSecOps teams perform static analysis and security scans before release, while SecOps handles runtime vulnerability detection. The problem? These efforts often operate in silos, leaving gaps where undetected vulnerabilities persist across production systems. A modern ICS framework unifies these processes, ensuring a seamless vulnerability lifecycle—detect, prioritize, and remediate vulnerabilities at every stage of software delivery.

AI-driven vulnerability management revolutionizes how organizations prioritize risk. Instead of overwhelming security teams with thousands of common vulnerabilities and exposures (CVEs), AI helps determine which vulnerabilities present an actual business risk based on exploitation likelihood, asset criticality, and adversarial behaviors. AI-assisted tools don't just flag vulnerabilities; they contextualize them, highlight remediation steps, and, in some cases, even automate patching workflows, ensuring minimal disruption to operations.

Leading solutions such as Qualys VMDR, Tenable.io, and Rapid7 InsightVM demonstrate how AI supercharges vulnerability management. Qualys VMDR offers AI-driven risk scoring, prioritizing vulnerabilities based on their likelihood of exploitation. Tenable.io applies ML to assess attack paths, predicting which vulnerabilities attackers are most likely to target. Rapid7 InsightVM goes a step further, recommending tailored remediation strategies that align with an organization's unique infrastructure.

Consider the MOVEit ransomware attack, where attackers exploited an unpatched vulnerability in managed file transfer software, compromising sensitive data across thousands of organizations. If AI-driven vulnerability management had been in place, automated scanners would have flagged the vulnerability during CI/CD testing, correlating the risk with real-world exploitation trends. Instead of waiting for an exploit to surface in production, an ICS-integrated vulnerability management system could have triggered an automated patching workflow, neutralizing the risk before attackers had the chance to strike.

Zero Trust Architecture

A Zero Trust architecture fundamentally shifts security away from perimeter-based models, assuming that no entity—whether inside or outside the network—should be trusted by default. This model enforces continuous verification of identities, devices, and transactions, making it a cornerstone of ICS frameworks. By integrating Zero Trust principles, ICS ensures that security is dynamically enforced based on real-time risk assessments, not just static access policies.

The power of a Zero Trust architecture in ICS lies in its ability to limit attack surfaces and contain threats before they escalate. Traditional network security models rely on implicit trust, meaning once an attacker breaches the perimeter, they often have unrestricted lateral movement. AI-driven Zero Trust approaches continuously validate user behaviors, device integrity, and network activity. If an anomaly is detected—such as a sudden login from an unrecognized location—AI can trigger step-up authentication, quarantine sessions, or even revoke access dynamically.

Industry-leading solutions such as Microsoft Azure AD Conditional Access, Google BeyondCorp, and Zscaler Zero Trust Exchange embody this approach. Microsoft Azure AD applies AI-driven risk-based authentication (RBA), adapting access controls in real time. Google BeyondCorp eliminates the concept of a corporate network, enforcing access decisions based on identity and device posture. Zscaler extends Zero

Trust to cloud environments, ensuring encrypted, authenticated connections regardless of user location.

Consider the case of Colonial Pipeline, where a compromised password led to a devastating ransomware attack that shut down fuel distribution across the East Coast of the United States. A Zero Trust model would have prevented lateral movement, ensuring that even if credentials were stolen, attackers couldn't escalate privileges unchecked. AI-driven identity verification and network segmentation could have isolated affected systems before critical infrastructure was impacted, demonstrating the vital role a Zero Trust architecture plays in ICS security.

Secrets Management

Secrets management is the foundation of secure access in an ICS framework, ensuring that credentials, API keys, and cryptographic tokens remain protected from exposure. Without a centralized approach to handling secrets, organizations risk credential leaks, unauthorized access, and privilege escalation attacks. An ICS-driven approach to secrets management ensures that sensitive data is stored, rotated, and accessed securely throughout the software lifecycle, from development to production environments.

AI-enhanced secrets management goes beyond static vaulting. It actively detects secrets sprawl, enforces access policies dynamically, and integrates with automated security workflows. ML models can identify anomalies in credential usage, flag unauthorized access attempts, and trigger real-time revocation processes when breaches occur. This ensures that security teams are always in control of sensitive data, even in highly dynamic cloud native environments.

Popular tools such as HashiCorp Vault, AWS Secrets Manager, and CyberArk Conjur exemplify AI-driven secrets management. HashiCorp Vault provides automated secret rotation and fine-grained access controls. AWS Secrets Manager integrates with cloud native security policies, allowing automatic credential updates. CyberArk Conjur ensures secure access for DevOps pipelines by managing secrets dynamically in containerized environments.

A real-world example of the risks of poor secrets management is the Uber breach, where attackers gained access to the company's internal systems using hardcoded credentials found in source code repositories. A properly implemented ICS framework with AI-enhanced secrets management could have detected unauthorized access attempts in real time, rotated compromised credentials automatically, and prevented lateral movement within the network before attackers could escalate their privileges.

Identity and Access Management

Identity and access management (IAM) plays a fundamental role in securing ICS frameworks, ensuring that users, services, and applications have appropriate access without exposing critical systems to unauthorized entities. Traditional access management often struggles with identity sprawl and misconfigurations, creating vulnerabilities that attackers exploit. ICS-driven IAM frameworks enforce least privilege access, integrate AI-driven behavioral analytics, and automate access policy enforcement across hybrid environments.

AI-enhanced IAM revolutionizes authentication and authorization by detecting anomalous behavior in real time. Instead of static, role-based access controls, AI-powered IAM solutions implement adaptive authentication, stepping up security measures when risky behavior is detected. For instance, an unusual login attempt from a new location may trigger multifactor authentication (MFA) or a temporary access block. These capabilities ensure that access decisions are context aware and dynamically adjusted based on real-time risk factors.

Solutions such as Okta Adaptive MFA, Microsoft Entra ID, and CyberArk Identity Security exemplify AI-driven IAM. Okta Adaptive MFA uses ML to assess login risk levels and apply step-up authentication only when necessary. Microsoft Entra ID integrates AI-driven anomaly detection to flag potential credential misuse. CyberArk Identity Security ensures that privileged access management (PAM) is enforced dynamically, preventing lateral movement in compromised environments.

A prime example of the necessity of AI-enhanced IAM is the Uber breach, where attackers used social engineering to compromise an employee's credentials and gain access to internal systems. AI-driven IAM could have detected abnormal authentication patterns, triggered an adaptive access control response, and restricted lateral movement, stopping the breach before it escalated.

Immutable Infrastructure as Code

Immutable Infrastructure as Code (IaC) represents a fundamental shift in how systems are deployed and managed within an ICS framework. Rather than allowing incremental changes to existing infrastructure, immutable infrastructure enforces a policy where new deployments replace old ones, ensuring consistency, security, and minimal drift. This approach significantly reduces the risk of configuration drift, where unauthorized or accidental changes introduce vulnerabilities. When combined with ICS, immutable infrastructure ensures that security policies, compliance standards, and hardened configurations are enforced at every deployment.

AI plays a key role in monitoring and validating IaC templates, ensuring that security misconfigurations are detected before deployment. ML models analyze infrastructure changes, flagging potential security issues based on past incidents and known vulnerabilities. Automated security testing in IaC pipelines further enhances security, allowing vulnerabilities to be identified and resolved before infrastructure reaches production.

Solutions such as Terraform with Sentinel, AWS CloudFormation Guard, and Google Cloud Security Command Center enable AI-enhanced immutable infrastructure. Terraform with Sentinel enforces security and compliance policies in code, preventing misconfigured infrastructure from being deployed. AWS CloudFormation Guard automatically validates infrastructure templates, detecting security issues early. Google Cloud Security Command Center provides real-time risk insights, ensuring that IaC adheres to security best practices.

A strong example of the need for immutable infrastructure is the Capital One breach, where an attacker exploited a misconfigured AWS instance to gain access to sensitive data. Had Capital One employed a fully immutable infrastructure model, automated compliance checks and AI-driven validation could have prevented misconfigurations from being deployed, eliminating the attack vector entirely.

Secure Software Supply Chain

The modern software supply chain is riddled with security risks, from vulnerable third-party dependencies to compromised CI/CD pipelines. ICS frameworks strengthen software supply chain security by integrating continuous verification, automated dependency scanning, and AI-assisted risk analysis. Organizations can no longer afford to treat supply chain security as an afterthought—attackers actively exploit weak links in the software ecosystem to distribute malware and backdoors.

AI-powered supply chain security ensures that every component of the software lifecycle is verified. This means using ML to assess the integrity of open source libraries, analyzing contributor behavior for anomalies, and scanning container images for vulnerabilities before they reach production. ICS frameworks also enforce signed artifacts and immutable builds, preventing tampered dependencies from entering the release pipeline.

Tools such as Cycode, GitHub Dependabot, and Google's Binary Authorization provide automated supply chain security. Cycode integrates directly into developer workflows, automatically flagging risky dependencies. GitHub Dependabot continuously scans repositories for outdated and vulnerable packages. Google's Binary Authorization enforces cryptographic signing of containerized workloads, ensuring integrity at runtime.

A real-world example is the EventStream npm package compromise, where attackers inserted malicious code into a widely used open source library. An ICS framework with AI-driven supply chain security would have flagged this anomaly by analyzing behavioral changes in the repository, identifying suspicious dependencies before they could propagate into enterprise applications.

Security Observability

Security observability extends beyond traditional monitoring by providing real-time, AI-enhanced visibility into security posture across an organization. Unlike static logging, observability correlates data across multiple sources, detecting threats that would otherwise remain hidden. ICS frameworks integrate security observability directly into DevSecOps and runtime operations, ensuring that anomalies are identified in real time rather than post-breach.

AI takes observability to the next level by automating threat detection, contextualizing alerts, and reducing false positives. Traditional security monitoring floods analysts with noise, making it difficult to differentiate between genuine threats and benign activity. AI-driven observability tools dynamically adjust baselines, recognize behavioral anomalies, and prioritize security events based on their actual risk.

Leading tools include Splunk Security Cloud, Datadog Security Monitoring, and Elastic Security. Splunk Security Cloud aggregates and analyzes security logs with AI-driven anomaly detection. Datadog Security Monitoring provides real-time visibility into cloud native applications. Elastic Security integrates security information and event management (SIEM) and endpoint security into a unified platform for threat hunting and forensic analysis.

Consider the Capital One AWS breach where an attacker exploited a misconfigured firewall rule to access customer data. AI-driven security observability could have detected abnormal traffic patterns and unauthorized access attempts in real time, triggering automated containment actions before data exfiltration occurred.

Detection Engineering

Detection engineering is a critical component of an ICS framework, focusing on proactively designing and fine-tuning security detections to stay ahead of adversaries. Traditional security monitoring often relies on static rules and signature-based alerts, which struggle to keep pace with evolving threats. Detection engineering transforms this reactive approach into a continuous process of improving detection efficacy by leveraging AI-driven behavioral analytics and threat modeling. This ensures that security teams can detect sophisticated attacks before they escalate.

AI-enhanced detection engineering continuously refines security rules by identifying patterns in attack behaviors and adapting to new tactics, techniques, and procedures (TTPs). ML models analyze telemetry data from logs, endpoint activity, and network traffic to uncover anomalies indicative of potential breaches. AI also helps prioritize alerts, reducing noise and ensuring that security teams focus on high-risk incidents instead of drowning in false positives.

Leading tools such as MITRE ATT&CK Navigator, Splunk Security Essentials, and Elastic Security Detection Rules provide frameworks for AI-driven detection engineering. MITRE ATT&CK Navigator helps security teams map adversary behavior and create detections based on real-world threats. Splunk Security Essentials automates the tuning of security alerts to match organizational risk levels. Elastic Security Detection Rules applies ML-based analytics to refine threat detection in SIEM environments.

A prime example of the importance of detection engineering is the Okta breach where attackers leveraged compromised credentials to move laterally within enterprise environments. AI-powered detection engineering could have identified unusual authentication patterns, triggering early warnings and automated mitigation actions. By dynamically refining detection logic, an ICS framework ensures that even sophisticated attackers face increased difficulty in bypassing security controls.

Security Monitoring

Security monitoring in an ICS framework goes beyond traditional SIEM-based log analysis by incorporating AI-driven analytics, behavioral profiling, and automated response mechanisms. Traditional monitoring often results in alert fatigue, where security teams struggle to differentiate real threats from benign anomalies. ICS frameworks address this by integrating AI to correlate threat signals, contextualize security alerts, and automate response workflows.

AI-powered security monitoring improves visibility across cloud, on-premises, and hybrid environments by dynamically adjusting to evolving threats. ML models assess real-time security logs, detect deviations from normal behavior, and reduce reliance on static correlation rules. This means security teams can focus on high-priority incidents rather than sifting through an endless stream of false alarms.

Tools such as Microsoft Sentinel, Google Security Operations, and IBM QRadar exemplify AI-driven security monitoring. Microsoft Sentinel leverages AI to detect multistage attacks and provide automated investigation paths. Google Security Operations applies ML to analyze massive datasets at scale, identifying emerging threats. IBM QRadar integrates advanced analytics with automated threat hunting, reducing response time.

Consider the Equifax breach where attackers exploited a known vulnerability and maintained network persistence for months before detection. AI-powered security monitoring could have identified abnormal data exfiltration patterns and unauthorized access attempts, enabling faster containment. By continuously refining detection capabilities, ICS frameworks ensure that organizations remain resilient against evolving cyber threats.

Automated Security Testing

Automated security testing is essential in an ICS framework to identify vulnerabilities early in the software development lifecycle and ensure Continuous Security validation across applications and infrastructure. Traditional manual testing approaches are slow and resource intensive, often failing to keep up with rapid DevOps release cycles. AI-driven automation transforms security testing by enabling continuous assessment, reducing human intervention, and providing real-time risk insights.

AI-powered security testing enhances static and dynamic analysis by intelligently detecting vulnerabilities and generating remediation recommendations. ML models analyze code repositories, identify insecure coding patterns, and automate penetration testing workflows. This ensures that security is embedded at every stage of development, from initial code commits to production deployments.

Leading solutions such as Synopsys Coverity, Burp Suite Enterprise Edition, and OWASP ZAP showcase AI-driven automated security testing. Synopsys Coverity applies AI to detect software vulnerabilities in source code. Burp Suite Enterprise Edition automates web application security scanning using AI-driven attack simulations. OWASP ZAP provides Continuous Security testing for DevSecOps pipelines, integrating with CI/CD workflows.

A real-world example demonstrating the importance of automated security testing is the Log4j vulnerability crisis. Organizations that employed AI-powered security testing tools were able to detect and patch vulnerable dependencies before adversaries could exploit them. By integrating Continuous Security validation, ICS frameworks ensure that security is not an afterthought but an inherent part of software development.

Conclusion

The ICS technology frameworks outlined in this section provide a robust foundation for integrating security into every phase of the software lifecycle. From threat intelligence and vulnerability management to security monitoring and automated security testing, each framework ensures that security is proactive, adaptive, and driven by AI-enhanced automation. By leveraging AI to detect patterns, enforce security controls, and continuously validate defenses, organizations can build resilient systems that withstand modern cyber threats.

As organizations continue to evolve their security strategies, the need for advanced security testing tools becomes increasingly critical. "ICS Testing Tools" on page 161 explores the specialized solutions designed to assess, validate, and reinforce security across DevSecOps and runtime environments, ensuring continuous protection against ever-evolving threats.

ICS Testing Tools

Ensuring the security of modern applications, infrastructure, and services requires more than just best practices; it demands rigorous and continuous validation. In an ICS framework, testing tools play a crucial role in identifying vulnerabilities before attackers can exploit them, enforcing compliance with security policies, and validating security controls under real-world conditions. Without automated and AI-augmented security testing, organizations are left exposed to evolving threats, struggling to keep pace with attackers who relentlessly probe for weaknesses.

ICS testing tools, shown in Figure 7-2, bridge the gap between DevSecOps and SecOps, providing proactive security validation across the entire software development lifecycle. Whether it's scanning code for vulnerabilities, stress-testing applications under high loads, or simulating attack scenarios, these tools ensure that security is integrated, measurable, and continuously improving. The following sections explore key ICS testing tools, their capabilities, and real-world applications that demonstrate their effectiveness in mitigating security risks before they escalate into costly breaches.

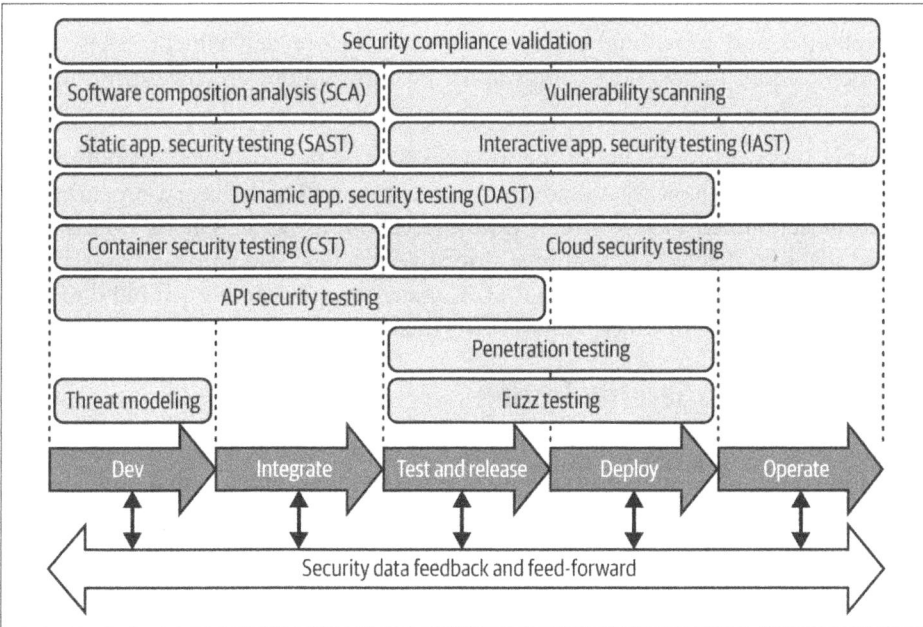

Figure 7-2. ICS testing tools in relation to application lifecycle

Software Composition Analysis

Software composition analysis (SCA) is a critical security testing tool designed to analyze open source and third-party components used in modern applications. With the growing reliance on open source libraries, organizations need a way to identify vulnerabilities, licensing risks, and outdated dependencies lurking in their codebases. SCA tools automate this process by scanning software packages, detecting security flaws, and ensuring compliance with open source policies. In the realm of ICS, SCA provides real-time risk insights, making security an ongoing practice rather than a one-time audit.

SCA helps organizations mitigate supply chain risks by continuously monitoring dependencies and alerting developers when vulnerabilities emerge. Traditional security tools often struggle with third-party risks because they focus on custom code rather than external libraries. SCA fills this gap by integrating directly into DevSecOps pipelines, scanning for vulnerabilities in real time, and suggesting automated remediations. AI-powered SCA solutions further enhance this process by predicting which vulnerabilities are most likely to be exploited and prioritizing fixes accordingly.

Several leading tools provide robust SCA capabilities. Cycode integrates seamlessly into CI/CD pipelines, detecting vulnerabilities and offering automatic fixes. Sonatype Nexus Lifecycle tracks dependency risks and enforces security policies across the software supply chain. JFrog Xray takes things a step further by analyzing artifacts for vulnerabilities and providing impact assessments before deployment. These tools help organizations maintain a strong security posture without slowing down software delivery.

A striking real-world example of the need for SCA is the Log4j vulnerability crisis. When a zero-day exploit was discovered in the popular Log4j library, organizations worldwide scrambled to assess their exposure. Those using SCA tools were able to quickly identify affected applications, prioritize patches, and mitigate risks before attackers could exploit them. Without SCA, many companies were left blind to their risk exposure, leading to widespread security incidents.

Static Application Security Testing

Static application security testing (SAST) is a foundational security practice that examines source code for vulnerabilities before an application is deployed. Unlike dynamic testing which evaluates running applications, SAST works early in the development lifecycle, helping developers catch security flaws before they make it into production. By analyzing code syntax and structure, SAST tools detect common security weaknesses such as SQL injection, cross-site scripting (XSS), and buffer overflows.

SAST enhances ICS by shifting security left, integrating security checks into development rather than waiting for security teams to test applications later. Traditional approaches to security testing often slow down software development, but AI-powered SAST tools reduce friction by learning from past scans and minimizing false positives. This allows developers to receive actionable security feedback in real time without being overwhelmed by excessive alerts.

Some of the most effective SAST tools include Synopsys Coverity, which provides deep code analysis with AI-powered recommendations, and Checkmarx SAST and Checkmarx ONE, which leverage ML to detect insecure coding patterns and integrate into version management systems. Veracode SAST offers cloud-based scanning with integration into DevSecOps workflows. These solutions help development teams enforce security best practices without requiring security expertise from every developer.

A real-world case demonstrating the importance of SAST is the Equifax data breach. Attackers exploited an unpatched vulnerability in the Apache Struts framework, compromising the personal data of millions. If robust SAST practices had been in place, Equifax could have identified the insecure code dependency early, ensuring timely remediation before the breach occurred.

Container Security Testing

Container security testing (CST) ensures that containerized applications, images, and runtime environments are secure before deployment. Unlike traditional security testing, CST is tailored for containerized workloads, scanning images, configurations, and Kubernetes deployments for vulnerabilities, misconfigurations, and compliance risks. It identifies insecure base images, outdated dependencies, excessive privileges, and runtime threats, helping organizations secure containers from build to production.

CST strengthens ICS by embedding security into the container lifecycle, ensuring that vulnerabilities are detected and remediated before deployment. AI enhances CST by automating anomaly detection, reducing false positives, and identifying emerging threats based on behavioral analysis. AI-powered CST tools correlate security findings across multiple containers and environments, allowing for proactive risk mitigation rather than reactive patching.

Several tools leverage AI for CST. Aqua Trivy and Anchore Grype provide automated vulnerability scanning, integrating with CI/CD pipelines to block insecure images. Sysdig Secure and Aqua Security use AI-driven runtime threat detection, learning normal container behavior to detect anomalies, privilege escalations, or exploit attempts in real time. Deepfence ThreatMapper applies AI to prioritize container vulnerabilities based on actual exploitability in production environments.

A real-world example of CST in action is the detection of supply chain attacks in public container registries. Attackers inject malware into widely used container images, compromising entire ecosystems. AI-driven CST tools continuously scan registries for malicious code patterns, preventing compromised images from reaching production. By integrating AI-powered CST into DevSecOps workflows, organizations can enhance security automation, reduce human effort, and proactively defend against evolving threats.

Dynamic Application Security Testing

Dynamic application security testing (DAST) is an essential security practice that evaluates applications in their running state to identify vulnerabilities that static analysis might miss. Unlike SAST, which examines code before execution, DAST simulates real-world attack scenarios, testing how applications respond to malicious input, misconfigurations, and authentication flaws. In an ICS framework, DAST plays a crucial role by detecting runtime security issues before attackers can exploit them.

DAST enhances ICS by ensuring that security is continuously validated during development, staging, and production. AI-powered DAST tools use ML to generate attack scenarios, analyze responses, and prioritize risks based on real-world exploitability. This approach eliminates guesswork and helps organizations fix security flaws that might only become apparent in a live environment.

Some of the most effective DAST tools include Burp Suite Enterprise Edition, which automates security scanning of web applications; Acunetix, which leverages AI for deep vulnerability analysis; and OWASP ZAP, an open source tool that integrates seamlessly into DevSecOps workflows. These tools provide dynamic insights into an application's security posture without requiring access to source code.

A real-world example showcasing the need for DAST is the Capital One breach, where a misconfigured web application firewall allowed an attacker to exfiltrate sensitive data. A well-implemented DAST strategy could have detected this misconfiguration before deployment, triggering alerts and automated remediation steps to prevent exploitation.

Interactive Application Security Testing

Interactive application security testing (IAST) blends the benefits of SAST and DAST by monitoring applications during execution to detect security vulnerabilities in real time. Unlike traditional testing approaches, IAST instruments applications at runtime, analyzing how code interacts with data flows and external systems. This allows organizations to detect security flaws with high accuracy and low false positives, making IAST a valuable addition to ICS frameworks.

IAST enhances ICS by providing real-time, contextual security insights during development and testing phases. AI-driven IAST tools continuously monitor application behavior, identifying vulnerabilities as they occur rather than relying on periodic scans. This ensures that security feedback is immediate, allowing developers to address issues more quickly and reducing the time-to-fix window.

Leading IAST tools include Contrast Security, which uses runtime instrumentation to detect vulnerabilities with minimal performance impact; HCL AppScan, which integrates IAST with AI-driven analytics; and Synopsys Seeker, which provides dynamic security insights tailored to DevSecOps environments. These tools help bridge the gap between static analysis and real-world threat detection.

A key use case demonstrating the value of IAST is the Uber API breach, where attackers exploited weak authentication mechanisms to access sensitive data. IAST could have detected these authentication flaws in real time, providing immediate remediation guidance before attackers found and exploited the vulnerability.

Fuzz Testing

Fuzz testing, or *fuzzing*, is a powerful security testing technique used to uncover vulnerabilities by bombarding applications with malformed, unexpected, or random inputs. The goal is to identify flaws that could lead to crashes, memory leaks, or exploitable vulnerabilities. In the context of ICS, fuzz testing is crucial for identifying security weaknesses in software that traditional testing methods may overlook, particularly in complex systems such as APIs, Internet of Things (IoT) devices, and network protocols.

AI-powered fuzz testing enhances ICS by automating the process of generating and evaluating test cases. Instead of relying on human testers to craft malicious inputs manually, ML models analyze historical vulnerabilities and generate tailored attack patterns. This approach improves testing efficiency, reduces false positives, and enables security teams to focus on high-risk findings rather than sifting through irrelevant results.

Leading fuzz testing tools include AFL (American Fuzzy Lop), which optimizes input mutation to maximize code coverage; Microsoft OneFuzz, an open source, scalable fuzzing platform; and Google OSS-Fuzz, which continuously fuzz-tests open source software at scale. These tools help organizations proactively discover security weaknesses before attackers can exploit them.

A striking real-world example of fuzz testing's impact is the discovery of Heartbleed, a critical OpenSSL vulnerability that allowed attackers to extract sensitive data from memory. Had systematic fuzz testing been applied earlier, this flaw might have been detected before it was widely exploited, saving organizations from significant security incidents and data breaches.

Penetration Testing Automation

Penetration testing automation (or *automated pentesting*) accelerates the process of simulating real-world attacks against systems to identify security weaknesses. Traditional penetration testing is labor intensive, requiring skilled ethical hackers to manually probe defenses. Automated penetration testing tools streamline this process by using AI and scripting to mimic attack behaviors at scale, providing continuous validation of security controls in ICS environments.

Automated penetration testing enhances ICS by ensuring that security assessments occur regularly and consistently rather than relying on periodic manual testing. AI-driven penetration testing tools adapt to evolving threats by dynamically generating attack paths, detecting misconfigurations, and prioritizing critical vulnerabilities for remediation. This enables organizations to strengthen security defenses without waiting for annual security audits.

Some of the top automated penetration testing tools include Pentera, which simulates adversary behaviors across an organization's infrastructure; Metasploit Pro, an industry-standard framework for penetration testing; and Cobalt Strike, which enables red teams to emulate sophisticated attack scenarios. These tools integrate into security workflows, providing actionable insights to security teams.

A real-world case demonstrating the importance of penetration testing is the Colonial Pipeline ransomware attack, where attackers exploited a weak VPN credential to gain access to critical infrastructure. Had automated penetration testing been part of the organization's ICS strategy, it could have identified the insecure access control and prompted remediation before an attacker took advantage of it.

Vulnerability Scanning

Vulnerability scanning is a core security practice that systematically identifies security weaknesses in software, networks, and cloud environments. Unlike penetration testing, which simulates attacks, vulnerability scanners automatically scan systems for known vulnerabilities, misconfigurations, and missing patches. ICS frameworks leverage vulnerability scanning to maintain Continuous Security hygiene across enterprise environments.

AI-powered vulnerability scanning enhances ICS by using ML to prioritize vulnerabilities based on exploitability and business risk. Instead of overwhelming security teams with thousands of alerts, AI-driven scanners categorize threats based on real-world attack likelihood, ensuring that remediation efforts focus on the most pressing risks first.

Top vulnerability scanning tools include Tenable Nessus, which detects vulnerabilities across IT and IoT environments; Qualys VMDR, which integrates AI-driven risk scoring into vulnerability management; and Rapid7 InsightVM, which provides continuous visibility into security posture. These tools help organizations proactively mitigate risks before attackers exploit them.

A prime example of the necessity of vulnerability scanning is the WannaCry ransomware outbreak. Attackers exploited a Microsoft SMB vulnerability that had already been patched, but many organizations had not applied the fix. Regular vulnerability scans could have flagged the missing patch, allowing security teams to close the security gap before it was too late.

Threat Modeling

Threat modeling is a proactive security process that helps organizations identify potential threats, attack vectors, and vulnerabilities in their systems before they can be exploited. Threat modeling encourages teams to think like attackers, mapping out risks and mitigating them early in the development lifecycle instead of waiting for security flaws to emerge in production. ICS frameworks rely on threat modeling to prioritize security efforts and ensure that high-risk scenarios are addressed before deployment.

AI-powered threat modeling enhances ICS by automating risk assessments and suggesting remediation strategies based on historical attack patterns. ML algorithms analyze previous breaches, system architectures, and industry-specific threats to help security teams create effective defense strategies. This ensures that organizations remain one step ahead of attackers by designing security into their systems rather than retrofitting it later.

Popular threat modeling tools include Microsoft Threat Modeling Tool, which helps teams identify and mitigate threats during the design phase; OWASP Threat Dragon, an open source tool that provides structured risk assessments; and IriusRisk, which automates threat modeling and integrates with DevSecOps workflows. These tools ensure that security considerations are embedded in every stage of software development. A word of caution, though, about the inherent challenges of biased models: threat models can often create a bias and lead teams to overlook other potential threats that were not identified during this activity. Expert opinions and analysis need to be in place to eliminate biased models.

In early 2024, several ransomware groups exploited a critical vulnerability in VMware ESXi hypervisors, identified as CVE-2024-37085. This flaw allowed attackers to gain full administrative access to domain-joined ESXi hosts by manipulating Active Directory group memberships, specifically targeting a group named "ESX Admins." By creating or modifying this group and adding themselves as members, threat actors obtained elevated privileges, enabling them to deploy ransomware and encrypt virtual machines hosted on the compromised hypervisors. To mitigate such risks, it is imperative for organizations to implement robust security practices, including regular vulnerability assessments.

API Security Testing

API security testing is a crucial practice in ICS that ensures that APIs remain secure from common attack vectors such as injection flaws, authentication bypasses, and data leakage. With the rise of microservices and cloud native applications, APIs have become a prime target for attackers, making rigorous security testing essential. ICS frameworks incorporate API security testing to detect vulnerabilities before they are exploited, ensuring that robust authentication, authorization, and input validation mechanisms are in place.

AI-powered API security testing enhances ICS by automating the identification of security flaws and predicting potential attack scenarios. These tools analyze API traffic, detect anomalies, and recommend remediation steps in real time. By integrating with CI/CD pipelines, AI-driven API security testing prevents insecure APIs from reaching production, reducing the attack surface significantly.

Leading API security testing tools include Postman Security Testing, which automates API vulnerability scans; 42Crunch, which provides AI-driven API risk analysis; and Burp Suite, which simulates API attacks to uncover security weaknesses. These tools help organizations continuously validate their API security posture.

A real-world example of the importance of API security testing is the Facebook API breach, where poorly secured API endpoints exposed user data to unauthorized third parties. AI-driven API security testing could have identified weak authentication mechanisms and prevented this data exposure before attackers exploited it.

Cloud Security Testing

Cloud security testing evaluates cloud-based applications, configurations, and infrastructure for security vulnerabilities. As organizations shift to cloud computing, securing cloud environments becomes increasingly complex. ICS frameworks integrate cloud security testing to continuously validate the security of cloud workloads, ensuring compliance with security policies and regulatory requirements.

AI-driven cloud security testing enhances ICS by automating misconfiguration detection, access control validation, and anomaly detection. These tools provide real-time insights into cloud security posture, enabling security teams to respond to threats proactively. By leveraging AI-driven security assessments, organizations can prevent cloud breaches before they occur.

Top cloud security testing tools include Palo Alto Prisma Cloud, which continuously monitors cloud environments for security risks; AWS Security Hub, which provides AI-driven security insights for AWS workloads; and Microsoft Defender for Cloud, which protects multicloud and hybrid environments. These solutions help organizations secure their cloud infrastructure efficiently.

A major cloud security failure was the Capital One data breach, where a misconfigured AWS firewall allowed an attacker to access sensitive customer data. AI-powered cloud security testing could have detected this misconfiguration before exploitation, preventing one of the largest cloud breaches in history.

Load Testing for Security

Load testing for security assesses how an application or system performs under extreme conditions while maintaining security resilience. Traditional load testing focuses on performance metrics, but in an ICS framework, security is a critical component. Attackers often exploit high-traffic situations, such as peak load times, to launch denial-of-service (DoS) attacks or exploit resource exhaustion vulnerabilities.

AI-enhanced load testing helps ICS by simulating traffic spikes, monitoring for unusual behaviors, and stress-testing security controls under extreme loads. This ensures that applications not only remain performant but also resist attacks during high-traffic scenarios. AI-driven anomaly detection can identify security weaknesses that emerge only under stress conditions.

Popular load-testing tools with security capabilities include Apache JMeter, which simulates high-traffic loads while analyzing system stability; LoadNinja, which integrates AI-driven performance and security testing; and Gatling, which tests API resilience under heavy loads. These tools help organizations validate their security posture in high-demand situations.

A real-world example of load testing for security is the Dyn DDoS attack, where attackers exploited IoT devices to launch a massive distributed denial-of-service (DDoS) attack, disrupting major internet services. AI-powered load testing could have detected weak points in infrastructure resilience and guided mitigation strategies before attackers capitalized on them.

SQL Injection Testing

SQL injection testing is a specialized security practice aimed at detecting vulnerabilities that allow attackers to manipulate database queries through user input fields. SQL injection remains one of the most dangerous and frequently exploited vulnerabilities in web applications. ICS frameworks incorporate automated SQL injection testing to prevent data breaches and unauthorized database access.

AI-powered SQL injection testing strengthens ICS by dynamically analyzing database queries, predicting potential injection points, and suggesting real-time fixes. ML models can recognize patterns indicative of SQL injection attempts, enabling proactive mitigation measures. This ensures that security teams can patch vulnerabilities before attackers exploit them.

Leading SQL injection testing tools include SQLMap, which automates SQL injection detection and exploitation; HCL AppScan, which provides AI-driven SQL injection analysis; and Acunetix, which integrates SQL vulnerability testing into DevSecOps workflows. These tools help organizations continuously assess and secure their database interactions.

A major case highlighting the importance of SQL injection testing is the Sony PlayStation Network breach, where attackers exploited an SQL injection flaw to access user data. If AI-driven SQL injection testing had been implemented, the vulnerability could have been identified and remediated before the breach occurred.

Security Compliance Validation

Security compliance validation ensures that organizations adhere to regulatory standards and industry best practices, such as the General Data Protection Regulation (GDPR), Health Insurance Portability and Accountability Act (HIPAA), Payment Card Industry Data Security Standard (PCI DSS), and those from the National Institute of Standards and Technology (NIST). Compliance is not just about meeting legal requirements; it is fundamental to maintaining a strong security posture. ICS frameworks incorporate continuous compliance validation to ensure that security controls align with evolving regulatory expectations.

AI-powered compliance validation enhances ICS by automating compliance assessments, monitoring security controls, and generating real-time compliance reports. AI-driven tools analyze security configurations and flag noncompliant elements, enabling organizations to remediate issues proactively. This reduces the risk of regulatory penalties and strengthens overall security governance.

Top security compliance validation tools include Tenable.sc, which provides continuous compliance assessments; Qualys Policy Compliance, which automates policy enforcement; and AWS Audit Manager, which monitors cloud security compliance in real time. These solutions ensure that organizations meet compliance standards efficiently.

A significant example of compliance failures is the Marriott data breach, where a lack of robust compliance validation resulted in the exposure of millions of customer records. AI-driven security compliance validation could have detected misconfigurations and data protection gaps, preventing regulatory violations and reputational damage.

Conclusion

ICS testing tools are fundamental to maintaining a proactive and resilient security posture. They enable organizations to detect, mitigate, and prevent security vulnerabilities across applications, cloud environments, and APIs before they can be exploited. From API security testing to cloud security assessments, these tools ensure that security is not just an afterthought but an integral part of software development and operational workflows. AI-driven testing solutions further enhance this by automating detection, improving accuracy, and reducing the time needed to identify security gaps.

As organizations continue to evolve their ICS strategies, the need for integration platforms becomes critical. ICS testing tools generate vast amounts of security data, which must be correlated, analyzed, and acted upon in real time. "ICS Integration Platforms" explores how organizations can streamline security operations by connecting testing tools, monitoring solutions, and automation frameworks into a unified security ecosystem.

ICS Integration Platforms

In the evolving landscape of ICS, managing security across development and operations is no small feat. Organizations often struggle with fragmented security tools, inconsistent data flows, and disjointed automation efforts. An ICS integration platform, illustrated in Figure 7-3, serves as the technology backbone of a unified security strategy, enabling seamless automation and coordination between DevSecOps and SecOps. These platforms integrate security testing tools, threat detection mechanisms, and automated response workflows into a cohesive ecosystem, allowing security teams to act more quickly and more effectively.

By embedding security policies, centralizing security metrics, and automating threat responses, ICS integration platforms transform reactive security into a proactive, intelligent defense mechanism. They provide a common framework that enables Continuous Security feedback, ensuring that vulnerabilities are addressed early in the development lifecycle while also maintaining vigilance in runtime environments. Whether through do-it-yourself (DIY) platforms, CI/CD integrations, or advanced security orchestration tools, these platforms help organizations streamline security workflows, minimize risks, and maintain compliance in an increasingly complex threat landscape. The following sections explore the key technologies and best practices that make ICS integration platforms a game-changer for modern security operations.

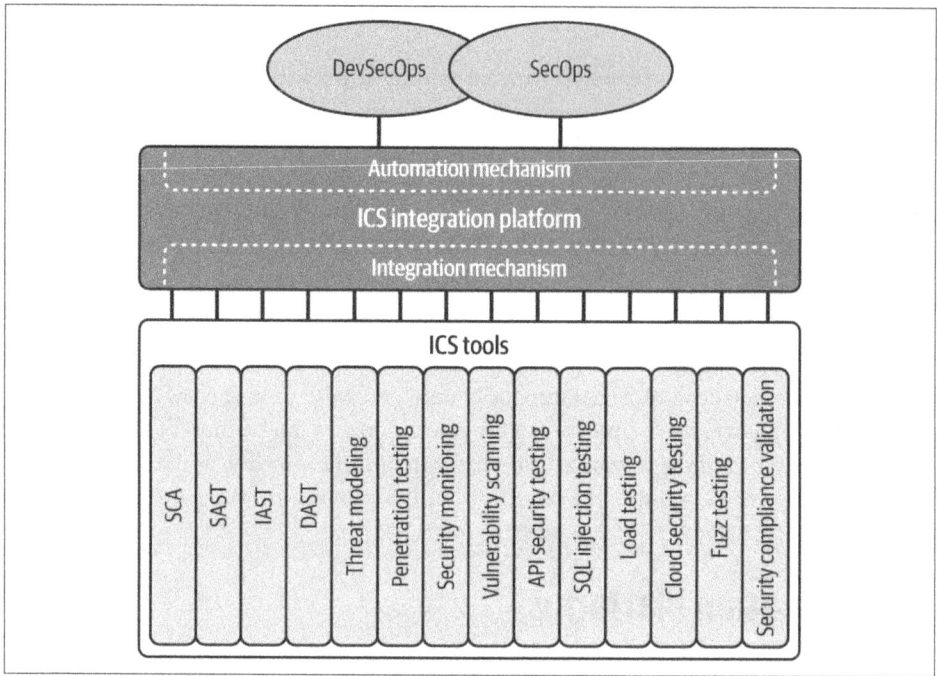

Figure 7-3. ICS integration platform

DIY Platforms: Custom-Built ICS Integration

Building an ICS integration platform from scratch offers organizations full control over security automation and workflow orchestration. DIY platforms leverage open source tools, scripting, and IaC to tailor security processes to specific business needs. Unlike off-the-shelf solutions, DIY platforms enable organizations to integrate security into both DevSecOps and SecOps workflows, ensuring a unified approach across development and operations.

This flexibility comes at a cost: DIY solutions require dedicated expertise to design, implement, and maintain integrations. However, organizations that invest in custom platforms can optimize security controls, automate repetitive tasks, and respond to threats with greater agility. AI-driven automation enhances DIY platforms by accelerating the development of custom workflows, analyzing security logs, and predicting attack patterns before they materialize.

Many enterprises build their own security automation stacks using Terraform for cloud security provisioning, Ansible for configuration management, and Jenkins for automated security testing. For example, a global financial services firm developed an internal security orchestration framework using Python-based automation and

Kubernetes-native security controls. This approach allowed the organization to detect threats in real time and enforce security policies dynamically.

CI/CD Platforms: Embedding Security in Software Delivery

CI/CD platforms serve as the foundation for DevSecOps, automating the build, test, and deployment pipeline. Security testing tools integrate directly into these pipelines, enabling early detection of vulnerabilities. This reduces the risk of security flaws making it to production, minimizing both exposure and remediation costs.

By embedding security scanning tools, such as static code analysis, dependency checks, and container vulnerability assessments, CI/CD platforms shift security left. AI-driven automation optimizes pipeline efficiency by suggesting remediation actions, prioritizing high-risk vulnerabilities, and reducing false positives. The result is faster, more secure software delivery.

Popular CI/CD platforms such as GitLab CI/CD, Jenkins, Azure DevOps, and CircleCI integrate security controls at multiple stages of development. A leading ecommerce company uses GitLab's security scanning features to enforce compliance in every deployment. By integrating AI-powered risk assessments, the platform dynamically adjusts security policies based on detected threats.

Value Stream Management Platforms: Security as a Business Function

Value stream management platforms (VSMPs) provide a high-level view of an organization's software delivery lifecycle, including security workflows. These platforms connect security events, risk metrics, and compliance data across development and operational teams, ensuring that security is treated as a business priority rather than an afterthought.

VSMPs integrate security metrics into value stream dashboards, enabling teams to track vulnerabilities, compliance status, and risk exposure in real time. AI-powered insights analyze historical security data, identify bottlenecks, and recommend optimizations to reduce mean time to detect (MTTD) and mean time to repair (MTTR).

Organizations such as Plutora, Tasktop Viz, and Jira Align use VSMPs to integrate security governance into their workflows. A major healthcare provider leveraged Tasktop Viz to monitor security risks across its software supply chain, reducing breach incidents by 40% by identifying weak points early in development.

Automated Release Orchestration Platforms: Secure Deployments at Scale

Automated release orchestration (ARO) platforms streamline the release process, ensuring that security policies are enforced at deployment. These platforms coordinate software releases across multiple environments, validating security controls before production rollout.

ARO platforms enhance security by integrating compliance checks, vulnerability assessments, and runtime security validation into deployment workflows. AI-driven release orchestration helps predict deployment risks, automate rollback strategies, and enforce policy-based security gating.

Companies use CloudBees CD/RO, Microsoft Release Manager, and Octopus Deploy to integrate security into their release pipelines. A fintech startup adopted an ARO solution to automate compliance validation in its cloud native applications, reducing deployment-related security incidents by 60%.

Platform Engineering: Security as a Service Capability

Platform engineering creates internal platforms that provide developers and security teams with self-service access to security tools, infrastructure, and automation workflows. These platforms standardize security integration, ensuring consistency across DevSecOps and SecOps practices.

By leveraging IaC and AI-powered automation, platform engineering teams deliver Security as a Service, eliminating ad hoc security implementations. AI-driven insights optimize security configurations, detect misconfigurations, and suggest best practices.

Tools such as Spotify's Backstage, HashiCorp Terraform Enterprise, and Humanitec provide platform engineering solutions tailored for security. A media streaming service built a security-centric platform using Spotify's Backstage, allowing teams to deploy security-compliant workloads without manual approvals.

SIEM: Centralized Threat Visibility

SIEM platforms aggregate and analyze security event data, providing organizations with real-time threat detection and forensic analysis capabilities. These platforms correlate logs, detect anomalies, and generate security alerts, enabling proactive incident response.

AI-powered SIEMs enhance threat detection by analyzing vast amounts of security telemetry, identifying suspicious behavior patterns, and recommending remediation steps. ML models continuously refine detection capabilities, reducing false positives and improving response accuracy.

Industry-leading SIEM solutions such as Splunk, IBM QRadar, and Elastic Security help organizations maintain security visibility across hybrid cloud environments. A retail chain implemented Splunk's AI-driven SIEM solution to detect fraud patterns in payment transactions, preventing millions of dollars in potential losses.

Security Orchestration, Automation, and Response: Automating Incident Response

Security Orchestration, Automation, and Response (SOAR) platforms automate incident response workflows, integrating with security tools to detect, triage, and remediate threats. These platforms reduce response time by coordinating security operations, automating repetitive tasks, and enabling analysts to focus on high-priority incidents.

AI-driven SOAR solutions improve security posture by analyzing historical incident data, suggesting response actions, and automating playbooks. Integration with SIEM platforms allows for immediate response to detected threats, reducing the impact of security incidents.

SOAR platforms such as Palo Alto Cortex XSOAR, Splunk Phantom, and IBM Resilient enable rapid incident response. A multinational bank deployed a SOAR platform to automate fraud detection and customer account protection, reducing investigation time from hours to minutes.

Conclusion

These ICS integration platforms provide the backbone for modern security operations, ensuring that security is not just an add-on but a fully integrated part of DevSecOps and SecOps workflows. The next section explores ICS dashboards, demonstrating how organizations can visualize security insights and drive continuous improvement in their security posture.

ICS Dashboards

Security teams today are overwhelmed with fragmented data spread across multiple tools and platforms. Without a unified way to visualize security posture, critical vulnerabilities can go unnoticed, compliance gaps can widen, and incident response can slow down when every second counts. ICS dashboards address these challenges by consolidating security insights into a centralized, interactive interface, and by emphasizing outcomes that are most important to the business mission.

These dashboards integrate data from DevSecOps and SecOps workflows, providing real-time visibility into security risks, threat detection, compliance status, and operational performance. More than just a reporting tool, an ICS dashboard serves as a command center for decision making, ensuring that teams can act on security intelligence quickly and effectively.

By leveraging automation and AI-driven analytics, ICS dashboards transform raw security data into actionable insights. ML models can highlight anomalies, predict emerging threats, and even suggest remediation strategies. This capability is essential for organizations that want to stay ahead of attackers rather than reacting to breaches after the damage is done.

A well-designed ICS dashboard enables Continuous Security improvement, fostering collaboration between development, security, and operations teams. The following sections explore key use cases, technical and functional requirements, implementation strategies, and best practices for designing and maintaining an effective ICS dashboard.

Figure 7-4 illustrates some of the benefits and values of well-engineered ICS dashboards.

Benefit	Key value proposition
Centralized visibility	Unified view of security metrics across the lifecycle
Real-time insights	Faster, data-driven decision making during incidents or vulnerability management
Improved collaboration	Aligns DevSecOps and SecOps workflows for seamless security management
Proactive threat detection	Early identification risks to reduce incident impact
Continuous compliance	Automated tracking and reporting of compliance adherence
Metrics-driven performance tracking	Data for continuous improvement and strategic alignment
Reduced alert fatigue	Prioritization of alerts based on severity and context
Workflow automation	Increased efficiency and reduced manual errors
Scalability and adaptability	Handles dynamic and growing infrastructures effectively
Faster root cause analysis	Accelerated resolution of security issues
Strategic business alignment	Links security efforts to organizational goals
Predictive security	Proactive risk management with AI/ML insights
Cost optimization	Efficient use of resources and reduction in redundant tools/processes

Figure 7-4. ICS dashboards

ICS Dashboard Requirements

An ICS dashboard must provide real-time visibility, actionable insights, and seamless integration across DevSecOps and SecOps workflows. To achieve this, organizations need to design dashboards with both functional and technical requirements in mind. Functionally, an ICS dashboard should enable real-time monitoring, drill-down capabilities, compliance tracking, and cross-team collaboration. These features allow security, operations, and development teams to respond to threats proactively and ensure compliance with security policies. Technically, the dashboard must support integration with ICS tools, scalability, robust data security, and advanced data analytics to process high volumes of security events efficiently.

A well-designed ICS dashboard consolidates critical security data into a single pane of glass, reducing information overload and improving decision making. Security teams must be able to customize views based on their roles, ensuring that developers, security engineers, and compliance officers see only the most relevant data. Actionable alerts should be prioritized based on severity, enabling faster incident response. Additionally, the ability to automate compliance reporting simplifies regulatory adherence by aggregating security logs, vulnerability scans, and audit results into structured reports.

The 2023 MOVEit ransomware attack illustrates the importance of an ICS dashboard in detecting and mitigating threats. The attack exploited a zero-day vulnerability in Progress Software's MOVEit Transfer, compromising over 2,000 organizations and affecting 60 million individuals. If an ICS dashboard had been in place with AI-driven threat detection, it could have flagged unusual access patterns and alerted security teams to the exploit before widespread damage occurred. Integration with SIEM tools such as Splunk or QRadar could have correlated logs from different systems to detect the anomaly early. Furthermore, a well-implemented ICS governance framework would have ensured continuous monitoring and automated patch management, reducing exposure to such vulnerabilities.

ICS Dashboard Solutions and Best Practices

An ICS dashboard must be more than just a collection of security metrics—it should provide actionable intelligence that drives security decision making. Organizations must decide whether to use prebuilt dashboards in security platforms (e.g., SIEM tools such as Splunk or QRadar), leverage custom dashboards via business intelligence tools such as Power BI or Tableau, or develop DIY dashboards using open source solutions such as Grafana and Kibana. Each approach has trade-offs: prebuilt dashboards offer quick implementation but may lack flexibility, custom dashboards allow greater adaptability but require integration effort, and DIY dashboards provide cost savings but need significant maintenance. The ideal solution depends on the organization's security maturity and the complexity of its DevSecOps and SecOps workflows.

Best practices for creating effective ICS dashboards start with defining clear objectives—what problems the dashboard should solve and who will use it. Prioritizing usability ensures that security teams can quickly extract insights without excessive complexity. Organizations should standardize data sources to ensure consistency across security reports and focus on key metrics rather than overwhelming users with unnecessary data. Custom views for different roles, automation of insights and alerts, and integration of feedback loops are critical elements of a mature ICS dashboard. Finally, security teams must harden the dashboard against unauthorized access by enforcing role-based access controls and encrypting sensitive data.

The SolarWinds Sunburst attack exposed weaknesses in traditional security monitoring, highlighting the importance of AI-driven dashboards with predictive analytics. Attackers inserted a backdoor into SolarWinds' Orion software, compromising thousands of organizations. A well-configured ICS dashboard with behavioral anomaly detection could have identified unexpected data exfiltration and unauthorized access patterns early in the attack lifecycle. If organizations had implemented automated correlation between security logs and cloud API activity, they could have flagged suspicious behavior before attackers gained persistent access. The lesson from this incident is clear: ICS dashboards must evolve beyond static monitoring into real-time, AI-enhanced threat detection systems.

ICS Dashboard Challenges, Pitfalls, and Solutions

Building an effective ICS dashboard requires careful planning to overcome challenges such as data silos, information overload, and complex integration. A poorly designed dashboard can lead to fragmented security insights, where teams struggle to correlate threats across DevSecOps and SecOps environments. Without a unified data model, organizations risk inconsistent security reporting and missed alerts. Information overload is another challenge—too many alerts can desensitize teams, making it difficult to prioritize critical security incidents. Additionally, complex integration arises when legacy systems lack APIs or require custom connectors to work with modern security analytics platforms.

To address these challenges, organizations should standardize security data sources and enforce structured logging across ICS tools. Automated correlation and AI-driven analytics help security teams focus on the highest-priority threats instead of manually sifting through logs. Role-based customization ensures that each team member sees only the information relevant to their function, preventing cognitive overload. Dashboards should also support drill-down capabilities, allowing teams to analyze security incidents at different levels of granularity. Implementing continuous feedback loops enables teams to refine dashboard configurations over time based on real-world security incidents.

Real-World Example: The MOVEit Ransomware Attack

The 2023 MOVEit ransomware attack exposed weaknesses in security visibility and incident response. Attackers exploited a zero-day vulnerability in the MOVEit Transfer software, compromising over 2,000 organizations and 60 million individuals. Many affected companies lacked centralized threat intelligence, preventing them from detecting anomalous behavior before the breach escalated. An ICS dashboard with AI-driven anomaly detection could have identified suspicious file transfers and unauthorized access attempts, enabling security teams to react sooner.

Organizations that had integrated ICS dashboards with their SIEM platforms (such as Splunk or QRadar) were able to correlate logs across endpoints, detect the attack earlier, and contain the damage. The key takeaway: ICS dashboards must be designed for proactive threat detection, not just passive monitoring.

An ICS dashboard is a critical tool for monitoring, analyzing, and responding to security threats across DevSecOps and SecOps environments. Effective dashboards provide real-time visibility, actionable insights, and seamless integration with security tools. The most successful implementations leverage AI-driven analytics, automated threat correlation, and customizable views to help security teams focus on the most pressing risks.

This section examined different approaches to building ICS dashboards, from prebuilt security platforms (e.g., SIEM tools such as Splunk) to custom and open source solutions (e.g., Power BI, Grafana, Kibana). Best practices include standardizing data sources, automating insights, prioritizing key metrics, and enabling cross-team collaboration. However, dashboards are effective only if they overcome data silos, prevent alert fatigue, and integrate seamlessly into security workflows. Real-world incidents, such as the MOVEit ransomware attack and the SolarWinds Sunburst breach, highlight the importance of proactive security monitoring and the role of ICS dashboards in early threat detection and incident response.

While ICS dashboards provide visibility and actionable intelligence, they are only part of the broader security strategy. Organizations must also establish ICS technology governance to ensure that security tools, policies, and processes are aligned with business objectives. "ICS Technology Governance Tools" explores ICS governance frameworks, risk management strategies, and compliance best practices to help organizations maximize the value of their ICS investments.

ICS Technology Governance Tools

ICS technology governance is essential for ensuring that security tools, policies, and processes align with business objectives. Without a structured framework, organizations risk inconsistent security controls, compliance failures, and an inability to measure the effectiveness of their security investments.

Figure 7-5 illustrates the elements of an ICS technology governance framework.

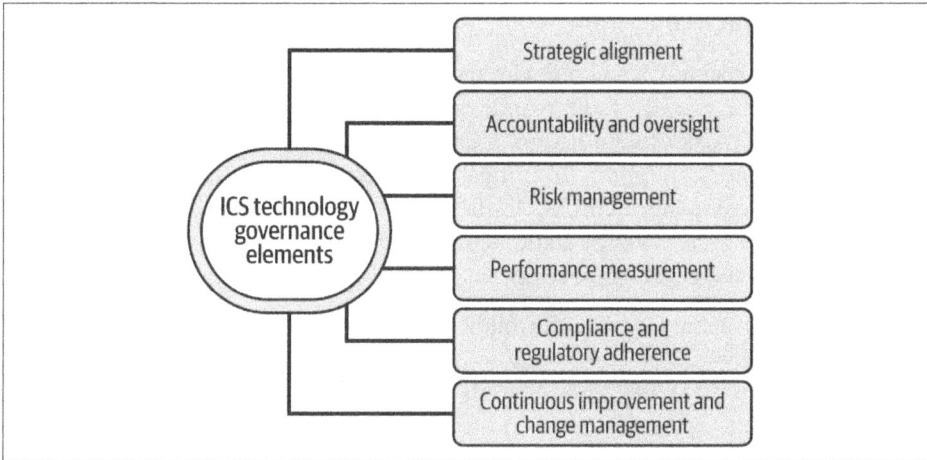

Figure 7-5. ICS technology governance elements

Governance provides a standardized approach to adopting, integrating, and managing ICS tools across DevSecOps and SecOps workflows. A robust governance model helps unify these practices, ensuring that security is embedded into the entire software lifecycle rather than treated as an afterthought.

To achieve effective governance, organizations must focus on the following key areas:

- Strategic alignment between security initiatives and business objectives
- Accountability and oversight to enforce security ownership
- Risk management to identify, assess, and mitigate security threats
- Compliance and regulatory adherence to meet industry standards
- Continuous improvement to adapt to emerging security threats

By implementing a governance model that prioritizes automation, AI-driven insights, and measurable security outcomes, organizations can maximize the value of ICS tools, reduce risk exposure, and streamline compliance reporting.

The SolarWinds Sunburst attack was a wake-up call for security governance failures. Attackers inserted a backdoor into the SolarWinds Orion software, compromising thousands of organizations, including government agencies. The breach exposed weaknesses in supply chain security, threat detection, and governance oversight. Had a structured ICS governance framework been in place, organizations could have implemented continuous monitoring of third-party software, automated compliance enforcement, and AI-driven anomaly detection to flag suspicious activity before it escalated. This incident highlights the need for proactive security governance, not just reactive incident response.

Governance Practices

Effective governance of ICS technologies requires organizations to establish clear policies and integrate security tools seamlessly into workflows. However, governance challenges such as lack of automation, inconsistent security controls, and resistance to change can hinder adoption. To mitigate these issues, organizations must implement automated compliance checks, AI-driven threat detection, and structured audit trails. Governance should not be static—continuous adaptation is required to address emerging threats and compliance requirements.

Key governance practices include the following:

- Automation of compliance checks, vulnerability scanning, and security validations
- AI-driven analytics for real-time threat detection and predictive risk modeling
- Policy enforcement through structured frameworks that align with security objectives
- Integration with DevSecOps pipelines to embed security governance into CI/CD workflows

Governance Challenges

Despite these best practices, organizations still face challenges such as fragmented security tools, lack of visibility, and slow response times to threats. Establishing unified governance across DevSecOps and SecOps is critical to closing these gaps.

In October 2023, the British Library experienced a significant cyberattack attributed to the Rhysida ransomware group, believed to be based in Russia. The attackers encrypted, destroyed, and exfiltrated approximately 600 gigabytes of data, including sensitive personal information. They demanded a £600,000 ransom, which the library refused to pay. The attack severely damaged the library's server infrastructure, resulting in an estimated £7 million in rebuilding costs.

This incident underscores the critical importance of robust security governance. Despite the library's efforts to maintain cybersecurity measures, the attack exploited vulnerabilities that could have been mitigated through more stringent governance practices. Implementing automated compliance checks, continuous vulnerability scanning, and real-time threat detection analytics could have enhanced the library's defenses. Furthermore, integrating security governance into DevSecOps workflows ensures that security considerations are embedded throughout the development and operational lifecycle. The British Library's experience highlights the necessity for organizations to adopt comprehensive, governance-driven security strategies that extend beyond basic compliance requirements, aiming to proactively identify and address potential threats before they materialize.

In summary, ICS technology governance establishes the policies, processes, and controls necessary to ensure effective adoption, integration, and management of security tools across DevSecOps and SecOps workflows. By aligning security governance with business objectives, organizations can enhance automation, streamline compliance, and mitigate risks associated with ICS adoption. Best practices include automating compliance checks, leveraging AI-driven threat detection, and enforcing policy frameworks to maintain a strong security posture. Real-world incidents, such as the SolarWinds Sunburst and MOVEit ransomware attacks, underscore the need for proactive governance to prevent security gaps rather than reacting to breaches after they occur.

However, governance alone is not enough. Organizations must also focus on the definition, selection, onboarding, operation, and evolution of ICS tools. The next section explores ICS technology transformation tools, outlining how organizations can effectively choose, implement, and optimize ICS solutions to maximize security impact.

ICS Technology Transformation Tools

Transforming to ICS technologies requires more than just selecting security tools. It demands a structured approach to defining requirements, selecting the right solutions, onboarding effectively, monitoring performance, and sustaining long-term effectiveness. Without the right transformation tools, organizations risk investing in ICS solutions that fail to meet business objectives, create unnecessary complexity, or introduce security gaps. To maximize the value of ICS technologies, we need a disciplined process supported by research, analytical frameworks, and performance tracking mechanisms.

Defining ICS Technology Solution Requirements and Priorities

Before evaluating ICS technologies, organizations must define their security needs and priorities. The right tools can help teams articulate what problems they are solving, which security gaps must be addressed, and how success will be measured. Research tools such as industry reports, analyst recommendations, and benchmarking studies provide insight into emerging security trends and best practices. Structured assessment frameworks, such as spreadsheets with weighted scoring models, help teams prioritize requirements based on business impact, regulatory compliance, and integration complexity. Organizations that rely solely on vendor marketing materials often end up with solutions that look good on paper but fail to deliver meaningful improvements. A data-driven approach, supported by structured evaluation tools, ensures that ICS investments align with both security and business objectives.

Selecting ICS Technology Solutions

Once priorities are established, the next challenge is selecting the right ICS tools from an increasingly crowded marketplace. Comparison tools such as feature matrix templates, vendor evaluation scorecards, and proof-of-concept (PoC) testing frameworks allow teams to assess multiple solutions objectively. The selection process must account for technical compatibility, scalability, ease of integration, and vendor stability. Security teams that rely on unstructured evaluation methods often make decisions based on gut instinct or vendor relationships rather than measurable performance indicators. Using structured selection tools ensures that decisions are based on clear, defensible criteria, reducing the risk of costly mistakes.

Acquiring a tool is only the beginning. Onboarding and deployment determine whether an ICS solution delivers value. Organizations that take an ad hoc approach to onboarding often face delays, misconfigurations, and user resistance. Deployment planning tools, such as roadmap templates, workflow automation platforms, and structured training modules, help organizations accelerate adoption and minimize operational disruptions. Security teams must also establish knowledge-sharing processes, ensuring that new tools integrate seamlessly into existing workflows rather than operating in isolation. Onboarding tools create a repeatable, scalable approach to deploying ICS technologies without introducing unnecessary risk or inefficiencies.

Monitoring and Operating ICS Technology Solution Performance

Once an ICS solution is in place, continuous monitoring tools are essential to track performance, detect inefficiencies, and measure security impact. Dashboards, telemetry platforms, and AI-driven anomaly detection tools provide real-time visibility into system performance and threat detection efficacy. Organizations that fail to monitor ICS tools effectively often experience degraded performance over time, increased security gaps, and reduced return on investment (ROI). Performance tracking must go beyond uptime metrics to assess false positive rates, incident response times, and automation effectiveness. Using structured monitoring frameworks allows security teams to optimize ICS technologies continuously, ensuring that they evolve with the organization's needs.

Sustaining and Evolving ICS Technology Solutions

ICS technologies are not static. They must evolve to address emerging threats, regulatory changes, and shifts in business priorities. Sustaining long-term effectiveness requires regular reassessment of security capabilities, structured feedback loops, and investment in continuous improvement. Organizations that rely on one-time tool evaluations often find themselves locked into outdated security solutions that no longer meet evolving requirements. Ongoing tool assessments, including structured review cycles, benchmarking studies, and upgrade roadmaps, upgrade roadmaps allow security teams to adapt ICS solutions proactively rather than reactively. Successful ICS transformations are not defined by the initial implementation but by the organization's ability to sustain and enhance security effectiveness over time.

In summary, transforming to Intelligent Continuous Security technologies requires a structured approach that goes beyond tool selection. Research tools help define requirements and priorities, comparison frameworks ensure informed decision making, structured onboarding minimizes deployment risks, monitoring tools optimize performance, and continuous improvement processes sustain long-term value. Organizations that invest in structured transformation tools reduce risk, improve security outcomes, and maximize the effectiveness of ICS solutions. In the absence of clear evaluation, monitoring, and evolution strategies, even the most advanced ICS tools can fail to deliver meaningful security improvements. By adopting a disciplined approach to ICS technology transformation, security leaders can ensure that their investments drive continuous, measurable security enhancements.

Summary

ICS technologies are a foundational shift in cybersecurity, enabling organizations to move from reactive security postures to proactive, AI-driven, and continuously adaptive security frameworks. This chapter explored ICS technology frameworks, which integrate AI-powered threat intelligence, a Zero Trust architecture, and vulnerability management into DevSecOps and SecOps processes. It then examined ICS technology governance, outlining structured approaches for aligning security tools, policies, and processes with business objectives to prevent compliance gaps and operational inefficiencies. Finally, the chapter covered ICS technology transformation tools, which guide organizations through the definition, selection, onboarding, monitoring, and evolution of ICS solutions to ensure Continuous Security improvement.

Key takeaways include the importance of structured governance, automation, and AI-enhanced decision making in ICS adoption. Organizations that leverage research tools for technology selection, structured onboarding frameworks, and AI-driven monitoring solutions can achieve real-time security visibility, automated compliance, and proactive risk management. Real-world incidents, such as the SolarWinds Sunburst and MOVEit ransomware attacks, demonstrate the necessity of Continuous Security evolution and intelligent governance. Chapter 8 explores ICS testing tools, focusing on how organizations can validate, assess, and reinforce ICS security measures using automated security testing, AI-driven validation frameworks, and continuous compliance assessments.

Real-World Applications and Use Cases

In today's digital landscape, security threats evolve at an unprecedented pace, targeting organizations across every industry and technology domain. Traditional security approaches—focused on periodic assessments, manual compliance checks, and reactive defenses—are no longer sufficient to protect businesses operating in complex, dynamic environments. From cloud-first enterprises to heavily regulated financial institutions, from AI-driven workloads to critical infrastructure operations, organizations face an ever-expanding attack surface. Intelligent Continuous Security (ICS) emerges as the necessary paradigm shift, enabling near-real-time risk assessment, automated threat mitigation, and proactive security enforcement that adapt to the evolving threat landscape.

This chapter explores 13 critical use cases where ICS practices are essential for strengthening cybersecurity postures, ensuring regulatory compliance, and maintaining operational resilience. Each use case presents unique security challenges, ranging from software supply chain vulnerabilities in DevOps pipelines to nation-state cyber threats against government institutions. Examining real-world security incidents and industry-specific risks highlights how ICS frameworks integrate AI-driven anomaly detection, Zero Trust security models, and automated compliance validation to protect modern enterprises from cyber threats.

Despite the diversity of these industries and technologies, a common theme emerges; security must be continuous, intelligent, and embedded into every phase of operations. Whether securing multicloud environments, protecting AI models from adversarial attacks, or mitigating financial fraud, ICS transforms security from a reactive, after-the-fact function into an integrated, always-on defense mechanism. By leveraging automation, real-time threat intelligence, and predictive analytics, ICS empowers organizations to detect, respond to, and prevent security incidents before they cause significant damage.

The following sections provide a deep dive into each use case, illustrating how ICS practices can be applied to solve real-world security challenges. By examining security concerns, real-world breach examples, and ICS-driven transformations, this chapter serves as a practical guide for organizations looking to modernize their cybersecurity strategies. Each use case demonstrates how ICS fortifies enterprise resilience, ensuring that security is not a bottleneck but a fundamental enabler of innovation and operational excellence.

Large Enterprises with Siloed DevSecOps and SecOps Teams

In large enterprises, security practices often evolve independently within different teams, leading to fragmentation between DevSecOps (which focuses on security within the development lifecycle) and SecOps (which manages security operations, monitoring, and response), as illustrated in Figure 8-1. These silos emerge naturally as organizations scale, driven by differences in team structures, priorities, and toolchains.

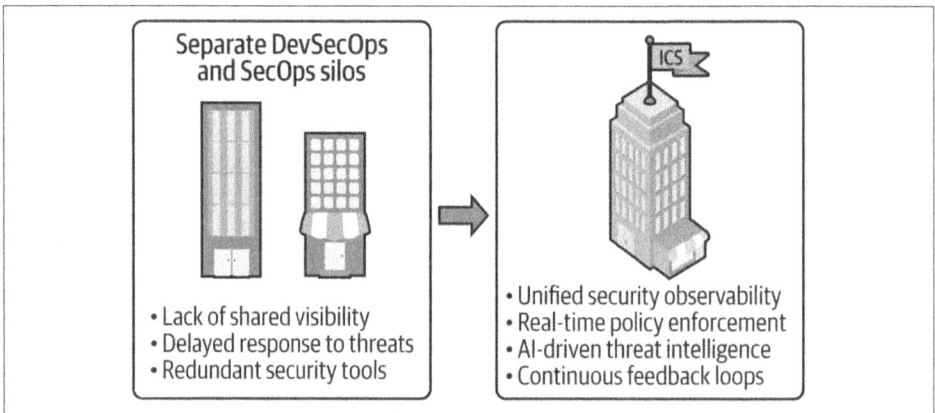

Figure 8-1. Siloed DevSecOps and SecOps

DevSecOps teams prioritize speed and agility, embedding security into Continuous Integration and Continuous Deployment pipelines to prevent vulnerabilities early. SecOps teams, however, are reactionary by design, focused on monitoring production environments, analyzing threats, and responding to security incidents. This disconnect often results in inconsistent security policies, redundant tools, and delays in addressing threats that could have been mitigated earlier in the software lifecycle.

Security Concerns in Typical DevSecOps and SecOps Practices

The separation between DevSecOps and SecOps manifests in several critical security challenges. Development teams may prioritize feature velocity over security rigor, relying on automated scanners without integrating security insights from SecOps teams. Meanwhile, SecOps teams struggle to enforce security controls post-deployment, often discovering vulnerabilities too late to prevent incidents.

Alert fatigue compounds the issue. DevSecOps tools produce volumes of vulnerability reports, while SecOps tools generate thousands of security alerts. Without coordination, false positives flood both teams, obscuring real threats. Furthermore, fragmented governance leads to misaligned security policies, with different teams interpreting compliance requirements in conflicting ways.

These inefficiencies create blind spots that adversaries can exploit, allowing attackers to bypass fragmented defenses and move laterally through an enterprise's infrastructure. The absence of unified security observability leaves teams reacting to breaches rather than preventing them.

Real-World Organizations That Match This Use Case

Large enterprises in financial services, healthcare, retail, and government sectors often suffer from this disconnect. Banks with legacy IT environments maintain dedicated Security Operations Centers (SOCs) but struggle to integrate security practices within cloud native development teams. Healthcare organizations managing sensitive patient data must comply with regulations such as the Health Insurance Portability and Accountability Act (HIPAA), but they face challenges aligning cloud security controls with DevSecOps automation. Even global technology firms, despite their emphasis on modern engineering practices, frequently experience fragmentation due to acquisitions, diverse product portfolios, and competing security priorities.

A notable example of the dangers of siloed security teams is the 2019 Capital One data breach. The breach exposed sensitive customer data, including Social Security numbers and bank account details, affecting over 100 million users. The attacker, a former Amazon Web Services (AWS) employee, exploited a misconfigured Amazon S3 bucket due to a weakly secured web application firewall (WAF) instance.

The underlying problem stemmed from poor coordination between DevSecOps and SecOps teams. The misconfiguration should have been caught during development, but the security operations team lacked visibility into cloud infrastructure changes. Meanwhile, DevSecOps teams focused on automating security within Continuous Integration/Continuous Delivery (CI/CD) pipelines but failed to align with SecOps on cloud security enforcement. The lack of unified security observability meant the breach was discovered after data exfiltration had occurred.

How ICS Practices Improve Security for Large Enterprises

Transforming from siloed security teams to Intelligent Continuous Security requires breaking down barriers between DevSecOps and SecOps by integrating AI-driven security automation, continuous risk assessment, and real-time feedback loops. With ICS in place, security insights flow bidirectionally. DevSecOps pipelines incorporate automated threat intelligence from SecOps, dynamically adjusting security policies based on live attack patterns. SecOps gains real-time visibility into software and infrastructure changes, leveraging AI-driven anomaly detection to predict and prevent misconfigurations before they reach production.

Centralizing security governance through Policy as Code (PaC) ensures consistent security policies across development, testing, and production. Security observability platforms unify logs, vulnerability reports, and runtime alerts, providing a single source of truth for risk assessment and compliance.

By integrating ICS, organizations eliminate security silos, enabling faster vulnerability detection, improved compliance adherence, and proactive threat mitigation. Development teams deliver software with security baked in from the start, while operations teams monitor software with contextual security insights, reducing noise and response time.

Instead of reacting to breaches, enterprises operate in a state of Continuous Security, where AI-driven automation enforces policies dynamically and predictive analytics preemptively neutralizes emerging threats. This shifts security from a bottleneck to a competitive advantage, ensuring resilience against supply chain attacks, misconfigurations, and cloud native threats.

Software Suppliers Separated from Their Customers

In the modern software ecosystem, many software vendors develop and deliver software to customers but do not operate or monitor it directly, as illustrated in Figure 8-2. This is especially common in on-premises enterprise software, packaged applications, and software components embedded in third-party systems. Unlike cloud-based software as a service (SaaS) providers that maintain direct control over security monitoring and updates, these software suppliers often lose visibility into how their software is deployed, configured, and secured by their customers.

This separation creates a disconnect between security responsibility and operational security reality. Suppliers may build security controls into their products, but customers are ultimately responsible for secure deployment, patching, and ongoing threat monitoring. This dynamic often results in delayed vulnerability discovery, inconsistent patching, and an increased risk of software supply chain attacks.

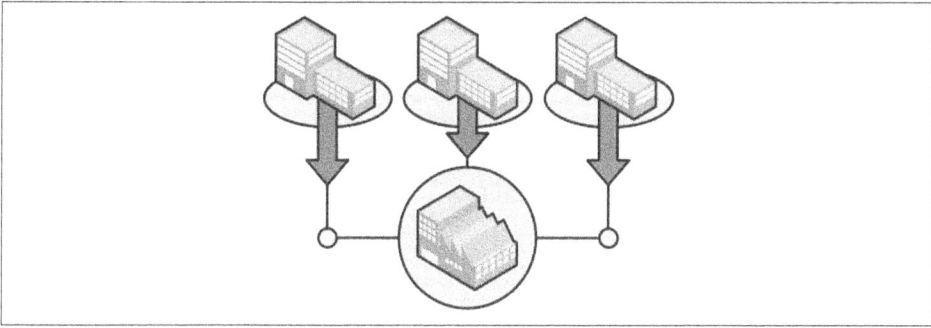

Figure 8-2. Security collaboration between vendors and customers

Security Concerns in Typical DevSecOps and SecOps Practices

When software suppliers and customers operate in separate security silos, several challenges emerge:

Delayed vulnerability detection
Software vendors often lack real-time feedback on how their products are being exploited in customer environments, leading to slow response times when vulnerabilities are discovered.

Inconsistent patching and security updates
While vendors may release security patches, customers may fail to apply them promptly due to operational constraints, fear of breaking integrations, or simple oversight.

Supply chain security risks
Attackers increasingly target software suppliers to inject vulnerabilities before software reaches customers (e.g., SolarWinds Sunburst attack).

Limited security monitoring capabilities
Customers often lack deep insights into vendor-supplied software, preventing proactive security monitoring and anomaly detection.

Regulatory and compliance challenges
Vendors must balance security transparency with intellectual property protection, while customers need assurance of software integrity for compliance with regulations like the General Data Protection Regulation (GDPR), HIPAA, and those from the National Institute of Standards and Technology (NIST).

Real-World Organizations That Match This Use Case

Industries with complex software supply chains, such as the following, commonly face this issue:

Enterprise software vendors
> Companies such as Microsoft, Oracle, SAP, and VMware supply on-premises enterprise software that customers must maintain securely.

Embedded software and Internet of Things (IoT) vendors
> Chipmakers (Intel, AMD), industrial automation firms (Siemens, Schneider Electric), and automotive software providers deliver firmware and applications that customers must secure independently.

Software component providers
> Open source maintainers (e.g., Apache Foundation, Log4j developers) and proprietary component vendors provide software that integrates into customer applications, creating hidden dependencies that are difficult to monitor for security risks.

The 2020 SolarWinds Sunburst attack exemplifies the risks of software suppliers being separated from their customers. Attackers compromised the SolarWinds Orion software update process, injecting a backdoor into the product before it reached customers. Because SolarWinds did not have visibility into how its software was being monitored or deployed, the malicious code remained undetected for months as it infiltrated government agencies, Fortune 500 companies, and critical infrastructure providers. This supply chain attack demonstrated the dangers of weak security oversight in vendor-supplied software. Customers relied on SolarWinds for security updates, but the attack exploited the disconnect between the supplier (SolarWinds) and the customer (end users), enabling widespread, undetected compromise.

How ICS Practices Improve Security
for Software Suppliers and Customers

The ICS model bridges the gap between software suppliers and customers by introducing real-time security intelligence sharing, automated patch validation, and AI-driven supply chain security monitoring:

Security telemetry integration
> ICS enables vendors to receive anonymized security telemetry from customer environments, improving threat intelligence and response times without compromising privacy.

AI-assisted supply chain security
> AI-powered risk assessment tools proactively analyze software dependencies and vendor-supplied updates before deployment, reducing supply chain attack risks.

Zero Trust–based update mechanisms
ICS enforces cryptographic integrity checks on software updates to prevent tampering before updates reach production environments.

Continuous patch monitoring and enforcement
Instead of relying on manual updates, ICS introduces automated patch validation, ensuring that customers apply security fixes without operational disruptions.

By embedding ICS practices into the software development and delivery lifecycle, vendors can proactively monitor risks and strengthen customer security postures without direct access to their environments. For software vendors, ICS practices reduce security blind spots, accelerate vulnerability response, and strengthen customer trust. Instead of waiting for customers to report issues, vendors receive Continuous Security insights, enabling them to predict and mitigate threats before widespread exploitation. For customers, ICS provides real-time assurance that vendor software remains secure, ensuring faster patch deployment, early threat detection, and automated supply chain risk management. This shifts security from reactive to proactive, reducing the likelihood of another SolarWinds-style compromise.

Government and Military Institutions Where Software Suppliers Are Separate from End Applications

In government and military environments, illustrated in Figure 8-3, software procurement follows a structured process where third-party vendors develop and supply software but do not operate or monitor it in real time. Unlike commercial enterprises where software suppliers may maintain ongoing security oversight, military and government institutions deploy software in highly controlled environments—often classified, air-gapped, or on specialized hardware.

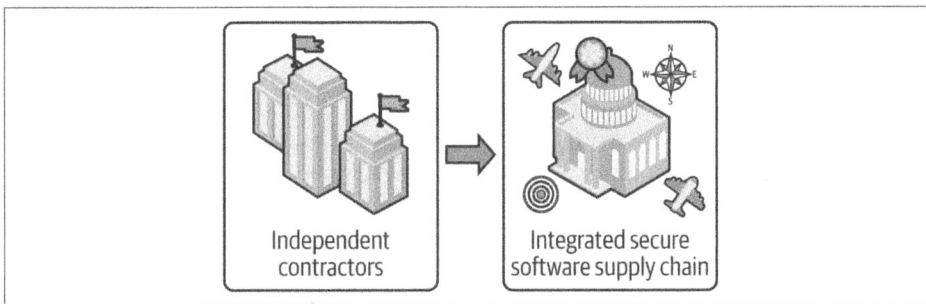

Independent contractors

Integrated secure software supply chain

Figure 8-3. Government and military supply chains

This separation is intentional. Governments require strict control over software deployment, data security, and operational secrecy, which limits direct vendor involvement. However, this also creates security challenges, as vendors are often unaware of how their software is configured, secured, or exploited in the field. The lack of real-time feedback and continuous monitoring leads to delayed vulnerability detection, inconsistent security updates, and exposure to supply chain attacks.

Security Concerns in Typical DevSecOps and SecOps Practices

The disconnect between software suppliers and government/military environments results in several security risks:

Supply chain vulnerabilities
> Without continuous vendor oversight, compromised software components can infiltrate mission-critical systems. Nation-state adversaries target suppliers (e.g., weapon system firmware, logistics software) as a means to introduce backdoors into government infrastructure.

Delayed patching and vulnerability management
> Unlike commercial environments where vendors issue frequent security updates, government software often remains unpatched for extended periods due to testing, certification, and deployment restrictions. This increases zero-day exploit risks.

Lack of security telemetry sharing
> In air-gapped or classified environments, threat detection and security insights do not flow back to vendors, making it difficult to improve software security based on real-world attack data.

Inconsistent security policy enforcement
> Government agencies and military units often interpret security policies differently, leading to fragmented security postures across various operational environments.

Nation-state espionage and cyberwarfare
> Adversaries exploit long software development cycles, embedded vulnerabilities, and weak software supply chains to plant long-term cyber threats in government systems.

These risks make software security in government and military environments uniquely challenging, requiring a structured yet adaptive approach to security monitoring and risk mitigation.

Real-World Organizations That Match This Use Case

The following are examples of this use case:

- US Department of Defense (DoD) and military contractors (e.g., Lockheed Martin, Northrop Grumman, Raytheon) develop mission-critical software for fighter jets, missile defense systems, and cyberwarfare tools.

- National intelligence agencies (e.g., NSA, GCHQ, FSB, MSS) use highly classified software systems for cyber operations, intelligence gathering, and national defense.

- Critical infrastructure agencies (e.g., US Cybersecurity and Infrastructure Security Agency [CISA], NATO, European Defense Agency) procure software for power grids, emergency response, and secure communications.

The Kaspersky NSA contractor breach in 2015 illustrates the risks of software suppliers being separated from end applications in government environments. An NSA employee took classified cyber-espionage tools home and installed them on a personal computer running Kaspersky antivirus software. Due to the lack of software monitoring and controlled vendor access, Kaspersky's scanning algorithms identified and uploaded NSA malware to its cloud-based threat detection system. Nation-state actors allegedly intercepted this data, gaining access to classified NSA hacking tools. This incident highlights how government security isolation can backfire. Without controlled software telemetry and intelligence-sharing mechanisms, software security risks can go unnoticed until adversaries exploit them.

How ICS Practices Improve Security for Government and Military Environments

Intelligent Continuous Security practices provide a structured yet adaptive security framework that allows software vendors and government institutions to collaborate securely without compromising operational secrecy:

Zero Trust–based secure software supply chain
ICS enforces end-to-end cryptographic integrity checks, provenance tracking, and automated threat detection at every stage of software procurement and deployment.

AI-powered risk assessment before deployment
Instead of relying on static security reviews, ICS introduces AI-driven software risk scoring, predicting vulnerabilities before deployment in government environments.

Secure feedback loops without exposing sensitive data
ICS enables controlled security telemetry sharing, allowing vendors to receive real-time insights on vulnerabilities without violating government data secrecy policies.

Automated security policy standardization
ICS applies PaC to enforce consistent security configurations across different military and intelligence units, reducing security gaps caused by inconsistent policy enforcement.

Real-time threat intelligence integration
ICS connects government security operations with global cyber threat intelligence, ensuring early detection of nation-state cyberattacks targeting military software.

By embedding ICS automation, AI-driven risk assessments, and Zero Trust controls into government procurement and cybersecurity workflows, government agencies can achieve real-time security assurance while maintaining operational secrecy.

For government institutions, ICS eliminates blind spots in software security, accelerates threat response, and enforces continuous risk monitoring. Software vendors gain better insights into security risks without direct access to classified systems, enabling faster vulnerability remediation and long-term supply chain resilience. ICS transforms government cybersecurity from a reactive, compliance-driven model to a proactive, intelligence-driven defense strategy, ensuring that mission-critical software remains secure even against advanced nation-state adversaries.

Network Software Manufacturers Separated from Network Systems Operators

Network software manufacturers develop routing, switching, firewall, and security software that powers modern enterprises, ISP, and telecommunications networks. These software products are embedded in network appliances, virtualized network functions (VNFs), and cloud native networking solutions that rely on their products, as shown in Figure 8-4.

This separation between the software suppliers and the network operators creates significant security challenges. Manufacturers release network software updates, but operators bear the responsibility of applying patches, securing configurations, and responding to active threats. In large-scale environments such as telecom networks, data centers, and critical infrastructure, this separation results in delayed vulnerability response, inconsistent security patching, and blind spots in network threat intelligence.

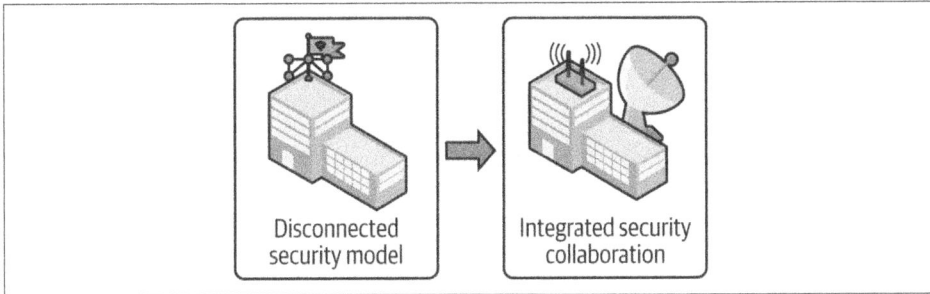

Figure 8-4. Network manufacturers and operators

Security Concerns in Typical DevSecOps and SecOps Practices

The lack of real-time collaboration between network software manufacturers and network operators introduces several persistent security issues:

Delayed security patch adoption
Network operators often delay installing software updates due to concerns about service disruptions, compatibility issues, or lack of internal change control processes. This delay exposes networks to known vulnerabilities long after patches are available.

Configuration drift and mismanagement
Operators may modify default security settings, disable security features, or apply inconsistent configurations across network environments, creating security gaps.

Supply chain security risks
Attackers target network software updates at the source (e.g., the software vendor) or during deployment (e.g., compromised firmware, unauthorized backdoors).

Fragmented security intelligence sharing
Network vendors lack visibility into real-time attack patterns affecting their software in customer environments, making it difficult to proactively improve security controls.

Compliance and regulatory challenges
Telecommunications providers, government networks, and cloud operators must adhere to strict regulatory standards (e.g., NIST, GDPR, FCC security requirements), yet inconsistent vendor–operator coordination makes compliance complex.

Without a continuous feedback loop between network software suppliers and network operators, security remains reactive, increasing the likelihood of successful attacks.

Real-World Organizations That Match This Use Case

The following are examples of this use case:

Network equipment vendors
> Companies such as Cisco, Juniper Networks, Arista, Huawei, and Nokia develop software that runs routers, switches, and firewalls used by enterprises and ISPs.

Telecommunications providers
> AT&T, Verizon, Deutsche Telekom, and China Mobile operate large-scale networks that rely on vendor-supplied networking software but must independently maintain security.

Cloud network operators
> AWS, Microsoft Azure, and Google Cloud run virtualized networking software stacks (e.g., SD-WAN, cloud firewalls) that depend on software updates from third-party vendors.

A major example of network software vulnerabilities being exploited is the Cisco ASA and Firepower VPN vulnerability (CVE-2020-3452). Cisco released an advisory for critical vulnerability in its Adaptive Security Appliance (ASA) and Firepower Threat Defense (FTD) VPN products, which affected enterprise networks, cloud security gateways, and government organizations.

However, because network operators were responsible for patching these vulnerabilities, many organizations failed to apply updates on time. Attackers quickly exploited unpatched systems, gaining unauthorized access to network infrastructure and exfiltrating sensitive data. The issue was not that Cisco didn't provide a patch, but that the operators didn't (or couldn't) apply it quickly enough due to operational concerns. This highlights the danger of separating network software vendors from real-time network security operations.

How ICS Practices Improve Security for Network Software and Network Operators

ICS integrates security automation, AI-driven monitoring, and real-time collaboration between software vendors and network operators. This enables the following:

Automated patch verification and deployment
> ICS ensures secure, automated testing and deployment of network software patches, reducing the risk of service disruptions and enabling faster vulnerability mitigation.

AI-powered configuration drift detection
> ICS continuously monitors network device configurations, alerting operators and vendors when security settings deviate from best practices.

Secure telemetry sharing between vendors and operators
ICS introduces privacy-preserving security intelligence sharing, allowing vendors to analyze real-time attack patterns across deployed environments without accessing sensitive operator data.

Zero Trust enforcement for network software updates
ICS applies cryptographic validation and behavioral anomaly detection to prevent supply chain attacks on network software updates.

PaC for network security compliance
ICS enforces regulatory security controls (e.g., NIST, GDPR, CISA directives) in network security policies, ensuring compliance across cloud, enterprise, and telecom environments.

By closing the security gap between network software manufacturers and network operators, ICS enables proactive threat prevention, continuous compliance, and faster incident response.

For network software vendors, ICS provides real-time visibility into security risks, allowing faster threat response and software hardening. For network operators, ICS automates security policy enforcement, ensures timely patching, and reduces the attack surface of critical network infrastructure. ICS eliminates reactive security gaps by transforming network security from a patch-driven, manual process into a predictive, AI-assisted security framework that continuously adapts to evolving threats.

Cloud Service Providers and the Need for ICS Practices

Cloud service providers (CSPs) such as AWS, Microsoft Azure, Google Cloud Platform (GCP), and Oracle Cloud, illustrated in Figure 8-5, deliver on-demand computing, storage, and networking services to enterprises. Unlike traditional software vendors, CSPs do not just provide software; they operate entire cloud environments, meaning they must secure both the underlying cloud infrastructure and the customer workloads running on their platforms.

Reactive cloud security

Proactive cloud security with AI and automation

Figure 8-5. Cloud service providers

However, security responsibilities in the cloud are shared between CSPs and their customers. CSPs secure the hardware, network, and hypervisor layers, while customers must secure their applications, data, and identity management. This Shared Responsibility Model creates complex security challenges, as threats can emerge from misconfigurations, insecure APIs, supply chain vulnerabilities, and insider threats.

Security Concerns in Typical DevSecOps and SecOps Practices

The scale and complexity of cloud security introduce several risks for both CSPs and their customers:

Cloud misconfigurations
Many breaches occur due to improperly configured cloud resources (e.g., exposed S3 buckets, open Remote Desktop Protocol [RDP] ports, weak identity and access management [IAM] policies).

Cloud supply chain risks
Attackers target cloud APIs, container registries, and software supply chains to inject malicious code into cloud workloads.

Shadow IT and uncontrolled access
Employees deploy unauthorized cloud services, bypassing security controls and exposing sensitive data.

Multitenancy threats
In public cloud environments, security gaps in one tenant can expose shared infrastructure risks across multiple customers.

Slow threat response
Traditional SecOps teams struggle with cloud-scale security, as manual processes cannot keep up with high-volume, high-speed cloud threats.

Without Continuous Security monitoring and automated policy enforcement, CSPs and their customers risk breaches, compliance violations, and operational disruptions.

Real-World Organizations That Match This Use Case

The following are examples of this use case:

Hyperscale cloud providers
AWS, Microsoft Azure, Google Cloud, and Oracle Cloud operate massive-scale cloud environments serving enterprises, governments, and startups.

Managed CSPs
IBM Cloud, Rackspace, and Alibaba Cloud offer custom cloud solutions and security management for enterprises.

Cloud native security vendors
Palo Alto Networks (Prisma Cloud), CrowdStrike (Falcon for Cloud), and Wiz specialize in cloud security observability and threat detection.

A major example of cloud security misconfiguration leading to a breach was the Capital One AWS S3 data breach of 2019. A former AWS employee exploited an improperly configured IAM role and a vulnerable WAF to gain access to Capital One's S3 storage. The attack exfiltrated over 100 million customer records, including credit card applications and Social Security numbers.

The root cause? Capital One misconfigured its AWS permissions, allowing an attacker to escalate privileges and access sensitive data. AWS secured the infrastructure, but the customer's security misconfigurations enabled the breach. This incident highlights the need for ICS to proactively detect misconfigurations and enforce cloud security best practices.

How ICS Practices Improve Security for CSPs

ICS integrates AI-driven threat detection, real-time policy enforcement, and automated remediation into cloud security operations, ensuring Continuous Security monitoring at scale:

AI-driven cloud security posture management (CSPM)
ICS automatically scans for cloud misconfigurations, excessive permissions, and insecure APIs, reducing human error risks.

Automated security policy enforcement (i.e., PaC)
ICS enforces security controls dynamically across cloud environments, preventing misconfigurations before deployment.

AI-assisted threat detection for cloud workloads
ICS continuously monitors serverless functions, containers, and cloud native applications, detecting anomalous behavior in real time.

Zero Trust access controls
ICS applies continuous identity verification to ensure that only authorized users and services interact with cloud resources.

Automated incident response with AI-powered SOAR
ICS enables SOAR, reducing mean time to detect (MTTD) and mean time to repair (MTTR) for cloud threats.

By embedding ICS into cloud security workflows, CSPs can proactively detect vulnerabilities, enforce best practices, and provide customers with automated security insights:

- For CSPs, ICS improves real-time threat detection, reducing attack dwell time; automated compliance enforcement, ensuring regulatory adherence (e.g., GDPR, Federal Risk and Authorization Management Program [FedRAMP], CISA Zero Trust); and customer security visibility, reducing misconfigurations and security blind spots.

- For cloud customers, ICS ensures stronger identity and access controls to prevent privilege escalation attacks; AI-driven cloud security monitoring, detecting threats before they escalate; and Continuous Security observability for hybrid and multicloud environments.

ICS transforms cloud security from a reactive process into an automated, intelligence-driven security framework, reducing operational risks and preventing large-scale breaches.

Financial Institutions Handling Large-Scale Transactions

Financial institutions, including banks, stock exchanges, payment processors, and insurance companies, operate high-value, high-frequency digital transactions that must be protected from cyber threats, fraud, and compliance violations, as illustrated in Figure 8-6. Unlike other industries, financial services demand real-time security monitoring, automated fraud detection, and strict regulatory compliance to maintain trust and prevent financial crime.

Figure 8-6. Large-scale financial institutions

With billions of dollars in daily transactions, these institutions are prime targets for nation-state attacks, organized cybercrime, insider threats, and sophisticated financial fraud schemes. Security failures in this sector can result in significant financial losses, regulatory fines, and erosion of customer trust.

Security Concerns in Typical DevSecOps and SecOps Practices

The financial industry faces unique security challenges due to its complex infrastructure, regulatory requirements, and evolving threat landscape. Common concerns include the following:

Transaction fraud and payment system attacks
   Adversaries exploit vulnerabilities in payment gateways, mobile banking apps, and real-time settlement systems to conduct fraudulent transactions or disrupt financial operations.

Advanced persistent threats (APTs) and insider risks
   Nation-state actors and cybercriminal groups target financial institutions for long-term infiltration, stealing financial data, manipulating markets, and disrupting payment networks.

Regulatory compliance and data protection
   Financial institutions must comply with the Payment Card Industry Data Security Standard (PCI DSS), GDPR, System and Organization Controls 2 (SOC 2), NIST, and banking regulations (e.g., Basel III, Dodd-Frank, PSD2 in Europe), requiring Continuous Security validation and reporting.

Cloud security and third-party risk management
   The rapid adoption of cloud banking, fintech integrations, and API-driven services increases supply chain security risks and the potential for data breaches through insecure third-party integrations.

High-speed cyberattacks targeting algorithmic trading
   Low-latency, automated trading systems introduce unique risks, as cybercriminals attempt to manipulate financial markets through data poisoning, distributed denial-of-service (DDoS) attacks, and AI-driven fraud.

Without Continuous Security monitoring, automated compliance enforcement, and AI-driven fraud detection, financial institutions risk monetary losses, reputational damage, and regulatory penalties.

Real-World Organizations That Match This Use Case

The following are examples of this use case:

Global banks
   JPMorgan Chase, Citibank, HSBC, and Bank of America operate large-scale financial networks requiring real-time security, risk modeling, and compliance enforcement.

Stock exchanges and trading platforms
   The New York Stock Exchange (NYSE), Nasdaq, and the London Stock Exchange handle trillions in daily trading volume, demanding high-speed, fraud-resistant cybersecurity solutions.

Payment processors and fintech companies
Visa, Mastercard, PayPal, and Stripe facilitate millions of transactions per second, requiring AI-powered fraud detection and real-time threat mitigation.

Central banks and financial regulators
The US Federal Reserve, the European Central Bank (ECB), and the Monetary Authority of Singapore (MAS) enforce financial cybersecurity frameworks and oversee national financial security resilience.

A major example of financial cybercrime was the Bangladesh Bank Heist in 2016, in which $81 million was stolen from the Federal Reserve Bank of New York using fraudulent SWIFT transactions.

Attackers compromised the Bangladesh Bank's SWIFT (Society for Worldwide Interbank Financial Telecommunication) system, bypassing security controls to send unauthorized wire transfer requests to the Federal Reserve. The funds were routed to fake accounts in the Philippines where they were quickly laundered and disappeared.

The root cause of the attack was weak endpoint security and a lack of real-time transaction monitoring. The Bangladesh Bank did not have AI-driven fraud detection or continuous monitoring, allowing attackers to manipulate SWIFT transactions without triggering alerts. This breach underscores the need for ICS-powered security solutions that provide real-time fraud prevention, AI-assisted transaction monitoring, and automated compliance enforcement.

How ICS Practices Improve Security for Financial Institutions

ICS integrates AI-driven risk management, automated fraud detection, and real-time compliance enforcement into financial security operations. ICS enhances financial cybersecurity in the following ways:

AI-powered fraud detection and risk scoring
ICS continuously analyzes transaction patterns, user behavior, and financial anomalies, detecting fraudulent activities in real time.

Automated compliance monitoring and reporting
ICS ensures that financial institutions remain compliant with PCI DSS, SOC 2, GDPR, and banking regulations, automatically validating security controls.

Zero Trust security for financial networks
ICS enforces continuous authentication and risk-based access control to prevent unauthorized financial transactions and insider threats.

Real-time anomaly detection for SWIFT, payment systems, and trading platforms
ICS applies machine learning (ML) and behavioral analytics to monitor high-speed financial transactions, detecting market manipulation, account takeovers, and unauthorized trading activities.

Cyber resilience and automated incident response
ICS integrates AI-powered SOAR to automate threat response in case of financial cyberattacks.

By embedding ICS-driven automation, AI-based fraud detection, and real-time compliance analytics, financial institutions can proactively mitigate threats, ensure regulatory compliance, and prevent large-scale financial cyberattacks.

For banks, stock exchanges, and payment processors, ICS provides real-time fraud prevention to reduce financial crime losses; continuous transaction monitoring to detect cyber threats at scale; automated regulatory compliance to eliminate manual audits and improve risk visibility; and proactive threat intelligence to ensure early detection of financial cyberattacks. ICS transforms financial security from a reactive, audit-driven process into an AI-powered, continuously adaptive security framework, ensuring that financial institutions remain resilient against cyber fraud, market manipulation, and regulatory breaches.

Healthcare and Pharmaceutical Sectors

The healthcare and pharmaceutical sectors handle some of the most sensitive and valuable data, including patient records, clinical research, drug formulas, and medical device software, as shown in Figure 8-7. Hospitals, research institutions, biotech firms, and pharmaceutical manufacturers all depend on highly regulated IT environments where security breaches can have life-threatening consequences.

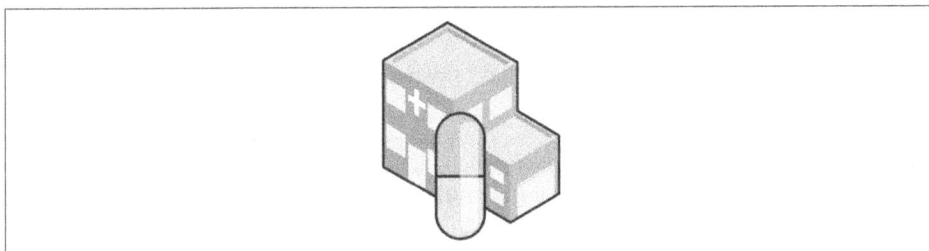

Figure 8-7. Healthcare and pharmaceuticals

Unlike other industries, healthcare security must balance three critical factors:

Patient safety
Cybersecurity incidents can disrupt hospital operations, delay treatment, or even compromise medical devices.

Data privacy
Regulations such as HIPAA, GDPR, and FDA cybersecurity guidelines require strict protection of patient data and intellectual property.

Supply chain integrity
Pharmaceutical companies rely on global supply chains for drug manufacturing, distribution, and clinical research, increasing the risk of supply chain attacks and counterfeit drugs.

Security Concerns in Typical DevSecOps and SecOps Practices

Healthcare and pharmaceutical organizations face unique security risks due to legacy systems, fragmented security operations, and an increasing attack surface:

Ransomware targeting hospitals and research institutions
Attackers target healthcare IT systems and medical devices, encrypting patient data and demanding ransom.

Pharmaceutical intellectual property theft
Nation-state actors and cybercriminal groups attempt to steal drug research and vaccine data from biotech companies.

Medical device security gaps
Many implantable devices, infusion pumps, and connected medical systems run on outdated, unpatched software, making them vulnerable to cyberattacks.

Insider threats in healthcare data breaches
Employees, contractors, or researchers misuse access privileges to steal or expose patient data.

Supply chain security for drug manufacturing
Counterfeit drugs, tampered drug formulations, and clinical trial data manipulation threaten pharmaceutical integrity and public safety.

Without Continuous Security monitoring, automated policy enforcement, and AI-driven anomaly detection, healthcare and pharmaceutical organizations risk cyberattacks that disrupt patient care, damage public trust, and compromise critical research.

Real-World Organizations That Match This Use Case

The following are examples of this use case:

Hospitals and healthcare providers
> Mayo Clinic, Johns Hopkins, NHS (UK), and Kaiser Permanente manage millions of patient records and connected medical devices.

Pharmaceutical giants
> Pfizer, Moderna, Johnson & Johnson, and AstraZeneca conduct high-stakes vaccine research, requiring strict intellectual property security.

Medical device manufacturers
> Medtronic, Siemens Healthiness, and GE Healthcare develop connected medical devices that must be secured against cyber threats.

Health insurance providers
> Blue Cross Blue Shield, UnitedHealth Group, and Cigna store financial and medical data, making them attractive cybercrime targets.

A high-profile cyberattack in 2020 targeted COVID-19 vaccine research. The European Medicines Agency (EMA) was breached, leading to the leak of Pfizer-BioNTech vaccine documents.

Attackers compromised a third-party IT vendor, gaining access to classified vaccine data that was later leaked on dark web forums. This breach exposed intellectual property theft risks in pharmaceutical supply chains, highlighting the urgent need for ICS-powered security frameworks in research environments.

How ICS Practices Improve Security for Healthcare and Pharmaceutical Sectors

Intelligent Continuous Security introduces AI-driven automation, Zero Trust policies, and continuous monitoring to protect patient data, medical devices, and pharmaceutical research:

AI-powered medical device security monitoring
> ICS continuously scans connected medical devices for vulnerabilities, preventing cyberattacks on life-critical systems.

Automated data loss prevention (DLP) for healthcare records
> ICS monitors electronic health record (EHR) systems, detecting unauthorized access and insider threats.

Zero Trust architecture for clinical research data
> ICS enforces strict authentication, least-privilege access, and continuous risk assessment for pharmaceutical IP protection.

Automated supply chain risk assessment for drug manufacturing
ICS applies AI-driven risk scoring to pharmaceutical suppliers, detecting counterfeit drugs and supply chain compromises.

Real-time threat intelligence for ransomware protection
ICS integrates AI-powered anomaly detection, preventing ransomware infections in hospital networks.

By embedding ICS automation, AI-driven risk analytics, and continuous compliance validation, healthcare and pharmaceutical organizations can proactively mitigate cyber threats while maintaining operational resilience.

For hospitals, pharmaceutical companies, and biotech firms, ICS provides continuous medical device security monitoring, ensuring patient safety; automated compliance enforcement for HIPAA, FDA, GDPR, and pharmaceutical security regulations; real-time anomaly detection, preventing ransomware and data breaches; and Zero Trust–based supply chain security, protecting vaccine research and drug development. ICS transforms healthcare cybersecurity from a fragmented, compliance-driven process into a proactive, AI-powered security model, protecting patient data, medical devices, and pharmaceutical innovation from cyber threats.

Critical Infrastructure Operators: Energy, Utilities, and Transportation

Critical infrastructure operators manage the essential services that power economies and societies, including electric grids, water systems, oil and gas pipelines, rail networks, and air traffic control systems, as illustrated in Figure 8-8. These systems rely on a combination of legacy industrial control systems, operational technology (OT), and modern IT solutions, creating a complex, interconnected environment.

Figure 8-8. Critical infrastructure

Unlike traditional IT environments, disruptions in critical infrastructure have real-world consequences—power outages, fuel shortages, water supply contamination, or transportation failures that can impact millions of people, national security, and economic stability. This sector is also a prime target for nation-state cyberattacks, ransomware campaigns, and insider threats.

Security Concerns in Typical DevSecOps and SecOps Practices

Critical infrastructure security presents unique challenges due to the mix of old and new technologies, physical security dependencies, and evolving cyber threats:

Legacy industrial control systems and Supervisory Control and Data Acquisition (SCADA) risks
Many critical infrastructure networks still rely on outdated SCADA systems, which lack modern cybersecurity protections and cannot be easily patched.

OT/IT convergence and increased attack surface
As OT systems connect to IT networks, cyberattack risks increase, because hacking IT systems can now disrupt physical operations.

Ransomware and nation-state attacks on energy and utilities
Critical infrastructure is a prime target for ransomware gangs and state-sponsored adversaries aiming to cause widespread disruptions or to exfiltrate sensitive operational data.

Insider threats in transportation and energy sectors
Employees and contractors with access to control systems, grid networks, or air traffic management can intentionally or unintentionally create security risks.

Regulatory compliance and national security considerations
Governments impose strict security mandates (e.g., NERC CIP, TSA Security Directives, CISA's Critical Infrastructure Security Guidance), but compliance is often manual and slow, leaving gaps in real-time security enforcement.

Without Continuous Security monitoring, automated policy enforcement, and AI-driven anomaly detection, critical infrastructure remains vulnerable to cyber-physical attacks, supply chain compromises, and operational disruptions.

Real-World Organizations That Match This Use Case

The following are examples of this use case:

Power grid operators
US National Grid, PJM Interconnection, and European power system operators manage electricity distribution, requiring strong cybersecurity protections.

Oil, gas, and water utilities
ExxonMobil, Chevron, Saudi Aramco, Shell, and water treatment plants world-wide depend on SCADA-controlled infrastructure that is vulnerable to cyberattacks.

Transportation infrastructure
Air traffic control (FAA, Eurocontrol), railway networks (Deutsche Bahn, Amtrak), metro systems (London Underground), and the 2021 Colonial Pipeline ransomware attack demonstrate how cyberattacks on critical infrastructure can disrupt entire economies.

A ransomware gang (Darkside) compromised Colonial Pipeline's IT network, forcing the company to halt fuel distribution across the East Coast of the United States. Although the OT systems were not directly hacked, Colonial shut down pipeline operations as a precaution, leading to fuel shortages, panic buying, and economic losses.

The root cause was weak IT security controls and lack of network segmentation, allowing attackers to breach corporate IT systems and indirectly impact OT operations. This attack highlights the need for ICS-driven Zero Trust security enforcement and real-time threat intelligence to protect critical infrastructure.

How ICS Practices Improve Security for Critical Infrastructure

Intelligent Continuous Security integrates AI-driven automation, Zero Trust policies, and real-time monitoring to protect power grids, utilities, and transportation networks from cyber-physical attacks:

AI-powered anomaly detection for SCADA and OT systems
ICS continuously monitors SCADA, ICS, and sensor telemetry to detect unauthorized changes, malware, and anomalous activity in critical infrastructure.

Zero Trust architecture for energy and transportation networks
ICS enforces strict authentication and least-privilege access, preventing unauthorized access to control systems and industrial networks.

Automated compliance enforcement for critical infrastructure regulations
ICS automates North American Electric Reliability Corporation's Critical Infrastructure Protection (NERC CIP), TSA Security Directives, and CISA cybersecurity compliance, ensuring Continuous Security validation.

Supply chain security for energy and utilities
ICS applies AI-driven risk assessments to third-party vendors, contractors, and industrial software suppliers, detecting supply chain compromises before deployment.

Automated incident response for ransomware and cyber-physical threats
ICS integrates AI-powered SOAR to automate threat containment and response before attacks spread.

By embedding ICS-driven automation, real-time risk analytics, and Zero Trust controls, critical infrastructure operators can proactively mitigate cyber threats, ensure operational resilience, and prevent large-scale disruptions.

The Benefits of ICS for Critical Infrastructure Security

For power grids, utilities, and transportation networks, ICS provides real-time threat detection for SCADA and industrial control systems; automated compliance validation, reducing regulatory risks; Zero Trust enforcement, preventing cyber-physical disruptions; and AI-driven anomaly detection, protecting against ransomware and nation-state cyberattacks. ICS transforms critical infrastructure cybersecurity from a reactive, manual process into an AI-powered security framework, ensuring resilience against cyber threats, operational disruptions, and regulatory compliance challenges.

Retail and Ecommerce Platforms

Retail and ecommerce platforms handle millions of financial transactions daily, processing sensitive customer data, payment details, and personal information, as illustrated in Figure 8-9. These platforms rely on highly dynamic digital infrastructure, including web applications, mobile apps, cloud services, APIs, and third-party integrations, to deliver seamless shopping experiences.

Figure 8-9. Retail and ecommerce

However, the rapid evolution of digital commerce introduces significant security risks, as retailers face high transaction volumes, seasonal traffic spikes, and extensive third-party dependencies. Attackers continuously target retail platforms, attempting credit card fraud, account takeovers, data breaches, and API abuse.

Security Concerns in Typical DevSecOps and SecOps Practices

Retail and ecommerce security must balance fraud prevention, payment security, and real-time application protection. Common security concerns include the following:

Payment card fraud and credentials theft
> Attackers exploit ecommerce checkout systems, POS terminals, and mobile payment APIs to steal credit card details and customer credentials.

Bot attacks and account takeovers
> Automated credential stuffing attacks use leaked passwords from previous breaches to hijack customer accounts and loyalty programs.

API and third-party security risks
> Ecommerce platforms integrate with payment gateways, logistics services, and customer analytics tools, increasing supply chain attack risks.

Cloud security misconfigurations
> Many retailers migrate to cloud environments without enforcing Zero Trust security, leading to exposed storage buckets, unsecured databases, and public APIs.

Ransomware and DDoS attacks on retail websites
> Hackers deploy ransomware to encrypt ecommerce databases or launch DDoS attacks to disrupt sales during peak shopping seasons.

Without Continuous Security monitoring, automated fraud detection, and AI-driven anomaly detection, ecommerce platforms risk financial losses, reputational damage, and regulatory fines.

Real-World Organizations That Match This Use Case

The following are examples of this use case:

Global ecommerce giants
> Amazon, eBay, Alibaba, and Walmart operate massive-scale retail platforms requiring real-time fraud prevention and cloud security monitoring.

Digital payment providers
> PayPal, Stripe, Square, and Klarna secure millions of digital transactions daily, requiring continuous fraud detection and compliance enforcement.

Retailers with online and physical presence
> Target, Best Buy, and Home Depot integrate ecommerce with in-store sales, increasing security risks across POS, mobile apps, and digital loyalty programs.

Luxury and high-end retailers
> Brands such as Louis Vuitton, Rolex, and Gucci face persistent cyber threats from counterfeiters, fraudsters, and digital piracy.

The British Airways data breach in 2018 is a prime example of a web skimming attack on an ecommerce platform. Attackers injected malicious JavaScript code into British Airways' website, allowing them to steal customer credit card details in real time during checkout. The breach compromised 400,000+ customer records, leading to a £183 million fine under GDPR. The root cause was a lack of real-time security monitoring and weak client-side security controls, allowing attackers to exploit third-party scripts without being detected.

This breach highlights the need for ICS-driven security solutions to monitor web traffic in real time, detect fraudulent transactions, and enforce Zero Trust API security.

How ICS Practices Improve Security for Retail and Ecommerce

Intelligent Continuous Security integrates AI-driven automation, real-time fraud prevention, and Zero Trust enforcement into retail cybersecurity operations:

AI-powered fraud detection and risk scoring
    ICS continuously analyzes transaction behavior, user activity, and payment anomalies, detecting fraudulent activities in real time.

Zero Trust API security for payment and checkout systems
    ICS enforces continuous authentication, API security validation, and transaction risk scoring to prevent card fraud and credential stuffing attacks.

Real-time threat intelligence for web skimming and magecart attacks
    ICS applies ML to ecommerce websites, detecting unauthorized script injections and client-side malware.

Automated compliance enforcement for PCI DSS and GDPR
    ICS ensures that retailers meet global security and privacy regulations, reducing the risk of legal penalties and data protection violations.

AI-driven anomaly detection for DDoS and ransomware prevention
    ICS integrates AI-powered SOAR to detect and mitigate large-scale cyberattacks before they disrupt ecommerce platforms.

By embedding ICS automation, AI-driven fraud prevention, and Zero Trust security policies, ecommerce platforms can proactively mitigate financial fraud, protect customer data, and ensure continuous regulatory compliance.

For ecommerce marketplaces, online retailers, and payment processors, ICS provides real-time fraud prevention and risk-based transaction monitoring; automated PCI DSS and GDPR compliance enforcement; Zero Trust protection for APIs and third-party payment integrations; and AI-powered anomaly detection to prevent bot attacks and account takeovers. ICS transforms retail cybersecurity from a reactive fraud-detection model into an AI-powered, continuously adaptive security framework, ensuring that ecommerce platforms remain resilient against cyber threats while maintaining seamless shopping experiences.

DevOps Teams in CI/CD Pipelines with High Deployment Frequencies

In modern software development, high-velocity DevOps teams deploy software multiple times per day using CI/CD pipelines, as illustrated in Figure 8-10. This approach enables rapid innovation, faster feature delivery, and improved responsiveness to customer needs.

Figure 8-10. CI/CD pipeline security

However, high deployment frequencies increase the risk of security misconfigurations, unpatched vulnerabilities, and inadvertent exposure of sensitive data. Without embedded security automation and real-time monitoring, DevSecOps and SecOps struggle to keep up, resulting in delayed security reviews, last-minute compliance roadblocks, and post-deployment security incidents.

Security Concerns in Typical DevSecOps and SecOps Practices

The fast pace of CI/CD pipelines introduces unique security risks that are difficult to address with traditional security models:

Lack of automated security testing in CI/CD pipelines
Many DevOps teams prioritize speed over security, leading to vulnerabilities slipping into production.

Secrets and credentials exposure
Hardcoded API keys, cloud access credentials, and private encryption keys often end up in source code repositories, making them prime targets for attackers.

Supply chain security risks in open source dependencies
  CI/CD pipelines automatically pull software components from open source repositories, increasing the risk of software supply chain attacks (e.g., Log4j, SolarWinds Sunburst).

Unverified Infrastructure as Code (IaC) configurations
  Misconfigurations in Kubernetes, Terraform, and cloud infrastructure templates can expose systems to attackers.

Manual compliance checks creating deployment bottlenecks
  Security teams lack automation to validate security policies, slowing down releases or forcing post-deployment fixes.

Without Continuous Security integration, automated compliance enforcement, and AI-driven risk assessment, DevOps teams risk deploying insecure code, exposing infrastructure misconfigurations, and introducing security gaps into production.

Real-World Organizations That Match This Use Case

The following are examples of this use case:

Tech giants and cloud native companies
  Netflix, Spotify, and Google deploy code hundreds of times per day, requiring automated security in every stage of CI/CD.

Financial institutions and fintech startups
  Banks such as Goldman Sachs, JPMorgan, and Stripe operate high-frequency CI/CD pipelines, demanding continuous compliance and security validation.

SaaS providers and AI/ML platforms
  Companies such as Salesforce, OpenAI, and GitHub rely on automated deployments, making software supply chain security a critical concern.

In 2019, Capital One suffered a major cloud security breach due to a misconfigured AWS IAM role in its CI/CD pipeline. An attacker exploited vulnerability in a public-facing application, escalating privileges to access Amazon S3 buckets containing customer financial data. The breach exposed over 100 million customer records, leading to a $190 million regulatory fine.

The root cause was a failure to integrate security into the CI/CD pipeline. The misconfigured IAM role should have been caught by automated security policy enforcement. This incident highlights the need for ICS-powered CI/CD security automation to prevent misconfigurations, secrets exposure, and unauthorized access.

How ICS Practices Improve Security for CI/CD Pipelines

ICS introduces AI-driven automation, Zero Trust enforcement, and continuous risk assessment into CI/CD security, enabling DevOps teams to deploy securely at high velocity:

AI-driven automated security testing in CI/CD
> ICS integrates static application security testing (SAST), dynamic application security testing (DAST), and software composition analysis (SCA) into CI/CD pipelines, ensuring secure code before deployment.

Automated secrets management and Zero Trust IAM controls
> ICS enforces real-time detection of exposed credentials, automating secrets rotation and role-based access control (RBAC).

Supply chain security validation for open source components
> ICS scans container images, libraries, and dependencies in real time, preventing malicious software from entering CI/CD pipelines.

PaC for automated compliance enforcement
> ICS validates IaC configurations (Terraform, Kubernetes, AWS CloudFormation) against security best practices before deployment.

Continuous threat monitoring and anomaly detection
> ICS applies ML-based behavior analytics to detect unusual changes in deployment environments, preventing code tampering and privilege escalation attacks.

By embedding ICS-driven automation, AI-powered security analytics, and Zero Trust access controls, DevOps teams can continuously deploy without increasing security risks.

The Benefits of ICS for High-Velocity DevOps Teams

For organizations with frequent deployments, ICS provides:

- Seamless security automation in CI/CD pipelines, eliminating bottlenecks
- Continuous compliance enforcement, preventing regulatory violations
- AI-driven code and dependency scanning, reducing software supply chain risks
- Automated secrets detection and policy enforcement, securing cloud credentials

ICS transforms CI/CD security from a fragmented, last-minute process into a proactive, AI-powered security framework, ensuring that DevOps teams deploy securely at scale.

Organizations with Strict Regulatory and Compliance Requirements

Organizations operating in heavily regulated industries such as finance, healthcare, government, energy, and defense must comply with stringent security and privacy regulations, as illustrated in Figure 8-11. These frameworks, including GDPR, HIPAA, PCI DSS, Sarbanes-Oxley (SOX), NIST 800-53, FedRAMP, and ISO 27001, impose strict data protection, auditability, and risk management requirements.

Figure 8-11. Governance, risk, and compliance

Unlike other businesses, these organizations cannot afford security lapses—noncompliance can result in legal penalties, financial fines, loss of public trust, and even operational shutdowns. However, traditional compliance approaches are slow, manual, and reactive, making it difficult for security teams to keep up with evolving threats and regulatory updates.

Security Concerns in Typical DevSecOps and SecOps Practices

Organizations with strict compliance mandates face unique security challenges due to complex audit requirements, frequent regulatory changes, and slow security enforcement:

Manual compliance audits lead to delays and errors
Many organizations still rely on spreadsheets and manual audits, leading to slow, reactive security processes that fail to detect real-time threats.

Compliance does not equal security
Passing a regulatory audit does not guarantee an organization is secure—many compliance programs focus on checklists rather than real-time risk mitigation.

Fragmented security and policy enforcement
> Security teams struggle to enforce standardized security policies across cloud, on-premises, and hybrid environments, increasing the risk of compliance violations.

Lack of continuous monitoring for regulatory violations
> Organizations often discover compliance failures after a breach or during an audit, rather than detecting and fixing risks in real time.

Data protection and privacy challenges
> Regulations such as GDPR, the California Consumer Privacy Act (CCPA), and HIPAA require continuous data protection, access control, and logging, but many organizations lack automated enforcement.

Without Continuous Security monitoring, automated policy enforcement, and AI-driven compliance validation, organizations struggle to keep up with regulatory requirements while maintaining strong cybersecurity postures.

Real-World Organizations That Match This Use Case

The following are examples of this use case:

Financial institutions
> Banks, stock exchanges, and payment processors must comply with PCI DSS, SOX, and Basel III regulations to protect financial transactions.

Healthcare and life sciences
> Hospitals and pharmaceutical companies must comply with HIPAA, GDPR, and FDA cybersecurity guidelines to protect patient data and medical research.

Government and defense contractors
> Companies working with government agencies must meet NIST 800-53, FedRAMP, and Cybersecurity Maturity Model Certification (CMMC) to ensure national security data protection.

Energy and critical infrastructure
> Power grid operators, oil and gas companies, and transportation networks must comply with NERC CIP, TSA Security Directives, and industry-specific cybersecurity mandates.

In 2020, Marriott International was fined £18.4 million for GDPR violations after a data breach exposed 339 million customer records. The breach stemmed from a failure to detect and secure sensitive customer data inherited from an acquired company. Marriott's security team did not continuously monitor data access, leading to prolonged undetected exposure. The root cause was a lack of automated compliance enforcement and real-time data protection, demonstrating why ICS-powered security automation is essential for regulatory compliance.

How ICS Practices Improve Security for Regulated Organizations

ICS integrates AI-driven automation, real-time compliance enforcement, and continuous risk assessment to ensure that organizations remain secure and audit ready at all times:

AI-powered continuous compliance monitoring
ICS automatically scans security configurations against PCI DSS, HIPAA, GDPR, NIST, and ISO 27001 requirements, ensuring continuous adherence.

Automated security policy enforcement (PaC)
ICS validates security policies dynamically, preventing misconfigurations that could lead to compliance violations.

Zero Trust–based data access controls
ICS enforces continuous authentication, least-privilege access, and real-time logging to prevent data breaches and unauthorized access.

Automated audit trail and incident reporting
ICS provides real-time compliance reporting and automated audit logs, reducing manual efforts and improving response times.

AI-driven risk assessment and threat detection
ICS applies ML to detect policy violations, ensuring that organizations stay ahead of regulatory changes and security risks.

By embedding ICS-driven automation, AI-powered security analytics, and real-time compliance validation, organizations can eliminate audit bottlenecks, enforce regulatory controls, and prevent costly noncompliance fines.

For financial institutions, healthcare providers, government agencies, and regulated enterprises, ICS provides:

- Real-time compliance monitoring, reducing manual audit overhead
- Automated regulatory enforcement, ensuring continuous adherence
- Zero Trust–based data security, preventing unauthorized data access
- AI-powered anomaly detection, detecting policy violations before audits

ICS transforms regulatory compliance from a reactive, checklist-driven process into a proactive, AI-powered security framework, ensuring continuous compliance enforcement while reducing operational risk.

Multicloud and Hybrid Cloud Environments

Organizations increasingly adopt multicloud and hybrid cloud architectures to improve scalability, redundancy, and cost efficiency, as shown in Figure 8-12. A multicloud strategy involves using multiple cloud providers (AWS, Microsoft Azure, Google Cloud, Oracle Cloud), while hybrid cloud environments integrate on-premises data centers with public or private cloud services.

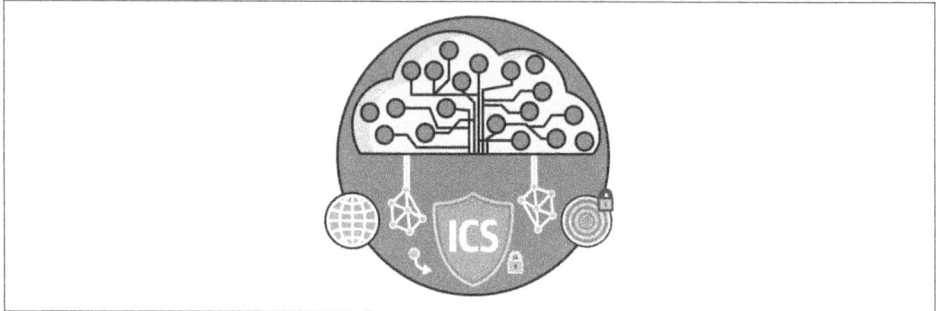

Figure 8-12. Cloud architectures

This approach provides flexibility and resilience, but it also expands the attack surface, complicates security policy enforcement, and increases the risk of misconfigurations. Without centralized visibility, automated security controls, and continuous monitoring, organizations struggle to maintain consistent security across multiple cloud platforms.

Security Concerns in Typical DevSecOps and SecOps Practices

Multicloud and hybrid cloud environments introduce complex security challenges due to varying cloud provider configurations, inconsistent security policies, and the difficulty of monitoring distributed assets:

Cloud misconfigurations leading to data breaches
> Many security incidents stem from improperly configured cloud services, such as publicly exposed S3 buckets, unrestricted IAM roles, and unencrypted databases.

Inconsistent IAM across clouds
> Security teams struggle to enforce least-privilege access when different cloud providers have unique IAM models, leading to privilege escalation risks.

Fragmented security visibility and incident response
> Organizations using multiple cloud security tools often experience delayed detection and response to security incidents.

Lack of unified compliance enforcement
Meeting regulatory requirements (PCI DSS, HIPAA, GDPR, SOC 2, NIST 800-53) becomes complex when security policies are inconsistently enforced across different cloud providers.

Insecure API integrations and third-party cloud services
Organizations rely on external SaaS and cloud APIs for operations, increasing the risk of API abuse, data leaks, and supply chain attacks.

Without Continuous Security monitoring, automated compliance enforcement, and AI-driven threat detection, multicloud and hybrid cloud architectures remain vulnerable to misconfigurations, insider threats, and cross-cloud cyberattacks.

Real-World Organizations That Match This Use Case

The following are examples of this use case:

Global enterprises with multicloud strategies
Companies such as Netflix, Goldman Sachs, and Boeing use multiple cloud providers to ensure redundancy, cost savings, and performance optimization.

Hybrid cloud-enabled financial institutions
JPMorgan Chase, Bank of America, and HSBC run critical workloads on premises while integrating with public cloud platforms for AI, big data, and customer services.

Government and defense agencies
The DoD, European Space Agency (ESA), and NATO NATO adopt hybrid cloud architectures for secure data management and mission-critical applications.

Ecommerce and retail platforms
Walmart, Target, and Alibaba use multicloud architectures to handle seasonal traffic spikes, real-time analytics, and fraud detection.

In 2019, Capital One suffered a cloud misconfiguration breach where an attacker exploited a misconfigured AWS S3 bucket to steal more than 100 million customer records. The attacker gained access through a misconfigured IAM role, escalating privileges to exfiltrate sensitive data stored in the cloud. This incident demonstrates the risks of misconfigured multicloud security settings, highlighting the need for ICS-powered security automation and continuous monitoring.

How ICS Practices Improve Security for Multicloud and Hybrid Cloud Environments

Intelligent Continuous Security integrates AI-driven automation, Zero Trust enforcement, and continuous monitoring to ensure real-time security, compliance, and risk mitigation across hybrid and multicloud environments:

AI-powered cloud misconfiguration detection and prevention
ICS continuously scans multicloud environments for misconfigurations, preventing publicly exposed data storage, weak IAM policies, and unencrypted assets.

Unified security policy enforcement across clouds
ICS applies PaC to enforce uniform security configurations, ensuring compliance with NIST, GDPR, PCI DSS, and other regulatory standards.

Zero Trust–based cloud IAM
ICS integrates continuous authentication and least-privilege access controls across multiple cloud platforms to prevent unauthorized access.

AI-driven threat intelligence for cross-cloud attacks
ICS applies behavioral analytics and anomaly detection to identify suspicious API calls, privilege escalation attempts, and lateral movement across cloud providers.

Automated incident response for multicloud security breaches
ICS enables AI-powered SOAR to contain cloud threats before they spread across environments.

By embedding ICS-driven automation, AI-based security monitoring, and real-time compliance validation, organizations can secure their multicloud and hybrid cloud environments while maintaining scalability and flexibility.

For enterprises, government agencies, and cloud-first organizations, ICS provides:

- Continuous cloud misconfiguration monitoring, preventing data leaks
- Automated compliance enforcement, ensuring regulatory adherence across clouds
- Zero Trust–based cloud security, reducing the attack surface and privilege escalation risks
- AI-powered anomaly detection, identifying cross-cloud threats in real time

ICS transforms cloud security from a reactive, manual process into an AI-driven, continuously adaptive security framework, ensuring resilient, scalable, and secure multicloud and hybrid cloud deployments.

AI and ML Workloads in Security-Sensitive Environments

AI and ML are transforming industries by enabling automated decision making, real-time data analysis, and predictive intelligence, as illustrated in Figure 8-13. Organizations in finance, healthcare, cybersecurity, national security, and autonomous systems increasingly rely on AI-driven applications to enhance efficiency and accuracy.

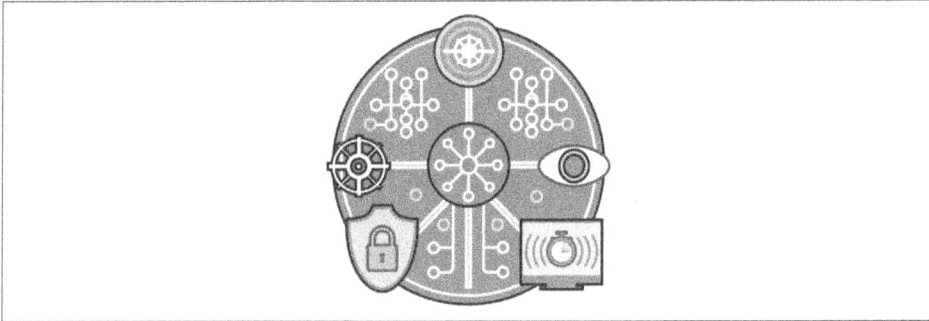

Figure 8-13. AI/ML security

However, securing AI/ML pipelines, data, and models is a major challenge. AI workloads involve large-scale data ingestion, model training, and inference across cloud, edge, and hybrid infrastructures, making them vulnerable to adversarial attacks, data poisoning, and unauthorized access. Unlike traditional applications, AI systems must maintain data integrity, explainability, and compliance with evolving regulatory frameworks while defending against sophisticated cyber threats.

Security Concerns in Typical DevSecOps and SecOps Practices

Organizations deploying AI/ML face unique security risks due to the complexity of AI models, data dependencies, and regulatory considerations:

AI model poisoning and data integrity attacks
   Attackers inject malicious or manipulated training data, causing AI models to produce incorrect predictions in critical applications such as fraud detection, medical diagnostics, and cybersecurity.

Adversarial ML attacks
   AttackersAdversarial ML attacks craft adversarial inputs that deceive AI models, bypassing facial recognition, spam filters, and AI-based fraud detection systems.

AI model theft and intellectual property risks
   AI models represent valuable intellectual property, making them targets for cyber espionage and insider threats. Attackers attempt to exfiltrate proprietary AI models from cloud environments.

Regulatory compliance for AI decisions
AI-driven applications in finance, healthcare, and law enforcement must meet strict compliance requirements for explainability, fairness, and data protection (e.g., EU AI Act, GDPR, NIST AI Risk Management Framework).

Cloud and edge security for AI deployments
AI models often run in cloud and edge computing environments (e.g., autonomous vehicles, IoT devices, industrial AI), increasing the attack surface for model manipulation, adversarial inputs, and data breaches.

API security risks in AI model access
Many AI models are exposed via APIs for real-time inference. Attackers can abuse, reverse-engineer, or manipulate API requests, leading to data leaks or malicious AI responses.

Without Continuous Security monitoring, automated compliance enforcement, and AI-driven anomaly detection, organizations risk AI-driven fraud, model corruption, regulatory violations, and operational disruptions.

Real-World Organizations That Match This Use Case

The following are examples of this use case:

Financial institutions and AI-driven fraud detection
Banks such as JPMorgan Chase, PayPal, and Visa use AI for fraud detection and risk scoring, requiring real-time model security and explainability.

Healthcare and AI-powered medical diagnostics
Organizations such as Mayo Clinic, IBM Watson Health, and Google DeepMind rely on AI for diagnosing diseases, processing medical images, and optimizing patient care.

Cybersecurity and AI-based threat detection
Companies such as CrowdStrike, Darktrace, and Palo Alto Networks use AI for detecting and mitigating cyber threats, requiring resilient, attack-resistant AI models.

Autonomous systems and AI in critical infrastructure
Tesla, NASA, and defense contractors rely on AI for autonomous decision making, requiring strong model security and real-time anomaly detection.

In 2020, Microsoft and OpenAI researchers identified vulnerabilities in AI models used for image recognition and cybersecurity threat detection. Attackers successfully manipulated AI inputs using adversarial ML techniques, causing incorrect classifications in cybersecurity software and misidentifications in facial recognition AI.

The root cause was a lack of AI-specific security controls, demonstrating how malicious actors can systematically fool AI models if organizations do not implement robust AI model security, continuous monitoring, and adversarial resilience testing. This incident highlights the need for ICS-powered security frameworks that protect AI models from tampering, adversarial inputs, and unauthorized access.

How ICS Practices Improve Security for AI/ML Workloads

ICS integrates AI-driven automation, Zero Trust enforcement, and continuous monitoring to ensure secure AI model development, deployment, and governance:

AI-powered adversarial attack detection and model hardening
   ICS continuously monitors AI training data, input data, and model responses, detecting manipulated inputs and adversarial threats.

Zero Trust–based model access and API security
   ICS enforces strict authentication and continuous verification for AI model access, preventing unauthorized inference and model theft.

Real-time model monitoring for bias, drift, and security violations
   ICS applies behavioral analytics to AI models, ensuring that models remain fair, unbiased, and resilient against manipulation.

Automated compliance validation for AI governance and regulations
   ICS ensures that AI models meet GDPR, NIST AI Risk Management Framework, EU AI Act, and other compliance standards.

Multicloud AI security integration
   ICS applies policy-based security enforcement across hybrid AI infrastructures, protecting AI models and data across cloud, edge, and on-premises environments.

By embedding ICS-driven automation, AI-based risk analytics, and real-time model security validation, organizations can deploy AI safely and prevent adversarial attacks, data breaches, and regulatory failures.

For financial institutions, healthcare providers, cybersecurity firms, and autonomous AI platforms, ICS provides:

- Continuous AI model security monitoring, detecting adversarial attacks in real time
- Automated AI compliance enforcement, ensuring regulatory adherence and explainability

- Zero Trust–based AI model access controls, preventing unauthorized model manipulation

- AI-powered anomaly detection, protecting AI workloads from poisoning attacks and data breaches

ICS transforms AI security from a reactive, fragmented process into a proactive, continuously adaptive security framework, ensuring that organizations can safely deploy AI at scale while maintaining trust, compliance, and security.

Summary

The 13 use cases examined in this chapter illustrate the broad and complex security challenges organizations face across industries, from cloud service providers and financial institutions to AI-driven workloads and critical infrastructure operators. Each scenario highlights how conventional security models—dependent on manual oversight, periodic assessments, and reactive defenses—fail to address the real-time nature of modern cyber threats. ICS provides the necessary paradigm shift, integrating AI-driven automation, continuous monitoring, and adaptive security policies to proactively protect assets, data, and users.

A recurring theme across these use cases is the need for security to be integrated, automated, and predictive rather than reactive. Whether mitigating software supply chain risks in high-velocity DevOps teams, securing multicloud and hybrid cloud environments, or preventing adversarial AI manipulation, organizations must embrace Zero Trust principles, AI-powered anomaly detection, and real-time compliance enforcement. These foundational elements ensure that security controls are continuous, self-adaptive, and resilient to emerging attack patterns.

Additionally, the chapter underscored how ICS reduces operational friction while strengthening security. Traditionally, security has been perceived as a bottleneck to innovation, slowing down deployment cycles, regulatory approval processes, and digital transformation efforts. ICS, however, enables seamless security enforcement without disrupting business agility, ensuring that organizations can deliver secure products and services, maintain regulatory compliance, and defend against sophisticated cyberattacks—all while optimizing performance and efficiency.

The real-world breaches and vulnerabilities explored in this chapter—such as the Capital One cloud misconfiguration breach, the SolarWinds supply chain attack, and the British Airways ecommerce data compromise—demonstrate the urgent need for ICS-driven defenses. In each use case, automated risk assessment, AI-driven policy enforcement, and continuous monitoring could have prevented or significantly mitigated the impact of the attack. By adopting ICS, organizations gain not just improved security posture but also operational resilience, regulatory alignment, and proactive threat mitigation—positioning them for long-term success in an increasingly hostile cyber landscape.

While this chapter has focused on securing diverse enterprise environments using ICS, Chapter 9 extends the discussion by examining AI-assisted attack prevention, defense, and response patterns. With AI-driven threats becoming more advanced—from deepfake phishing to autonomous malware and AI-powered cyberattacks—organizations must leverage AI not only for defense but also for predictive attack prevention. Chapter 9 explores how AI can dynamically detect, predict, and neutralize attacks before they escalate, transforming cybersecurity into an intelligent, proactive system capable of outpacing modern adversaries.

Metrics for Intelligent Continuous Security

Security is often described as a journey rather than a destination. Organizations invest heavily in security technologies, implement best practices, and train personnel, but without a structured way to measure success, they are flying blind. Metrics provide that structure. They translate security investments into measurable outcomes, helping security leaders make informed decisions, justify spending, and improve operations over time.

Intelligent Continuous Security (ICS) takes this further by integrating security across the entire software lifecycle, from development and deployment to operations and compliance. Unlike traditional security approaches, ICS embeds automation, AI-driven insights, and real-time risk management into every stage of software delivery and IT operations. To evaluate the effectiveness of ICS, security leaders need meaningful metrics that not only assess current security posture but also drive continuous improvement.

A Landscape View of ICS Metrics

Security metrics in ICS can be categorized into distinct classes, each serving a different purpose. These classes help measure security in business terms, evaluate ICS effectiveness, track transformation progress, assess risk exposure, and ensure compliance. Across all categories, metrics must consider people, processes, and technology to provide a complete picture of security maturity.

Business Outcome Metrics

At the highest level, organizations need to measure security in terms of business impact. Executives and board members don't focus on vulnerability counts or log entries; they care about how security influences revenue, risk, and compliance.

Business outcome metrics quantify security's contribution to organizational resilience and regulatory compliance.

For example, one relevant metric in this class is how security controls prevented financial losses. If an ICS solution detects and mitigates a security event before it escalates, the avoided financial impact should be measured. Other business outcome metrics might track security's role in customer trust, brand reputation, and operational uptime.

ICS Effectiveness Metrics

While business outcome metrics tie security to financial and strategic goals, ICS effectiveness metrics evaluate whether the security program itself is working as intended. These metrics measure how well ICS solutions reduce risk, detect threats, and automate response.

One example is mean time to detect (MTTD) and mean time to respond (MTTR) to security incidents. If ICS enables faster detection and response through AI and automation, these times should decrease. Other effectiveness metrics might assess the accuracy of security alerts, the success rate of automated threat containment, or the percentage of vulnerabilities detected before production deployment.

ICS Transformation and Improvement Metrics

Adopting ICS is a transformational effort. Organizations need metrics to track their progress in implementing security automation, shifting security left in the development pipeline, and improving overall security posture. These metrics ensure that ICS initiatives stay on course and continue to mature over time.

An example in this class is the percentage of applications fully integrated with automated security testing. If a company aims to embed security earlier in the development lifecycle, tracking adoption rates of security automation tools provides insight into progress. Other transformation metrics may focus on security training adoption, policy compliance across teams, or the reduction of manual security processes through automation.

Risk and Threat Exposure Metrics

Understanding an organization's security risk is critical to prioritizing defenses and reducing attack surfaces. Risk and threat exposure metrics measure how vulnerable systems, applications, and infrastructure are against known and emerging threats.

For example, the percentage of critical vulnerabilities detected but not yet remediated within service level agreements (SLAs) is a key metric in this category. It helps organizations ensure that security gaps are identified and addressed in a timely manner.

Other metrics may assess phishing susceptibility, insider threat activity, or overall attack surface reduction.

Compliance and Governance Metrics

Regulatory and policy compliance is a fundamental requirement for many organizations. Compliance and governance metrics measure adherence to security policies, legal frameworks, and industry regulations such as the Payment Card Industry Data Security Standard (PCI DSS), Health Insurance Portability and Accountability Act (HIPAA), General Data Protection Regulation (GDPR), and those from the National Institute of Standards and Technology (NIST).

One example is the percentage of systems audited and fully compliant with security policies. This ensures that security controls are enforced and monitored continuously rather than just at audit time. Other compliance metrics may track policy violations, security exceptions, or the effectiveness of automated compliance enforcement mechanisms.

Aligning Metrics with ICS Goals

Each of these metrics classes serves a different audience and purpose, but together they form a comprehensive measurement strategy. Business leaders need outcome-driven insights, security teams need operational effectiveness indicators, transformation leaders need visibility into progress, risk managers need exposure assessments, and compliance teams need governance tracking. By defining and tracking the right metrics, organizations can ensure that their ICS initiatives deliver tangible and intangible improvements in security, efficiency, resilience, and satisfaction.

Business Outcome Metrics

Security is often seen as a cost center, an unavoidable expense required to minimize risk. However, in organizations with mature ICS implementations, security is recognized as a business enabler, as illustrated in Figure 9-1. Business outcome metrics provide the means to quantify the impact of security investments on operational efficiency, financial performance, and customer trust. These metrics shift the conversation from security as an overhead cost to security as a strategic asset, influencing executive decision making and long-term planning.

Measuring business outcomes helps align security initiatives with broader corporate goals. Instead of focusing on security for its own sake, organizations use these metrics to evaluate how ICS contributes to revenue protection, regulatory compliance, and brand reputation. By demonstrating tangible business benefits, security leaders can secure executive buy-in, justify investments, and ensure that security becomes an integral part of enterprise success.

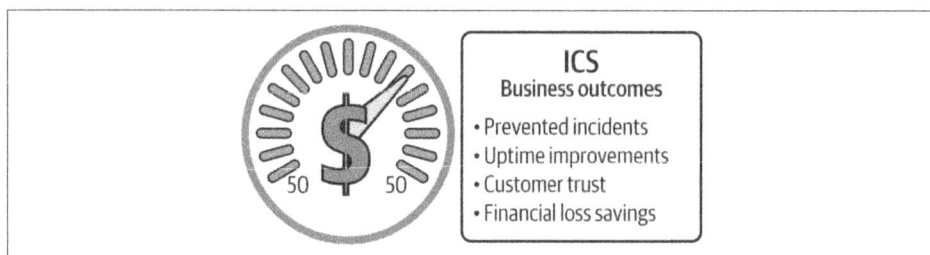

Figure 9-1. Business outcome metrics

One of the most significant business outcome metrics is financial losses prevented due to security controls. Organizations must not only prevent cyberattacks but also understand the economic impact of their security measures. This metric assesses the estimated financial damage that was avoided by ICS solutions, such as thwarting ransomware attacks or fraud attempts. It is measured by evaluating past incidents, estimating potential damages from similar threats, and comparing them to successfully prevented attacks. For instance, a financial institution that prevents a major fraud attempt through real-time security automation could document millions in avoided losses, directly proving the value of its security posture.

Another crucial metric is the reduction in business downtime due to security incidents. Downtime caused by cyberattacks or breaches results in lost productivity, revenue disruption, and operational inefficiencies. ICS helps mitigate these risks by enabling faster threat detection, automated response, and resilience measures, providing high availability levels and business continuity. Organizations track system availability before and after ICS implementation to assess improvements. For example, a cloud service provider (CSP) may reduce its quarterly security-related downtime from 6 hours to less than 30 minutes, translating directly into customer satisfaction and financial stability.

Regulatory compliance is another area where ICS provides measurable benefits. Compliance violation cost avoidance tracks the financial penalties and legal costs averted through proactive security measures. Regulations such as GDPR, HIPAA, and PCI DSS impose strict security requirements, and noncompliance can result in significant fines. By integrating automated compliance validation into ICS, organizations can measure how much financial liability they have prevented. A healthcare provider that avoids a multimillion-dollar HIPAA fine by implementing real-time compliance monitoring offers a concrete example of how security investments translate into financial savings.

Beyond financial considerations, customer retention and trust impact is an essential business outcome metric. Consumers and enterprise clients increasingly prioritize security when selecting service providers. By tracking customer churn rates, net promoter scores (NPS), and security-related feedback, organizations can measure how security improvements influence customer confidence. An ecommerce platform that strengthens its ICS framework and subsequently sees a 20% increase in NPS demonstrates a clear business advantage derived from security investments.

ICS Effectiveness Metrics

While business outcome metrics focus on the broader impact of security investments, ICS effectiveness metrics (Figure 9-2) measure how well security initiatives perform in reducing risk, detecting threats, and automating responses. These metrics provide insight into the operational efficiency of security controls, helping organizations assess whether ICS solutions truly improve their security posture or simply add complexity without meaningful impact.

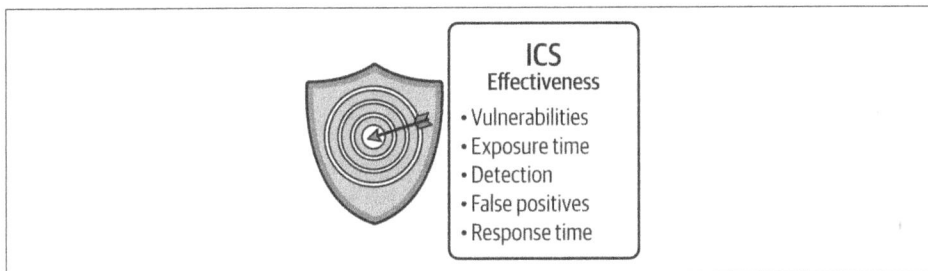

Figure 9-2. ICS effectiveness metrics

ICS effectiveness metrics allow security teams to fine-tune their defenses by identifying gaps in detection, response, and mitigation. They ensure that automation and AI-driven security technologies are achieving their intended goals rather than generating noise. By continuously evaluating security effectiveness, organizations can ensure that ICS not only meets compliance requirements but actively strengthens resilience against cyber threats.

Two of the most fundamental ICS effectiveness metrics are the MTTD and MTTR to security incidents. These metrics measure how quickly security teams can identify and remediate potential threats. A lower MTTD means threats are caught earlier, reducing the window of exposure. A lower MTTR means incidents are resolved more quickly, minimizing damage. ICS solutions that incorporate AI-driven threat detection should see both values improve over time. A technology company that reduces MTTD from 48 hours to under 5 minutes through automated anomaly detection provides a strong example of ICS improving security effectiveness.

Another critical metric is the accuracy of security alerts. Security teams are often overwhelmed by false positives, which consume valuable time and lead to alert fatigue. ICS solutions should not only generate alerts but ensure their relevance. Measuring the true positive rate versus false positive rate helps determine whether ICS is improving security efficiency. A financial institution that reduces false positives by

60% through an AI-driven ICS solution ensures that analysts focus on real threats rather than sifting through noise.

Additionally, organizations should measure the percentage of security vulnerabilities detected before production deployment. The earlier that vulnerabilities are found, the cheaper and easier they are to fix. ICS effectiveness is demonstrated when automated security testing, code analysis, and infrastructure scanning catch issues before they reach production. A software company that increases preproduction vulnerability detection from 40% to 90% significantly reduces its exposure to zero-day attacks.

ICS Transformation and Improvement Metrics

Transitioning to Intelligent Continuous Security requires fundamental changes in security processes, tooling, and culture. Measuring the progress of this transformation is critical to ensuring that ICS initiatives achieve their intended goals. Transformation and improvement metrics track the adoption of ICS practices, the maturity of automated security workflows, and the reduction of manual security efforts over time. These metrics provide visibility into whether an organization is successfully shifting security left, embedding security into the software development lifecycle, and continuously optimizing its defenses.

ICS transformation and improvement metrics are illustrated in Figure 9-3. One of the most revealing metrics in this category is the percentage of applications fully integrated with automated security testing. This metric measures the extent to which security checks are embedded into the development pipeline, reducing the reliance on post-deployment security reviews. Organizations tracking this metric can gauge their progress in proactively identifying vulnerabilities before they reach production. A company that increases its automated security coverage from 30% to 85% over two years demonstrates a clear commitment to ICS adoption.

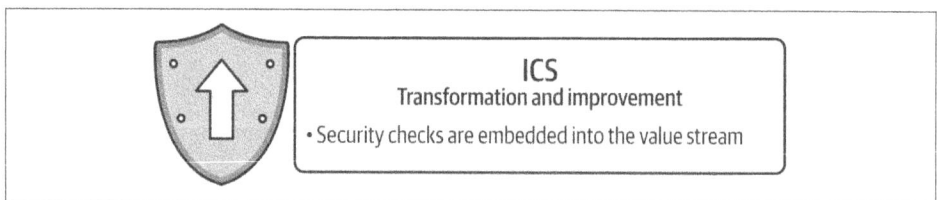

ICS
Transformation and improvement
• Security checks are embedded into the value stream

Figure 9-3. ICS transformation and improvement metrics

Another essential metric is the percentage of security processes automated through ICS solutions. Automation is a key enabler of ICS, reducing the burden of manual security checks and improving consistency. This metric assesses how much of the security workflow—from threat detection to incident response—is handled through automated tooling. A financial services company that automates 70% of its security alert triage within a year sees not only improved efficiency but also faster response times and reduced analyst fatigue.

Risk and Threat Exposure Metrics

While other metrics focus on security performance and transformation, risk and threat exposure metrics, illustrated in Figure 9-4, provide a real-time assessment of an organization's vulnerability to cyber threats. These metrics help security teams quantify risk, identify high-risk assets, and prioritize security investments based on actual exposure. Understanding an organization's risk profile allows for a more proactive approach to security, reducing the likelihood of breaches and minimizing potential impact.

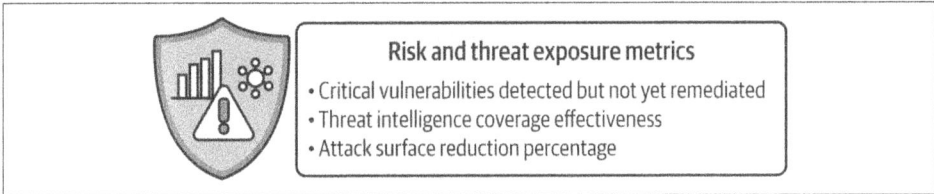

Risk and threat exposure metrics
- Critical vulnerabilities detected but not yet remediated
- Threat intelligence coverage effectiveness
- Attack surface reduction percentage

Figure 9-4. Risk and threat exposure metrics

Risk and threat exposure metrics allow organizations to shift from reactive security postures to predictive threat modeling. By continuously evaluating exposure levels, security teams can identify attack surface changes, emerging vulnerabilities, and gaps in security coverage. These metrics ensure that ICS is not just performing well but also effectively managing and mitigating organizational risk.

One of the most critical risk exposure metrics is the percentage of critical vulnerabilities detected but not yet remediated within SLAs. This metric highlights gaps in patching and remediation efforts, ensuring that security teams prioritize high-risk vulnerabilities before they can be exploited. It is measured by comparing the number of unresolved critical vulnerabilities against the total vulnerabilities identified. A financial institution that reduces its unpremeditated critical vulnerabilities from 30% to 5% within a year demonstrates an effective ICS implementation in minimizing exposure.

Another key metric is threat intelligence coverage effectiveness, which measures how well an organization integrates external threat intelligence feeds into its security operations. This metric evaluates the percentage of detected threats that align with known threat intelligence indicators, ensuring that ICS solutions leverage real-time threat intelligence to anticipate and defend against attacks. A multinational corporation that detects and blocks 90% of adversary tactics reported in its industry threat feeds ensures that its ICS framework remains ahead of evolving cyber threats.

Additionally, attack surface reduction percentage is a valuable metric for understanding security posture improvement. This measures the effectiveness of ICS efforts in reducing exposed assets, open ports, unprotected APIs, and other attack vectors. A cloud provider that reduces its externally exposed attack surface by 40% over a year demonstrates a proactive risk reduction strategy through Continuous Security monitoring and automation.

Compliance and Governance Metrics

Compliance and governance metrics are illustrated in Figure 9-5. One of the most essential compliance metrics is the percentage of systems audited and fully compliant with security policies. This metric helps organizations determine the extent to which their infrastructure, applications, and operational processes meet required security standards. It is measured by tracking completed audits against the total number of systems in scope. A healthcare provider that increases its system compliance rate from 75% to 98% through automated policy enforcement demonstrates the effectiveness of ICS in maintaining regulatory alignment.

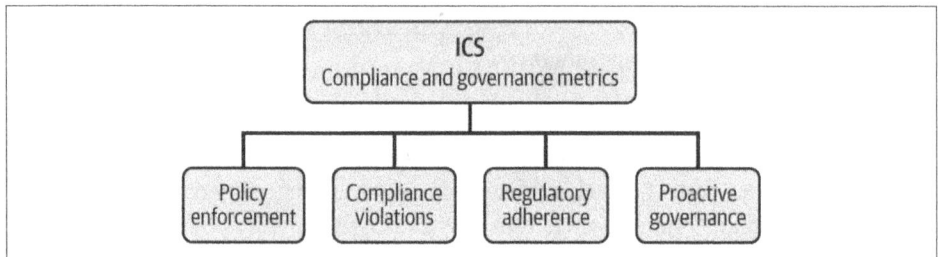

Figure 9-5. Compliance and governance metrics

Another crucial governance metric is the time to remediate compliance violations. Identifying a noncompliant system is only part of the challenge—organizations must also ensure timely remediation. This metric measures the average time taken to address security misconfigurations, policy violations, or audit failures. By reducing remediation times from months to days through automation, enterprises significantly lower their risk of noncompliance fines and security incidents.

Additionally, organizations should track the percentage of security controls automated for continuous compliance enforcement. Compliance is no longer just a matter of periodic audits; ICS enables real-time compliance monitoring and enforcement. This metric assesses how many security controls are automated versus manually enforced. A financial institution that automates 85% of its compliance checks eliminates much of the human error and inefficiency associated with traditional audits, improving both security and governance outcomes.

ICS Measurement Observability

ICS observability is the ability to monitor, analyze, and gain insights into the security posture of applications, development pipelines, and infrastructure elements, as illustrated in Figure 9-6. In the context of ICS, observability enables organizations to track key security metrics across the entire software lifecycle, ensuring that security issues are detected, measured, and acted upon in real time. Without strong observability, ICS metrics become unreliable, as gaps in monitoring lead to blind spots in security coverage.

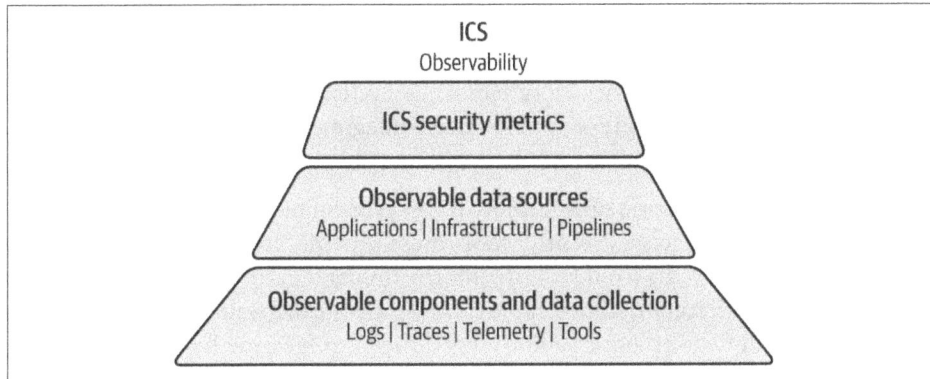

Figure 9-6. ICS observability

Observability plays a crucial role in making security measurable, actionable, and automated. It extends beyond basic logging and monitoring, requiring the collection and correlation of security-relevant data across applications, Continuous Integration/Continuous Delivery (CI/CD) pipelines, cloud and on-premises infrastructure, and runtime environments. Organizations implementing ICS must ensure that their observability strategies align with the security metrics they aim to measure, supporting proactive threat detection, compliance validation, and continuous improvement.

The Importance of ICS Observability

Without observability, ICS metrics are based on fragmented data, limiting their effectiveness in guiding security decisions. Observability ensures that security teams can collect meaningful telemetry from applications, pipelines, and infrastructure, transforming raw data into valuable security insights. This enables real-time risk detection, automated response, and ongoing compliance tracking. The ability to correlate security signals across different stages of the software lifecycle is essential for maintaining an accurate picture of an organization's security posture.

Effective observability also enhances incident response and forensic analysis. Security breaches often occur due to undetected misconfigurations or unnoticed security drift. ICS observability ensures that security teams have access to historical and real-time security data, allowing for rapid root cause analysis and remediation. This proactive approach minimizes the impact of security incidents and enables continuous refinement of security policies and controls.

Observability Requirements Across ICS Metrics Categories

Observability requirements vary depending on the type of ICS metric being measured. For business outcome metrics, observability focuses on collecting financial impact data, downtime tracking, and customer trust indicators. This requires monitoring systems that track financial loss avoidance, system availability, and compliance cost reductions. Observability solutions must integrate with business intelligence platforms to correlate security investments with tangible business outcomes.

For ICS effectiveness metrics, observability is centered on threat detection, alert accuracy, and response efficiency. Security tools must provide deep visibility into threat surfaces, correlating events from security information and event management (SIEM) systems, endpoint detection and response (EDR) platforms, and AI-driven security analytics. Without detailed observability, it is difficult to measure key indicators such as MTTD and MTTR.

In ICS transformation and improvement metrics, observability plays a role in tracking security automation adoption, manual intervention reductions, and process optimization. Organizations need insight into security workflows, developer adherence to secure coding practices, and the effectiveness of security automation pipelines. Observability solutions should integrate with DevSecOps tools, providing continuous feedback on security improvements over time.

For risk and threat exposure metrics, observability ensures comprehensive attack surface monitoring, vulnerability detection, and risk modeling. Organizations need telemetry from infrastructure components, cloud security posture management (CSPM) tools, and real-time threat intelligence feeds. Observability solutions must be capable of tracking risk levels, unpatched vulnerabilities, and lateral movement within an organization's environment.

For compliance and governance metrics, observability focuses on policy enforcement, audit readiness, and real-time compliance validation. Security teams require continuous visibility into policy adherence, regulatory compliance gaps, and automated audit logging. Observability solutions should seamlessly integrate with governance, risk, and compliance (GRC) platforms, ensuring that compliance is continuously measured rather than assessed periodically.

Designing an ICS Observability Strategy

When designing an ICS observability strategy, organizations must first identify which security signals are essential to their metrics framework. This involves evaluating the critical applications, infrastructure components, and development pipelines that require monitoring. Security teams should prioritize observability solutions that provide end-to-end visibility, data correlation, and real-time alerting.

A design team should also consider scalability and automation when selecting observability tools. ICS observability tools must support dynamic environments, including cloud native applications, containerized workloads, and hybrid infrastructure. Solutions should be capable of automated log collection, anomaly detection, and intelligent alerting, reducing the need for manual analysis. Integrating observability with AI-driven security analytics can further enhance the ability to detect and mitigate threats proactively.

Organizations must also focus on interoperability and integration. ICS observability solutions should seamlessly connect with SIEM platforms, security orchestration tools, DevSecOps pipelines, and compliance monitoring frameworks. Without interoperability, observability data remains siloed, limiting its usefulness for cross-functional security teams.

Real-Life Examples of ICS Observability Design

In the dimension of people, ICS observability enhances security operations by providing security analysts with real-time threat intelligence dashboards. A global financial institution implemented an observability platform that visualizes security risks across all cloud and on-premises environments. This empowered analysts to detect advanced threats more quickly and reduced incident response times by 50%.

In the process dimension, a software development company integrated observability solutions into its CI/CD pipelines. By embedding security monitoring at every stage of the development lifecycle, the company achieved automated vulnerability tracking and compliance validation. This resulted in a 70% reduction in post-deployment security issues, improving overall security efficiency.

In the technology dimension, a multinational corporation deployed an observability solution that continuously monitors API security, container security, and network traffic analytics. By using AI-powered detection models, the organization identified and mitigated potential breaches before attackers could exploit vulnerabilities, strengthening its overall ICS framework.

ICS observability is a fundamental enabler of effective security measurement. It ensures that security metrics are based on real-time, actionable insights rather than fragmented data. By implementing a well-designed observability strategy, organizations can enhance security visibility, automate compliance tracking, and improve risk detection, making ICS a fully measurable and continuously optimized security model.

ICS Security Architecture

As organizations adopt ICS, the volume and complexity of security data increase exponentially. Without a well-engineered ICS metrics architecture, as illustrated in Figure 9-7, organizations face challenges such as inconsistent data collection, lack of real-time insights, siloed data repositories, and inefficient query processing. These limitations hinder proactive security decision making and introduce delays in detecting and mitigating threats. A structured ICS security architecture ensures that data is collected, processed, and made actionable in a scalable and efficient manner.

A robust ICS security architecture eliminates fragmented data sources by providing a centralized and intelligent data management system. It enables organizations to collect logs from applications, CI/CD pipelines, and infrastructure; process and store them in a structured format; and apply AI-driven analytics to generate meaningful insights. Without this architectural foundation, organizations struggle with incomplete visibility into security threats and the inability to reliably measure security effectiveness.

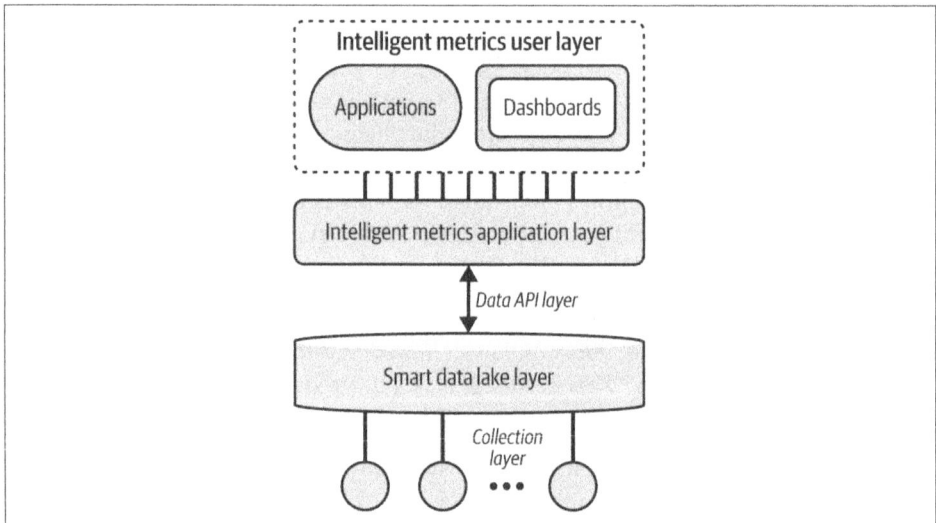

Figure 9-7. Five-layer ICS security architecture model

The Five-Layer ICS Security Architecture Model

A well-designed ICS security architecture consists of five interconnected layers, each serving a distinct function in collecting, processing, and delivering security insights.

Collection layer

The collection layer is responsible for gathering log data from applications, CI/CD pipelines, and infrastructure elements. This layer ensures that raw security data is consistently captured, formatted, and transmitted to a common data repository. Log data sources may include application runtime logs, build pipeline security scans, network logs, and cloud infrastructure telemetry.

Preprocessing in this layer involves standardizing log formats, applying basic filtering, and enriching data with contextual metadata. Efficient data transmission mechanisms ensure that logs reach the smart data lake layer without introducing bottlenecks and delays. Without this layer, security data remains fragmented, making it difficult to aggregate meaningful insights.

Smart data lake layer

The smart data lake layer serves as the centralized repository for all enterprise security data. Unlike traditional log storage, this layer incorporates a prescribed format with metadata tagging, allowing for efficient data cataloging and retrieval. The structured approach ensures that security teams can run predictive queries and historical analyses without excessive data retrieval delays.

The data lake stores information on security alerts, compliance audit logs, vulnerability assessments, and access logs, creating a single source of truth for security analytics. This structured storage approach enhances the ability to correlate security events across applications, pipelines, and infrastructures to detect complex attack patterns. Massively parallel processing (MPP) architecture is a type of computing architecture that is commonly used for big data analytics and data warehousing for query optimization and distributed processing.

Data API layer

The data API layer provides a structured interface for applications to query and interact with the smart data lake. Rather than requiring security analysts to manually retrieve data, this layer offers an intelligent data access framework that enables automated security analytics, dashboarding, and machine learning (ML) queries.

Through APIs, different security solutions, compliance tools, and DevSecOps workflows can seamlessly retrieve security data on demand. This layer supports automated, precompiled, precomputed correlation queries, security incident investigations, and compliance checks. Without it, accessing and analyzing security data becomes cumbersome and reliant on manual intervention.

Intelligent metrics application layer

The intelligent metrics application layer houses AI-driven security analytics, anomaly detection algorithms, and predictive modeling engines. This is where raw security data is transformed into actionable security insights.

Using ML models, this layer can identify security trends, detect insider threats, and forecast potential vulnerabilities based on historical data. Automated security rule engines ensure that threats are detected in real time, and AI-driven analysis helps security teams prioritize risk response.

Intelligent metrics user layer

The intelligent metrics user layer is responsible for customizing security data presentation based on user roles and requirements. Security insights are presented in role-specific dashboards, executive summaries, and real-time security feeds. This layer ensures that stakeholders—from security engineers to compliance officers—receive the most relevant security metrics in a format tailored to their needs.

This layer enables security teams to visualize compliance adherence, threat trends, security effectiveness, and overall risk posture. Organizations can design security dashboards that align with business objectives, making it easier to communicate the value of ICS investments.

Use Case: Custom Dashboards for ICS Metrics Categories

Consider a large financial institution adopting ICS security architecture to enhance its threat monitoring and compliance reporting. The organization requires customized dashboards to provide insights tailored to different stakeholders:

- The security operations team uses dashboards that visualize real-time threat intelligence, attack surface changes, and risk and threat exposure metrics.
- The compliance team accesses dashboards that track regulatory adherence, audit history, and compliance and governance metrics.
- The executive leadership team views high-level reports summarizing security effectiveness and risk mitigation.

By integrating custom dashboards into the intelligent metrics user layer, each stakeholder gains access to relevant security insights without needing to manually sift through raw data. This structured approach to ICS observability and security metrics architecture ensures that security decisions are data driven, proactive, and aligned with organizational goals.

A well-engineered ICS security architecture provides the foundation for scalable, real-time security insights. The five-layer model ensures that security data is collected, stored, analyzed, and presented in a structured and efficient manner. By integrating a smart data lake, intelligent analytics, and customizable dashboards, organizations can transition from reactive security practices to a predictive, AI-powered ICS model that enhances security maturity across the enterprise.

Sustaining a Reliable ICS Metrics Architecture

A well-designed ICS metrics architecture, illustrated in Figure 9-8, is valuable only if it remains sustainable, reliable, and adaptable over time. Security threats, compliance regulations, and technology landscapes are continuously evolving. An ICS architecture that cannot keep pace with these changes will quickly become outdated, unreliable, and unusable. Sustainability ensures that the architecture remains functional and cost-effective in the long run. Reliability guarantees that metrics provide accurate, consistent insights without system failures or performance degradation. Adaptability enables the architecture to evolve with new security challenges, business needs, and technological advancements.

Beyond these core attributes, an ICS metrics architecture must also be easy to onboard new users and new applications. Security teams, compliance officers, DevOps engineers, and business executives all rely on security metrics, but if the system is too complex or difficult to integrate with new applications, its effectiveness will be severely limited. Organizations should design their ICS metrics architecture so that new users can quickly access relevant insights and new security data sources can be integrated without excessive reconfiguration.

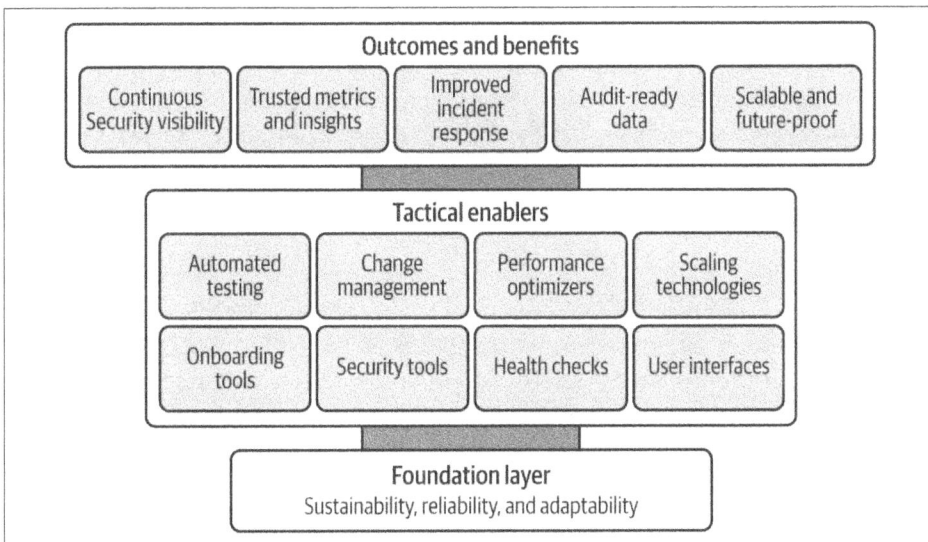

Figure 9-8. Sustainability, reliability, and adaptability of ICS metrics

Additionally, the architecture itself must adhere to best practices for security. A security observability system that is vulnerable to tampering, unauthorized access, or data corruption undermines the integrity of security metrics. Organizations must enforce access controls, encryption, logging, and continuous monitoring to ensure that the ICS security architecture is as secure as the systems it monitors.

Tactics for Ensuring Sustainability, Reliability, and Adaptability

To maintain an ICS metrics architecture that is effective over time, organizations must implement proactive strategies that sustain its long-term performance and usability. These strategies involve strong change control, automated testing, built-in health metrics, ease of onboarding, and enforcing security best practices.

Implement excellent change management

ICS metrics architectures must be resilient to change while ensuring that modifications do not disrupt security observability. Change control practices should include version control for metrics definitions, controlled deployments of observability updates, and rigorous testing of changes before production implementation. By maintaining traceability of modifications, organizations can ensure that security metrics remain accurate, standardized, and relevant.

Automate testing for all architecture components

Automated testing is crucial for maintaining the integrity of an ICS metrics architecture. Each component—from the collection layer to the intelligent metrics user layer—must undergo automated validation checks to ensure that data flows correctly, processing logic remains accurate, and dashboards display correct information. This includes automated regression testing, integration testing between layers, and continuous validation of data accuracy. Without automated testing, organizations risk introducing silent failures where incorrect security data goes undetected, leading to poor security decisions.

Embed built-in health metrics

An ICS metrics architecture must monitor its own health. Health metrics should track data ingestion rates, processing latencies, API response times, and error rates across all observability layers. Any deviation from expected values should trigger automated alerts and automated remediation, allowing teams to remediate issues before they impact security insights. If the architecture lacks internal health monitoring, organizations will not detect when security metrics are failing to provide accurate visibility.

Design for scalability, performance, and ease of onboarding

ICS metrics architectures must be built to handle growing data volumes and increasing complexity. As organizations expand their security monitoring scope, their architecture must scale horizontally to accommodate new data sources, support real-time analytics, and provide rapid query execution. Using cloud native technologies, distributed processing, and AI-driven anomaly detection enhances the scalability and performance of ICS observability systems.

Just as important as scalability is the ability to onboard new users and applications efficiently. A well-architected ICS observability system should provide self-service access to security dashboards, role-based access controls (RBACs), and standardized data integration points that make it easy for teams to extract security insights. If onboarding a new application or adding a new security team takes weeks, the architecture is failing in one of its most fundamental objectives: making security data accessible and actionable.

Treat an ICS metrics architecture as a product, not just a project

One of the most common pitfalls organizations face is treating ICS security metrics as a one-time implementation effort rather than an evolving product. A product mindset ensures that ongoing maintenance, iterative improvements, and continuous adaptation remain priorities. Organizations should establish dedicated teams responsible for refining security observability, incorporating feedback, and enhancing architecture capabilities over time. By shifting from a project-based mindset to a product-oriented approach, organizations sustain their ICS architecture's effectiveness and ensure long-term success.

Ensure security best practices for an ICS metrics architecture

A security monitoring system that lacks security itself is a contradiction. The ICS metrics architecture must follow security best practices to ensure data integrity, confidentiality, and availability. This includes RBACs, encryption of security logs, multi-factor authentication (MFA) for administrative access, tamper-proof audit logging, and real-time anomaly detection to prevent unauthorized modifications. A compromised ICS observability system can introduce false metrics, obfuscate security incidents, or allow attackers to evade detection. Ensuring end-to-end security for ICS observability infrastructure is critical to maintaining the trustworthiness of security metrics.

The Consequences of Failing to Maintain a Sustainable ICS Metrics Architecture

When an ICS metrics architecture is not designed for sustainability, reliability, or adaptability, its value degrades over time. Data inconsistencies, metrics inaccuracies, and system failures cause security teams to lose trust in the architecture, leading them to revert to manual processes and fragmented security measurements. Security teams may struggle with data silos, compliance blind spots, and ineffective security responses due to unreliable or outdated insights.

In worst-case scenarios, organizations may experience security blind spots that lead to breaches because their observability systems failed to detect early warning signs. Compliance violations can also arise when organizations are unable to generate accurate, audit-ready reports due to a lack of real-time security data. These risks make it imperative that ICS architectures are continuously evaluated, maintained, and improved.

Sustaining a reliable, adaptable, and well-managed ICS metrics architecture is essential for ensuring Continuous Security observability and proactive risk management. Organizations must implement structured change management, automated testing, built-in health monitoring, scalability mechanisms, and security best practices to prevent their security measurement framework from becoming obsolete. Most importantly, ICS security metrics must be treated as a long-term product that evolves alongside the business and the threat landscape. By embedding sustainability into ICS observability, organizations ensure that their security measures remain accurate, actionable, and resilient in the face of ongoing cybersecurity challenges.

Choosing ICS Metrics

Selecting the right security metrics for an ICS solution is crucial to ensuring actionable insights that improve security posture, operational efficiency, and compliance, as illustrated in Figure 9-9. Not all organizations require the same set of metrics—what works for a financial institution may not be as relevant for a cloud native software as a service (SaaS) provider or a government agency. The key to effective metrics selection is aligning security measurements with business objectives, operational risks, and compliance requirements.

Organizations should focus on metrics that are directly tied to their security goals and can drive measurable improvements. For example, if an enterprise prioritizes risk reduction, it should emphasize metrics related to vulnerability management, threat exposure, and security incident response. If regulatory compliance is a primary concern, the organization should prioritize compliance adherence, audit readiness, and policy enforcement metrics. Each selected metric must be relevant and measurable, and must contribute to decision making.

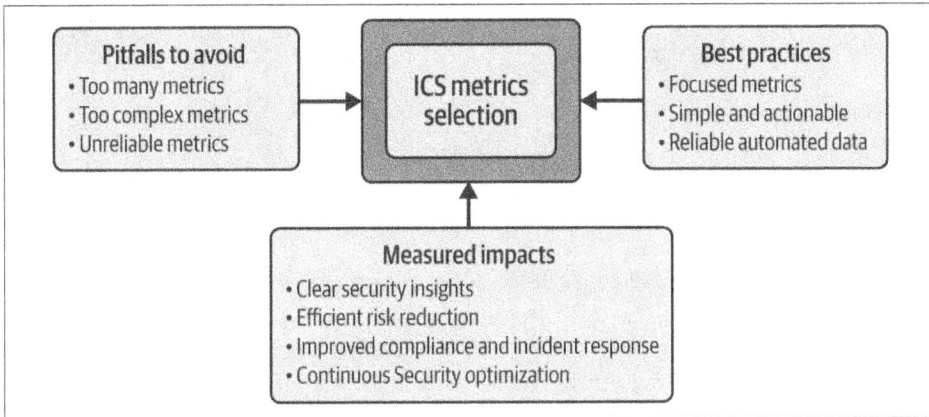

Figure 9-9. Selecting ICS metrics

Pitfalls to Avoid When Choosing ICS Metrics

Many metrics for ICS are possible. However, metrics must be chosen carefully because there are many ways you can run into problems with metrics, as explained in this section.

Choosing too many metrics

A common mistake is selecting an excessive number of metrics, leading to data overload and analysis paralysis. Security teams may struggle to interpret vast amounts of data, and decision makers may be unable to extract meaningful insights.

Real-world example: A multinational technology firm implemented over 100 different security metrics across its ICS framework. While the organization had extensive visibility into various aspects of security, security analysts found it overwhelming to track and respond to all indicators effectively. As a result, critical vulnerabilities were sometimes overlooked due to the sheer volume of data, leading to a major security incident when an unpatched vulnerability was exploited.

Selecting metrics that are too complex

Overly complex metrics that require excessive computation, specialized knowledge, or multiple layers of data transformation can become impractical. When metrics are difficult to calculate or interpret, security teams may fail to derive actionable insights in a timely manner.

Real-world example: A financial services company designed an intricate risk-scoring model that incorporated dozens of factors, each weighted differently. While it provided a sophisticated security posture analysis, engineers and security teams struggled to maintain the system, leading to misinterpretations of security trends.

Eventually, they replaced the system with simpler, real-time risk indicators that were easier to understand and act upon.

Using potentially unreliable metrics

Metrics must be based on high-quality, trustworthy data sources. If an organization selects metrics that depend on incomplete, inconsistent, or manipulated data, it risks making flawed security decisions.

Real-world example: A CSP relied heavily on self-reported compliance checks from individual teams to track its security posture. However, these manual reports were often outdated or inaccurately completed. When an external audit was conducted, significant security gaps were discovered, revealing that the metrics used for compliance tracking were not an accurate reflection of the organization's actual security posture.

Best Practices for Effective ICS Metrics Selection

To ensure that an ICS solution delivers relevant, actionable, and sustainable security insights, organizations should follow these best practices when selecting metrics:

Keep metrics focused and aligned with business priorities.
> Security metrics should directly support an organization's strategic objectives rather than tracking data for the sake of visibility.

Ensure that metrics are simple enough to understand and act upon.
> Metrics should not require excessive computation or expertise to interpret; instead, they should be practical for security teams and decision makers.

Validate the accuracy and reliability of data sources.
> Ensure that security metrics rely on real-time, consistent, and verifiable data sources.

Prioritize automation and real-time visibility.
> Metrics should be automated whenever possible to reduce manual reporting errors and ensure real-time insights.

Regularly review and refine metrics.
> As security threats evolve and business needs change, organizations should periodically reassess their security metrics to ensure continued relevance and effectiveness.

By following these best practices and avoiding common pitfalls, organizations can build an effective ICS metrics framework that provides clear security insights, supports decision making, and drives continuous improvement.

Summary

Measuring the effectiveness of Intelligent Continuous Security is essential for ensuring that security initiatives are delivering real value. ICS metrics provide visibility into security performance, business impact, transformation progress, risk exposure, and compliance adherence. Without a well-structured measurement framework, organizations risk operating in the dark, unable to assess the effectiveness of their security investments. The right metrics enable security leaders to make data-driven decisions, continuously improve security strategies, and align security objectives with business goals.

ICS metrics are not one-size-fits-all; they must be carefully selected to align with organizational needs. Business outcome metrics ensure that security investments contribute to financial stability and customer trust. ICS effectiveness metrics measure how well security processes detect and respond to threats. Transformation and improvement metrics track the adoption and maturity of ICS practices. Risk and threat exposure metrics help organizations understand their vulnerabilities, while compliance and governance metrics ensure adherence to regulatory standards. Selecting the right mix of these metrics is key to maintaining a proactive and adaptive security posture.

A robust ICS measurement architecture must be sustainable, reliable, and adaptable. This requires embedding automated validation, change management, built-in health metrics, and scalability. Organizations must avoid the pitfalls of selecting too many metrics, using overly complex indicators, or relying on unreliable data sources. Instead, best practices include focusing on clear, actionable metrics, ensuring simplicity in measurement, and integrating real-time observability. A well-designed ICS metrics system provides both real-time security insights and long-term strategic value.

As ICS continues to evolve, security observability and AI-driven analytics will play an increasingly significant role in ensuring accurate, actionable, and automated security measurement. The integration of AI for predictive risk modeling, automated response optimization, and real-time compliance tracking will further refine how organizations measure and respond to security threats. Forward-thinking organizations will embrace AI-powered metrics solutions to enhance their security capabilities and maintain resilience against evolving cyber threats.

With ICS metrics providing a foundation for continuous improvement, organizations must now look to the future of Intelligent Continuous Security. Chapter 10 explores how AI-driven security automation, predictive defense strategies, and self-healing security systems will redefine the next generation of cybersecurity, ensuring that ICS remains dynamic, adaptive, and capable of defending against the threats of tomorrow.

The Future of
Intelligent Continuous Security

The future of cybersecurity is not just about stronger firewalls, smarter detection systems, or faster incident response. It is about a fundamental shift in how security is embedded, automated, and continuously optimized across the digital landscape. As we move forward, the convergence of AI, machine learning (ML), and predictive analytics with security practices will redefine what it means to be secure. Intelligent Continuous Security (ICS) is not just an evolution of DevSecOps and SecOps. It is the next step in creating a security-first digital ecosystem that adapts, learns, and responds autonomously.

This book has explored the essential components of ICS, from its foundational principles to the tools and methodologies that enable real-time security monitoring, automation, and risk assessment. We have seen how AI and automation are transforming security operations, allowing organizations to detect threats earlier, respond more quickly, and manage vulnerabilities more effectively. However, the journey does not end here. The next frontier in ICS will focus on developing self-healing security systems, adaptive risk-based controls, and AI-driven security decision making that operate at machine speed. For example, SentinelOne Singularity already provides AI-driven endpoint detection and response/extended detection and response (EDR/XDR).

The need for this transformation is more urgent than ever. Cyber adversaries are not slowing down; they are leveraging AI, automation, and sophisticated attack strategies to exploit vulnerabilities more quickly than traditional security teams can respond. Organizations that continue to rely on outdated, reactive security models will find themselves increasingly vulnerable to breaches, regulatory penalties, and operational disruptions. The future of ICS lies in proactive, predictive, and autonomous security frameworks that empower security teams with the tools to outpace attackers.

This final chapter explores the trends shaping the next generation of ICS, the role of AI in security automation, and how organizations must prepare for the coming wave of cyber threats. It examines how businesses can build future-proof ICS strategies, leveraging emerging technologies while ensuring that they remain adaptable to shifting regulatory and technology landscapes. More importantly, it will challenge organizations to rethink their approach to security, not as a compliance requirement, but as a continuous, intelligent, and strategic advantage.

ICS is no longer an option for enterprises—it is a necessity. As we look ahead, the question is not whether organizations will adopt intelligent, AI-driven security solutions, but how quickly they can do so before they fall behind. By embracing the principles of ICS, leveraging AI-assisted security operations, and fostering a culture of continuous improvement, businesses can build a security model that is not just reactive, but predictive and resilient. The following sections will outline what this future looks like and what steps enterprises need to take to stay ahead in the evolving landscape of AI-assisted cybersecurity.

Emerging Trends in Intelligent Continuous Security

The field of Intelligent Continuous Security is undergoing a rapid transformation, driven by evolving threats, technological advancements, and shifting regulatory landscapes. Organizations that once relied on reactive security measures are now embracing proactive and predictive security approaches. The emergence of AI-driven security analytics, automated compliance enforcement, and real-time risk assessment is reshaping how enterprises defend against modern cyber threats. As ICS continues to mature, new trends are emerging that will define the next generation of cybersecurity strategies, from human-centric security innovations to highly autonomous, self-healing security architectures.

Understanding these trends is crucial for organizations looking to stay ahead of cyber adversaries. Many of the short-term trends discussed in this section are already being integrated into DevSecOps and SecOps workflows, helping businesses reduce risk exposure and improve security efficiency. At the same time, longer-term trends— such as AI-driven threat prediction, behavioral-based risk modeling, and fully autonomous security response systems—represent the future direction of ICS. While adoption of these technologies remains limited, research and pilot programs suggest that these innovations will soon become mainstream.

As illustrated in Figure 10-1, trends shaping ICS security can be broadly categorized into three areas: people, processes, and technology.

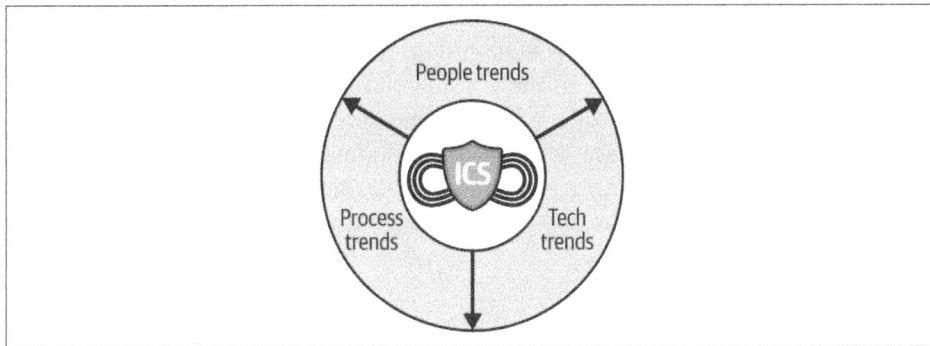

Figure 10-1. Security trends

The human element remains one of the most unpredictable variables in cybersecurity, necessitating greater investment in behavioral analytics, workforce security training, and cognitive risk assessments. Meanwhile, process innovations such as automated security policy enforcement, AI-driven compliance validation, and predictive risk modeling are transforming security operations. Finally, emerging technologies—ranging from AI-assisted threat intelligence to homomorphic encryption—are setting the stage for a new era of secure computing.

By exploring these trends, we gain insight into how ICS will evolve in both the immediate future and the long term. Some of these innovations are already driving measurable security improvements, while others remain largely experimental but have the potential to revolutionize how organizations approach cybersecurity. The following sections will examine the key short-term and long-term trends across human, process, and technology domains, providing real-world examples that illustrate their significance.

People: Emerging Trends

Security is fundamentally a human-driven discipline, and as organizations evolve their ICS strategies, they are placing greater emphasis on the intersection of human behavior, cybersecurity awareness, and operational resilience. In the short term, enterprises are adopting behavioral analytics and AI-assisted user activity monitoring to detect insider threats and security policy violations before they escalate. Unlike traditional rule-based monitoring, these approaches leverage ML to establish behavioral baselines and detect anomalies indicative of compromised credentials or malicious intent. This shift is particularly relevant considering recent security breaches, such as the 2023 MOVEit file transfer exploit where undetected compromised credentials were used to access sensitive systems for months.

Another short-term trend gaining traction is the integration of Continuous Security training into DevSecOps workflows. Rather than relying on annual training sessions, organizations are embedding real-time, context-aware security education directly into developer environments. Secure coding guidance powered by AI is being integrated into IDEs, allowing developers to receive immediate feedback when writing potentially vulnerable code. This practice is already seeing widespread adoption in financial services and healthcare, where compliance-driven security policies mandate rigorous coding standards.

Longer-term research is focusing on cognitive security models and neurobehavioral security profiling. The goal is to develop AI systems that can predict high-risk behavior patterns among employees and alert security teams before an insider threat materializes. This approach builds on psychology-based security risk assessment methodologies but applies ML to analyze decision-making tendencies under stress or time constraints. While still in its early stages, government agencies and critical infrastructure operators are investing in pilot programs to determine whether these predictive models can effectively reduce human-driven security incidents.

Another area of long-term exploration is the intersection of cybersecurity and workforce well-being. Research suggests that cognitive overload and burnout in security teams contribute to human error and alert fatigue, leading to overlooked threats. Organizations are experimenting with adaptive Security Operations Centers (SOCs) that adjust workflows based on individual analyst workloads, cognitive load assessments, and AI-driven prioritization of threats. This concept remains largely in the experimental phase, but major cloud providers and financial institutions are funding research into optimizing security team performance through human-aware cybersecurity automation. These trends are illustrated in Figure 10-2.

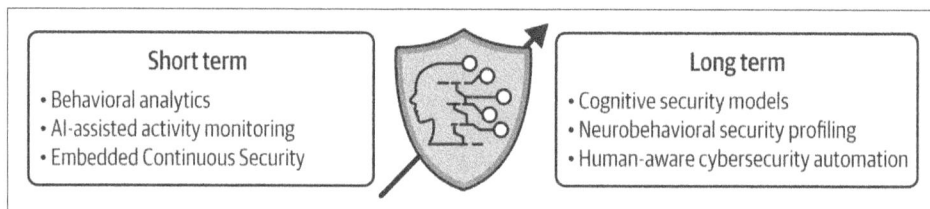

Short term	Long term
• Behavioral analytics • AI-assisted activity monitoring • Embedded Continuous Security	• Cognitive security models • Neurobehavioral security profiling • Human-aware cybersecurity automation

Figure 10-2. People security trends

Process: Emerging Trends

ICS practices are fundamentally reshaping security workflows and, in the short term, we are seeing the widespread adoption of security Policy as Code (PaC) and automated compliance validation. Organizations are shifting away from manually enforced security policies and instead are embedding security requirements directly into Infrastructure as Code (IaC) and Continuous Integration/Continuous Delivery (CI/CD) pipelines. By codifying security policies, enterprises ensure that every deployed system meets predefined compliance and security standards before it reaches production. This shift has been particularly critical for cloud native organizations that operate in highly dynamic environments. The 2022 Uber data breach, where misconfigurations in cloud identity and access management (IAM) policies exposed sensitive internal tools, reinforced the necessity of policy automation and continuous compliance enforcement.

Another key short-term trend is the rise of autonomous security remediation. Modern ICS platforms are integrating self-healing capabilities that automatically respond to security incidents without human intervention. When a misconfiguration or vulnerability is detected, these systems can automatically roll back to a secure state, apply necessary patches, or isolate affected workloads. This approach significantly reduces the time-to-remediation window and minimizes human error, particularly in large-scale cloud environments where security teams are managing thousands of assets in real time.

In the longer term, organizations are researching AI-driven security orchestration, where autonomous security decision-making processes can dynamically adjust security controls based on real-time risk assessments. This involves AI engines that ingest real-time security telemetry, assess business risk factors, adjust firewall rules, access policies, and set up workload configurations autonomously. While this concept is still in experimental phases, recent supply chain attacks, such as the 2023 SolarWinds successor attacks, have highlighted the need for adaptive security architectures that can self-modify defenses as new threats emerge.

These trends are illustrated in Figure 10-3.

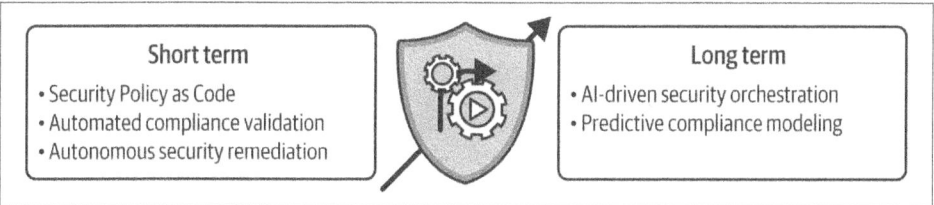

Figure 10-3. Process security trends

Another long-term process trend is predictive compliance modeling, where AI-driven simulations proactively assess security posture against future regulatory requirements. Instead of reacting to compliance changes when new laws take effect, organizations will leverage AI to continuously model upcoming regulatory shifts and proactively implement policy changes. This approach is gaining traction in finance and healthcare, where new regulations are emerging at an accelerated pace, making manual compliance strategies increasingly untenable.

Technology: Emerging Trends

ICS is shaped by rapid advancements in cybersecurity technology, and in the short term, we are seeing increased adoption of AI-assisted threat intelligence platforms that dynamically analyze global attack patterns and provide real-time risk scoring for enterprise environments. By leveraging AI-driven analytics, security teams can gain immediate insights into how evolving threats impact their specific infrastructure, allowing for proactive remediation. This approach gained significant traction following the Log4j vulnerability crisis, where organizations using real-time threat intelligence were able to mitigate risks far more effectively than those relying on static security policies.

Another short-term trend is the convergence of XDR with AI-driven behavioral analytics. Modern security platforms are evolving beyond simple log aggregation and moving toward intelligent detection engines that correlate disparate security signals to uncover sophisticated attack patterns. This shift is crucial in the face of advanced persistent threats (APTs), where attackers use low-and-slow techniques to evade traditional detection mechanisms. The 2022 Lapsus$ attacks, which involved highly coordinated social engineering and data exfiltration tactics, demonstrated the growing need for cross-platform security correlation that extends beyond endpoint detection alone.

Looking further ahead, security researchers are investigating fully homomorphic encryption (FHE) for secure cloud processing, which would allow organizations to perform computations on encrypted data without ever decrypting it. If successfully implemented at scale, FHE would revolutionize data privacy, allowing enterprises to outsource sensitive workloads to the cloud while maintaining Zero Trust encryption models. While FHE is still in early research phases, companies such as IBM and Google are actively investing in this space.

Finally, longer-term research is focusing on AI-powered deception technology—where advanced automated honeypots and decoy systems can autonomously mimic real production environments to lure and analyze attacker behavior. The concept is evolving beyond traditional honeypots, leveraging AI to create dynamic, self-adapting decoys that engage attackers for longer periods, gathering intelligence on emerging threat tactics. Recent state-sponsored cyber espionage campaigns have demonstrated the growing need for advanced cyber deception to misdirect and slow down adversaries in high-value environments. These trends are illustrated in Figure 10-4.

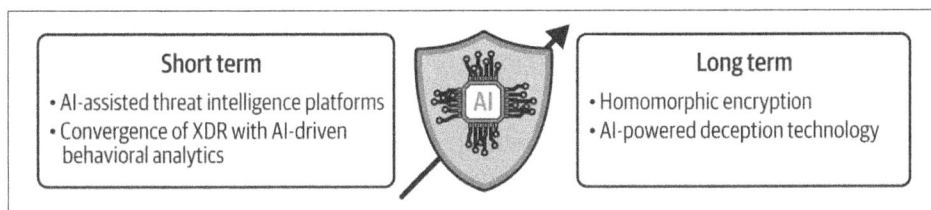

Short term		Long term
• AI-assisted threat intelligence platforms • Convergence of XDR with AI-driven behavioral analytics		• Homomorphic encryption • AI-powered deception technology

Figure 10-4. Technology security trends

As you have seen, the landscape of Intelligent Continuous Security is evolving at a remarkable pace, with new trends emerging across people, process, and technology domains. Short-term advancements—such as AI-driven user activity monitoring, automated security policy enforcement, and real-time threat intelligence—are already being integrated into ICS solutions, enhancing security visibility and operational resilience. Meanwhile, longer-term innovations—including predictive compliance modeling, neurobehavioral security profiling, and self-adapting deception technology—represent the future direction of cybersecurity. These developments indicate a clear shift from traditional, reactive security measures toward proactive, intelligent, and automated security frameworks.

As organizations prepare to adopt these trends, they must consider the challenges of implementation, including scalability, interoperability, and the need for cultural and operational shifts. While many organizations are already embracing ICS-driven transformation, others are still in the early stages of evaluating these innovations. "Preparing for Future Trends" explores strategies for preparing for the implementation of trends, focusing on how enterprises can successfully integrate emerging ICS practices into their existing security ecosystems.

Preparing for Future Trends

Successfully implementing emerging ICS trends requires careful planning, a deep understanding of organizational constraints, and a willingness to embrace continuous adaptation. While new security technologies and process improvements hold immense promise, their integration into existing security frameworks is rarely seamless. Organizations must anticipate operational challenges, ensure workforce readiness, and align their security strategies with business objectives. Without this structured approach, even the most advanced security innovations can fail to deliver meaningful impact.

One of the primary challenges organizations face is bridging the gap between emerging ICS capabilities and existing security operations. Many enterprises operate legacy systems that were never designed with Continuous Security in mind. The challenge lies in integrating modern, AI-driven security practices without disrupting core business functions. This requires a transition strategy that includes phased adoption, interoperability assessments, and rigorous testing of new security methodologies.

Another key consideration is the readiness of security teams and stakeholders. Security is not just about deploying new tools. It's about ensuring that people understand how to leverage the tools effectively. Organizations must develop tailored training programs that align with the specific trends they aim to implement, whether that involves AI-driven security orchestration, behavioral analytics, or automated compliance validation. A well-trained workforce is essential to maximizing the effectiveness of ICS investments.

Organizations must also be prepared to navigate regulatory and governance implications as they adopt emerging ICS trends. Compliance frameworks continue to evolve, and as security automation becomes more prevalent, regulators are adjusting their expectations. Ensuring that ICS implementations align with industry regulations and data protection requirements is crucial for both security effectiveness and legal adherence. Organizations that take a proactive approach to compliance—by embedding automated validation into their security pipelines—will find it easier to adapt to future regulatory shifts.

Preparing for People Trends

The human element in security is both a strength and a vulnerability, making the preparation for human-centered ICS trends a priority. As organizations integrate AI-assisted behavioral analytics and Continuous Security training, they must address key challenges such as user resistance, privacy concerns, and the difficulty of changing ingrained behaviors. Many employees see security measures as a hindrance to productivity, and without proper incentives, they may resist new security processes. Organizations can overcome this by embedding security within workflows rather than forcing it as an additional layer. Adaptive training programs that integrate with developer environments and Security Operations Center (SOC) dashboards can reinforce best practices in real time without disrupting daily tasks. It is important that people not only accept the change but also embrace it and support it.

Privacy concerns are another major hurdle, particularly with the adoption of AI-driven user behavior monitoring. Employees and stakeholders may fear that continuous monitoring infringes on their privacy, leading to reluctance in adopting these solutions. Organizations can counteract this concern by ensuring transparency—clearly communicating what is being monitored, how data is protected, and how it will be used strictly for security improvements rather than individual performance evaluation.

The long-term adoption of cognitive security models and neurobehavioral profiling poses even greater challenges, as these systems require massive datasets and a deep understanding of human psychology. The accuracy of these models depends on comprehensive training data, which many organizations lack. To prepare, enterprises must invest in collecting anonymized behavioral datasets while collaborating with research institutions specializing in cybersecurity psychology.

Preparing for Process Change Trends

Process-driven ICS trends, such as automated compliance enforcement and security PaC, require fundamental shifts in how security teams operate. The biggest challenge here is the cultural resistance from security and compliance teams accustomed to manual enforcement processes. Many security professionals still see security policies as static documents rather than dynamic, code-driven frameworks. Training teams to think about security in an automated and integrated way is a necessary step for success.

Security teams also struggle with process bottlenecks when integrating compliance automation into CI/CD pipelines. Some regulatory frameworks require human review at critical decision points, which can slow down the automation process. Organizations must develop hybrid models where automation handles routine compliance checks while human experts intervene in edge cases requiring judgment.

Longer-term process changes, such as AI-driven security orchestration and predictive compliance modeling, demand even more extensive preparation. Organizations need to establish a security data architecture that allows AI systems to make informed risk-based decisions. Without high-quality security telemetry, AI-driven process automation cannot function effectively. This means investing in security data lakes, standardized logging formats, and real-time threat intelligence feeds.

Preparing for Technology Trends

Technology-driven ICS trends require both infrastructure investment and organizational readiness. The shift toward AI-assisted threat intelligence platforms and XDR is already underway, but many enterprises struggle with the complexity of integration. Security tools often operate in silos, making it difficult for AI models to analyze threats holistically. The key to successful adoption is open security architectures that facilitate data sharing across different security platforms.

Longer-term advancements such as FHE and AI-driven deception technology present different challenges. FHE remains computationally expensive, and few enterprises have the infrastructure to support encrypted cloud workloads at scale. Organizations should monitor industry developments and prepare by exploring hybrid cryptographic models that balance security and performance.

AI-driven deception technologies require deep customization as they must mirror the specific characteristics of an organization's IT environment. The effectiveness of these technologies hinges on how convincingly they replicate production environments.

Organizations preparing for adoption should start by testing basic deception strategies, such as honeypots and decoy credentials, before moving toward fully autonomous deception frameworks.

The implementation of emerging ICS trends is a complex but necessary evolution for modern security programs. Organizations must prepare for challenges related to integration with existing systems, workforce adaptation, and regulatory alignment. By anticipating these obstacles and proactively developing transition strategies, enterprises can ensure that their ICS investments deliver long-term security and operational benefits.

The final section of this chapter provides a summary of key insights for ICS overall. This will consolidate the critical lessons learned throughout the book, offering a strategic perspective on the future of Intelligent Continuous Security and how organizations can sustain a proactive, AI-driven security posture.

Summary

The evolution of cybersecurity practices has made it clear that traditional approaches—such as siloed DevSecOps and SecOps methodologies—are no longer sufficient to defend against modern threats. ICS represents a transformative shift by embedding security directly into the software lifecycle, leveraging AI-driven automation, and prioritizing real-time threat intelligence. Unlike legacy models that treat security as a separate function, ICS unifies security across development, operations, and compliance, ensuring that organizations maintain a proactive and adaptive defense posture.

ICS is distinguished by several key practices that set it apart from traditional security models:

- Its integration across the entire software lifecycle allows security to evolve dynamically alongside applications and infrastructure.
- Its reliance on AI and automation reduces manual intervention, enabling security teams to focus on high-value activities such as risk management and threat analysis.
- Its emphasis on continuous monitoring and real-time analytics provides organizations with the agility to respond to emerging threats before they escalate into major security incidents.

A fundamental lesson from ICS adoption is the necessity of *continuous improvement and evolution*. Security is not a one-time investment; it is an ongoing discipline that must adapt to an ever-changing threat landscape. Organizations that fail to sustain and evolve their ICS practices risk falling behind attackers who continuously refine their tactics. This means that ICS is not just about implementing the latest tool; it is about fostering a security-first culture, enhancing collaboration across teams, and ensuring that security remains embedded in business operations.

Keeping up with emerging trends is a crucial part of maintaining a resilient ICS strategy. The rise of AI-powered deception technology, self-healing security architectures, and cognitive security analytics demonstrates that the field is still in its early stages of innovation. Organizations that stay informed and remain agile in adopting these new capabilities will be better positioned to defend against increasingly sophisticated threats. Adopting a forward-looking security mindset ensures that enterprises can leverage ICS not just as a defense mechanism, but as a strategic enabler of business resilience and growth.

As this book has outlined, ICS is more than a collection of tools or best practices—it is a fundamental shift in how security is approached. The integration of intelligent automation, Continuous Security validation, and AI-driven decision making allows organizations to move beyond the limitations of traditional security frameworks. By adopting ICS, enterprises can achieve greater efficiency, reduce risk exposure, and ensure long-term security sustainability.

Ultimately, the future of ICS lies in its ability to adapt, evolve, and sustain itself in response to an ever-changing cybersecurity landscape. As organizations embrace AI-assisted security, predictive analytics, and self-healing architectures, they will be better prepared to navigate the complexities of modern cybersecurity threats. Those that invest in ICS today will not only protect their systems from current risks but will also future-proof their security strategies for years to come.

Final Thoughts

If you've made it this far, you have taken a significant step toward advancing your understanding of Intelligent Continuous Security. The fact that you've committed time to exploring these concepts demonstrates that you recognize the importance of shifting beyond traditional security methods and embracing a more integrated, proactive approach. Cybersecurity is no longer a static field. It is a dynamic, evolving challenge that requires forward-thinking strategies, intelligent automation, and a commitment to continuous improvement.

ICS is not just a set of tools or methodologies. It is a *mindset shift* that fundamentally changes how security is embedded into the entire lifecycle. By leveraging AI-driven automation, real-time risk management, and continuous monitoring, organizations can move beyond reactive security models and take control of their security posture. But as with any transformative change, the real impact comes not from simply understanding these concepts, but from actively applying them. I encourage you to take what you've learned in this book and assess how it applies to your own organization, whether that means reevaluating your security strategies, implementing new automation capabilities, or driving cultural change to integrate security across teams.

The journey toward fully realizing ICS does not stop here. As cyber threats evolve, so too must our security strategies. Keeping up with emerging trends—such as AI-assisted threat intelligence, self-healing security architectures, and predictive risk modeling—will be essential for staying ahead of adversaries. I encourage you to remain engaged in the broader security community, explore ongoing advancements in AI-driven security, and continue refining your organization's approach to ICS.

As I've said many times, security is not an endpoint; it is a continuous process of adaptation, learning, and improvement. The most successful organizations are those that treat ICS as a core business enabler rather than just a compliance requirement. By making security an integral part of your operations, development practices, and executive decision making, you will not only strengthen your defenses but also enable innovation and resilience in the face of an increasingly complex digital landscape.

For those who wish to go deeper, I highly recommend exploring the Appendix, which provides references to best practices, tools, frameworks, and further readings to extend your competency in ICS. Whether you are looking for hands-on technical guidance or strategic leadership insights, these resources will help you refine your security strategies and drive meaningful transformation within your organization.

Thank you for taking this journey with me. I look forward to seeing how you apply ICS to shape the future of cybersecurity.

Resources for Further Learning

Security and DevOps professionals face an ever-expanding landscape of threats, tools, and best practices that continuously evolve. To navigate this complex terrain, a wealth of knowledge is available in the form of books, websites, articles, and professional courses that provide guidance on the principles and execution of Intelligent Continuous Security (ICS). This Appendix is a curated collection of essential resources for readers who want to deepen their understanding of ICS concepts, refine their security strategies, and stay ahead of emerging risks. The references provided here span a broad spectrum of topics, from foundational DevSecOps principles to advanced AI-driven security methodologies, equipping readers with the insights needed to implement robust and adaptive security measures.

This collection includes influential books that cover DevSecOps, risk management, compliance, and the intersection of AI with security, alongside trusted websites offering up-to-date industry insights and community discussions. A selection of authoritative articles and blogs provides real-world perspectives on security challenges and innovations, while professional certification courses offer structured learning paths for those seeking formal accreditation in cybersecurity. Whether readers are new to ICS or looking to refine their expertise, these resources will serve as a valuable reference point for continued learning and professional development.

Books

Continuous Testing, Quality, Security, and Feedback (Packt, 2024)

- *Author:* Marc Hornbeek
- *Description:* This book delves into the practices of continuous testing, emphasizing the integration of quality, security, and feedback mechanisms throughout the software development lifecycle.

Engineering DevOps (BookBaby, 2019)

- *Author:* Marc Hornbeek
- *Description:* A comprehensive guide that explores the principles and practices of DevOps, offering insights into engineering methodologies that enhance collaboration and efficiency.

Enterprise DevOps for Architects: Leverage AIOps and DevSecOps for a Secure and Agile Enterprise (Packt, 2021)

- *Author:* Jeeva S. Chelladhurai
- *Description:* This book provides an architectural overview of DevOps, AIOps, and DevSecOps, offering strategies to drive and accelerate digital transformation securely.

Generative AI Security: Theories and Practices (Springer, 2024)

- *Author:* Ken Huang
- *Description:* A practical exploration of real-world generative AI security challenges, offering insights into building resilient security programs and understanding global AI governance.

How to Measure Anything in Cybersecurity Risk (John Wiley & Sons Inc., 2016)

- *Authors:* Douglas W. Hubbard and Richard Seiersen
- *Description:* This book simplifies the challenging task of quantifying cybersecurity risks, providing a clear framework for measuring the likelihood and impact of threats.

Operationalizing Threat Intelligence: A Guide to Developing and Operationalizing Cyber Threat Intelligence Programs (Packt, 2022)

- *Authors:* Kyle Wilhoit and Joseph Opacki
- *Description:* A comprehensive guide offering actionable steps for building, implementing, and optimizing effective cyber threat intelligence programs.

Practical Cybersecurity Architecture: A Guide to Creating and Implementing Robust Designs for Cybersecurity Architects (Packt, 2023)

- *Authors:* Diana Kelley and Ed Moyle
- *Description:* This book covers the fundamentals of cybersecurity architecture, providing evergreen approaches adaptable to new and emerging technologies such as AI and machine learning.

Project Zero Trust: A Story About a Strategy for Aligning Security and the Business (Wiley, 2022)

- *Author:* George Finney
- *Description:* A hands-on guide presenting an effective and practical Zero Trust security strategy, illustrated through an engaging narrative.

The Art of Social Engineering: Uncover the Secrets Behind the Human Dynamics in Cybersecurity (Packt, 2023)

- *Authors:* Cesar Bravo and Desilda Toska
- *Description:* This book explores psychological principles exploited by attackers, offering insights into developing defensive strategies against social engineering attacks.

The DevSecOps Playbook: Deliver Continuous Security at Speed (Wiley, 2023)

- *Author:* Sean D. Mack
- *Description:* An expert analysis of maintaining security through the critical balance of people, processes, and technology within DevSecOps practices.

The Language of Deception: Weaponizing Next Generation AI (Wiley, 2023)

- *Author:* Justin Hutchens
- *Description:* An incisive look into how contemporary and future AI can be weaponized for malicious purposes, offering strategies for defense against AI-driven threats.

Websites

Cloud Native Now

- *URL: https://cloudnativenow.com*
- *Description:* A platform offering news, articles, and resources focused on cloud native technologies, including Kubernetes, microservices, and containerization.

Darktrace

- *URL: https://www.darktrace.com*
- *Description:* A leading cybersecurity company that leverages AI to detect and respond to cyber threats in real time.

DevOps.com

- *URL: https://devops.com*
- *Description:* A leading source for DevOps news, tutorials, and industry insights, covering topics from Continuous Integration to deployment practices.

DevSecOps.org

- *URL: https://www.devsecops.org*
- *Description:* A community-driven site promoting the integration of security into DevOps practices, offering resources, blog posts, and a comprehensive DevSecOps manifesto.

EngineeringDevOps.com

- *URL: https://engineeringdevops.com*
- *Description:* A resource hub providing insights, best practices, and tools for engineering DevOps solutions effectively.

Google Security Operations (SecOps)

- *URL: https://cloud.google.com/security/products/security-operations*
- *Description:* Google's intelligence-driven and AI-powered security operations platform empowers security teams to better detect, investigate, and respond to threats.

NIST AI Risk Management Framework

- *URL: https://www.nist.gov/itl/ai-risk-management-framework*
- *Description:* A framework developed to help organizations manage risks associated with AI, promoting trustworthy and responsible AI development.

NIST Computer Security Resource Center (CSRC)

- *URL: https://csrc.nist.gov*
- *Description:* Offers a comprehensive repository of the National Institute of Standards and Technology's cybersecurity and information security–related projects, publications, news, and events.

NIST Cybersecurity Framework

- *URL: https://www.nist.gov/cyberframework*
- *Description:* The National Institute of Standards and Technology's framework offering guidelines and best practices for managing cybersecurity-related risks.

NIST DevSecOps Project

- *URL: https://csrc.nist.gov/projects/devsecops*
- *Description:* Focuses on integrating security practices into DevOps processes, ensuring that security is addressed throughout the software development lifecycle.

Palo Alto Networks

- *URL: https://www.paloaltonetworks.com*
- *Description:* A global cybersecurity leader providing AI-driven security solutions to prevent successful cyberattacks across clouds, networks, and mobile devices.

PlatformEngineering.org

- *URL: https://platformengineering.org*
- *Description:* A community hub for platform engineers, providing resources, events, and discussions on building and managing internal developer platforms.

Recorded Future

- *URL: https://www.recordedfuture.com*
- *Description:* Provides real-time threat intelligence powered by machine learning to help organizations proactively defend against cyberattacks.

Security Boulevard

- *URL: https://securityboulevard.com*
- *Description:* A comprehensive site offering news, analysis, and insights on cybersecurity topics, including application security, cloud security, and data protection.

SentinelOne

- *URL: https://www.sentinelone.com*
- *Description:* An AI-powered cybersecurity platform offering autonomous threat detection and response across endpoints, containers, cloud workloads, and Internet of Things devices.

Techstrong.ai

- *URL: https://techstrong.ai*
- *Description:* A platform dedicated to AI and its intersection with various industries, providing articles, news, and resources on AI-driven innovations.

Vectra AI

- *URL: https://www.vectra.ai*
- *Description:* Specializes in AI-driven network detection and response, helping organizations identify and respond to hidden cyber threats.

Articles, Blogs, Ebooks, and Webinars

Engineering DevOps Consulting

- *Author:* Marc Hornbeek
- *URL: https://engineeringdevops.com*
- *URL: https://oreil.ly/bridging-the-dev-and-secops-gap*
- *Description:* Marc Hornbeek, known as "DevOps-the-Gray," shares his expertise through various articles, blog posts, and webinars focusing on DevOps, continuous testing, and DevSecOps practices.

DevOps.com

- *Author:* Marc Hornbeek
- *URL: https://devops.com/author/marc-hornbeek*

- *Description:* A platform where Marc contributes insightful articles on DevOps and security, offering practical guidance and industry perspectives.

Security Boulevard

- *Author:* Marc Hornbeek
- *URL: https://securityboulevard.com/author/marc-hornbeek*
- *URL: https://securityboulevard.com/?s=Intelligent+Continuous+Security*
- *Description:* Marc's articles on Security Boulevard delve into various aspects of cybersecurity, providing readers with strategies to enhance their security posture.

Techstrong.ai

- *Author:* Marc Hornbeek
- *URL: https://techstrong.ai/author/marc-hornbeek*
- *Description:* Marc explores the intersection of AI and security in his contributions to Techstrong.ai, discussing how AI can revolutionize security practices.

"Revolutionizing the Nine Pillars of SRE with AI-Engineered Tools"

- *Author:* Marc Hornbeek
- *URL: https://devops.com/revolutionizing-the-nine-pillars-of-sre-with-ai-engineered-tools*
- *Description:* An article discussing how AI-driven tools can enhance site reliability engineering (SRE) practices across nine foundational pillars.

"Embracing Chaos with AI: Reinventing SRE's Anti-Fragility Practices"

- *Author:* Marc Hornbeek
- *URL: https://oreil.ly/embracing-chaos-with-ai*
- *Description:* This article explores the role of AI in enhancing the resilience and anti-fragility of systems through improved site reliability engineering (SRE) practices.

"Strategic Roadmap for SREs: Software Deployments with AI"

- *Author:* Marc Hornbeek
- *URL: https://devops.com/strategic-roadmap-for-sres-software-deployments-with-ai*

- *Description*: An insightful piece on how AI can optimize software deployment strategies, minimizing risks and enhancing efficiency for site reliability engineering (SRE).

"Upgrade SRE Performance Management with AI"

- *Author*: Marc Hornbeek
- *URL*: *https://devops.com/upgrade-sre-performance-management-with-ai*
- *Description*: This article examines how AI-engineered tools can improve the performance management of applications and infrastructure within site reliability engineering (SRE) practices.

"Harnessing AI for Automated and Toil-Free SRE"

- *Author*: Marc Hornbeek
- *URL*: *https://devops.com/harnessing-ai-for-automated-and-toil-free-sre*
- *Description*: An exploration of how AI can reduce manual efforts (toil) in site reliability engineering (SRE) tasks, leading to more efficient and automated operations.

"Revolutionizing the Nine Pillars of DevOps with AI-Engineered Tools"

- *Author*: Marc Hornbeek
- *URL*: *https://oreil.ly/revolutionizing-the-nine-pillars-of-devops*
- *Description*: An article detailing how AI can transform DevOps practices across nine key pillars, enhancing efficiency and collaboration.

"How AI Transforms DevOps Infrastructure"

- *Author*: Marc Hornbeek
- *URL*: *https://devops.com/how-ai-transforms-devops-infrastructure*
- *Description*: This piece discusses the impact of AI on DevOps infrastructure, including automation and scalability improvements.

"Harnessing AI in Continuous Delivery and Deployment"

- *Author*: Marc Hornbeek
- *URL*: *https://devops.com/harnessing-ai-in-continuous-delivery-and-deployment*
- *Description*: An article exploring how AI can enhance Continuous Delivery and Continuous Deployment processes, leading to faster and more reliable releases.

"Design for DevOps—Best Practices"

- *Author:* Marc Hornbeek
- *URL: https://devops.com/design-devops-best-practices*
- *Description:* This article examines how AI can influence software design practices to better align with DevOps methodologies.

Courses and Certifications

DevSecOps Foundation

- *Provider:* DevOps Institute
- *URL: https://www.devopsinstitute.com*
- *Description:* This course introduces the principles of DevSecOps, emphasizing the integration of security practices into the DevOps pipeline to enhance the security posture of organizations.

DASA Intelligent Continuous Security Certification

- *Provider:* DevOps Agile Skills Association (DASA)
- *URL: https://www.dasa.org/products/talent-products/certification-programs/dasa-intelligent-continuous-security*
- *Description:* This certification program equips professionals with the skills and mindset to integrate security seamlessly into DevOps practices, addressing AI-driven risks and fostering proactive defense strategies.

Certified Information Systems Security Professional (CISSP)

- *Provider:* (ISC)²
- *URL: https://www.isc2.org/Certifications/CISSP*
- *Description:* A globally recognized certification that validates an individual's expertise in designing, implementing, and managing a best-in-class cybersecurity program.

Certified Ethical Hacker (CEH)

- *Provider:* EC-Council
- *URL: https://www.eccouncil.org/programs/certified-ethical-hacker-ceh*

- *Description:* This certification focuses on equipping professionals with the skills to think and act like a hacker, identifying vulnerabilities and weaknesses in systems to prevent potential attacks.

Certified Information Security Manager (CISM)

- *Provider:* ISACA
- *URL: https://www.isaca.org/credentialing/cism*
- *Description:* Designed for management-focused individuals, this certification emphasizes the relationship between an information security program and broader business goals and objectives.

Certified Information Systems Auditor (CISA)

- *Provider:* ISACA
- *URL: https://www.isaca.org/credentialing/cisa*
- *Description:* This certification is ideal for professionals who audit, control, monitor, and assess an organization's IT and business systems.

CompTIA Security+

- *Provider:* CompTIA
- *URL: https://www.comptia.org/certifications/security*
- *Description:* An entry-level certification that covers foundational cybersecurity skills, including network security, compliance, operational security, threats, and vulnerabilities.

Offensive Security Certified Professional (OSCP)

- *Provider:* Offensive Security
- *URL: https://www.offensive-security.com/pwk-oscp*
- *Description:* A hands-on certification that requires professionals to demonstrate their ability to identify and exploit vulnerabilities in various operating systems and applications.

Certified Cloud Security Professional (CCSP)

- *Provider:* (ISC)²
- *URL: https://www.isc2.org/Certifications/CCSP*
- *Description:* This certification is tailored for IT and information security leaders responsible for applying best practices to cloud security architecture, design, operations, and service orchestration.

Systems Security Certified Practitioner (SSCP)

- *Provider:* (ISC)²
- *URL: https://www.isc2.org/Certifications/SSCP*
- *Description:* Ideal for IT administrators, managers, and network security professionals, this certification focuses on hands-on operational IT roles and emphasizes practical security knowledge.

Glossary of Continuous Security Terms

Security terminology is constantly evolving, and in the field of Intelligent Continuous Security (ICS), many concepts go beyond standard industry definitions. This glossary is not intended to serve as a formal or comprehensive dictionary of security terms, but rather, as a practical reference for readers of this book. The explanations provided here are written in plain language to clarify how key security terms are used within the context of ICS, helping readers better understand their application in securing the software lifecycle.

Some of the terms included in this glossary may have different meanings in other contexts or industries but, in this book, they are defined in a way that aligns with ICS principles, AI-driven security automation, and Continuous Security practices. Readers should use this glossary as a companion resource to navigate the discussions and case studies presented throughout the book.

access control

> The practice of restricting access to systems, applications, or data based on user roles, policies, and authentication mechanisms to prevent unauthorized access.

adversarial AI

> Techniques used by attackers to manipulate or evade AI-driven security systems by injecting deceptive inputs or exploiting weaknesses in machine learning models. Adversarial AI is often trained in response to an existing security system.

AI-assisted security

> The integration of artificial intelligence to enhance security operations, automate threat detection, and improve response times in cybersecurity environments.

AI agents

> Autonomous systems that interact with their environment, make decisions, and take actions to achieve specific goals. AI agents are often powered by machine learning and large language models to adapt dynamically to different security scenarios. AI agents can act as *automated incident responders*, analyzing threats in real time and executing predefined countermeasures without human intervention.

attack surface

> The total set of vulnerabilities, entry points, and exposed systems that an attacker can exploit in an organization's infrastructure.

automated compliance enforcement

The use of software to continuously validate security controls against regulatory and policy requirements without manual intervention.

behavioral analytics

AI-driven analysis of user behavior to detect anomalies, insider threats, or compromised credentials by identifying deviations from normal activity patterns.

change control

To maximize the number of successful service and product changes by ensuring that risks have been properly assessed, authorizing changes to proceed, and managing the change schedule.

change management

The structured process of implementing changes in an IT environment while minimizing risks and ensuring security and compliance.

CI/CD pipeline

A set of automated processes and tools used to build, test, and deploy software in a Continuous Integration/Continuous Delivery workflow, ensuring frequent and reliable releases.

cloud security posture management (CSPM)

Automated tools and processes used to ensure that cloud environments remain configured securely and compliant with industry standards.

cognitive security models

AI-driven systems that assess human decision-making tendencies and predict potential security risks based on behavioral patterns and stress responses.

continuous authentication

A security mechanism that continuously verifies user identity throughout a session rather than relying solely on an initial login.

continuous compliance validation

The automated process of continuously verifying that security controls align with regulatory and policy requirements, reducing compliance drift.

Continuous Delivery (CD)

The practice of ensuring that software is in a deployable state, at all times, by automating testing and validation processes throughout the software lifecycle.

Continuous Deployment

The automated release of software updates directly into production without manual intervention, ensuring rapid iteration and delivery.

Continuous Integration (CI)

A software development practice where developers frequently merge code changes into a shared repository, triggering automated testing and validation.

continuous monitoring

The ongoing process of collecting, analyzing, and responding to security events in real time to detect potential threats or policy violations.

continuous testing

The practice of executing automated tests at every stage of the software development lifecycle to identify and remediate security vulnerabilities early.

cyber deception technology

AI-driven security tools that create decoys and honeypots to mislead attackers and gather intelligence on malicious tactics.

cyber resilience

An organization's ability to anticipate, withstand, recover from, and adapt to cyberattacks while maintaining operational continuity.

data lake for security

A centralized repository that collects and normalizes security telemetry data from various sources to support analytics, threat detection, and compliance.

data loss prevention (DLP)

Security measures designed to prevent unauthorized access, transfer, or destruction of sensitive information.

DevOps

A cultural and technical approach that integrates software development (Dev) and IT operations (Ops) to enable Continuous Delivery and improved collaboration.

DevSecOps

The practice of integrating security into the DevOps process to ensure that security considerations are embedded throughout software development and deployment.

dynamic application security testing (DAST)

A security testing approach that evaluates applications in a runtime environment to detect vulnerabilities in real-world conditions.

end-to-end encryption

A method of securing data in transit and at rest, ensuring that only authorized parties can access or decrypt the information.

extended detection and response (XDR)

A security approach that consolidates threat detection and response capabilities across multiple security layers, including networks, endpoints, and cloud environments.

fully homomorphic encryption (FHE)

A cryptographic technique that enables computations on encrypted data without requiring decryption, enhancing data privacy and security.

General Data Protection Regulation (GDPR)

An EU regulation that governs data protection and privacy for individuals within the European Union, setting strict guidelines on how organizations collect, process, and store personal data.

generative AI (GenAI)

A subset of AI focused on creating new content, such as text, images, code, or music, based on learned patterns from existing data. *Example ICS use case:* Generative AI can be used to create synthetic attack simulations that help security teams test their defenses against evolving cyber threats.

Health Insurance Portability and Accountability Act (HIPAA)

A US regulation that establishes national standards to protect sensitive patient health information from being disclosed without consent or knowledge.

ICS pillars of practice

The foundational principles and practices of Intelligent Continuous Security as defined in this book. These eight pillars ensure that security is embedded across the software lifecycle:

Continuous Security culture

Embedding security as a shared responsibility across development, security, and operations teams, fostering a proactive mindset and reinforcing security in all aspects of the organization.

Continuous Security awareness training

Providing ongoing security training and education, leveraging AI-driven learning modules to dynamically adapt training content based on evolving threats.

security integration across the lifecycle

Ensuring that security practices, policies, and automation are embedded at every stage of the software lifecycle, from design to deployment and beyond.

automated security testing

Using AI and automation to continuously test applications, infrastructure, and code for vulnerabilities, reducing manual testing efforts while increasing coverage and accuracy.

proactive security risk management

Leveraging predictive analytics and AI-driven risk assessment to anticipate threats and prioritize security efforts based on real-time risk intelligence.

rapid incident response

Implementing AI-powered Security Orchestration, Automation, and Response (SOAR) to automate detection, triage, and remediation of security incidents in real time.

Continuous Security monitoring and compliance

Continuously monitoring security events, integrating AI-driven anomaly detection, and automating compliance enforcement to align with regulatory requirements.

security feedback and continuous improvement

Leveraging real-time security insights, post-incident analysis, and AI-driven optimizations to ensure that security practices evolve in response to emerging threats.

identity and access management (IAM)

A framework of policies and technologies that ensure that users have appropriate access to systems and data while preventing unauthorized use.

Intelligent Continuous Security (ICS)

Applies AI-augmented security practices continuously across the entire software development lifecycle and operational environment. It leverages AI to ensure real-time threat detection, automated security testing, and seamless integration of security across development and operations.

interactive application security testing (IAST)

A security testing approach that combines static and dynamic testing by monitoring applications in real time to detect vulnerabilities.

intrusion detection and prevention systems (IDPSs)

Security tools that monitor network traffic for malicious activities and take automated actions to block or mitigate threats.

large language models (LLMs)

Advanced AI models trained on vast amounts of text data to understand and generate humanlike text, enabling tasks such as automated documentation, code generation, and chatbot interactions. *Example ICS use case:* LLMs can be applied to automated security policy generation, ensuring that compliance documentation is kept up-to-date with regulatory changes.

machine learning (ML)

A broad category of AI where algorithms learn from data to identify patterns, make predictions, and automate decision making. ML includes techniques such as supervised learning, unsupervised learning, and reinforcement learning. *Example ICS use case:* ML-driven anomaly detection systems can continuously monitor infrastructure logs and network traffic to detect early signs of security breaches.

machine learning security models

AI-driven models that analyze patterns in data to predict, detect, and respond to cyber threats autonomously.

penetration testing

A security assessment technique where ethical hackers attempt to exploit vulnerabilities in systems to identify weaknesses before malicious actors do.

Policy as Code (PaC)

The practice of defining security policies in a machine-readable format, allowing for automated enforcement and validation within DevSecOps workflows.

predictive compliance modeling

AI-driven simulations that anticipate future regulatory changes and proactively align security policies with evolving compliance standards.

proactive security posture

A security strategy focused on preventing incidents rather than responding reactively, using automation, intelligence, and predictive analytics.

real-time threat intelligence

Security insights generated from live attack data, allowing organizations to identify and mitigate threats before they escalate.

risk-based authentication (RBA)

A security approach that adjusts authentication requirements dynamically based on a user's risk level, such as login location, device, or behavior.

role-based access control (RBAC)

A security model that assigns system permissions based on user roles to enforce the principle of least privilege.

runtime application self-protection (RASP)

Security technology that embeds protection mechanisms directly into applications to detect and block threats in real time.

SecOps

The collaboration between security teams and IT operations to maintain real-time security monitoring and incident response across an organization.

SecDevOps

The evolution of DevSecOps with an increased focus on security-first principles, ensuring that security is embedded as a fundamental component of all development and operations activities.

security information and event management (SIEM)

A security solution that aggregates and analyzes log data from various sources to detect threats and provide incident response insights.

Security Operations Center (SOC)

A centralized team responsible for monitoring, detecting, analyzing, and responding to cybersecurity incidents in real time.

software composition analysis (SCA)

The automated process of identifying vulnerabilities in open source software components within applications.

static application security testing (SAST)

A security analysis technique that scans source code for vulnerabilities without executing the application.

synthetic data

Artificially generated data that mimics real-world data but does not contain any actual sensitive or personal information. Synthetic data is often used to improve security testing, particularly during design and delivery phases, without exposing real user data to security risks.

threat hunting

A proactive cybersecurity approach where analysts actively search for indicators of compromise (IOCs), anomalous behavior, or advanced threats within an organization's network before automated tools detect them.

threat modeling

A systematic approach to identifying potential threats, vulnerabilities, and attack vectors in an application or system before they are exploited.

value stream

A holistic view of processes and workflows that deliver value to an organization or its customers. A value stream encompasses all the activities, from initiation to completion, that contribute to the delivery of a product, service, or security outcome. Within a value stream, individual processes serve as building blocks, addressing specific functions but remaining part of the larger, integrated flow. *Example ICS use case:* In ICS, value streams help ensure that security is embedded across all stages of software development and IT operations. For example, an ICS-enabled security value stream ensures that automated security controls, risk assessments, and compliance enforcement mechanisms are continuously integrated into Continuous Integration/Continuous Delivery pipelines, infrastructure management, and runtime security monitoring.

Zero Trust architecture
A security model that assumes no user, device, or system is inherently trusted and enforces strict access controls and continuous authentication.

Index

A

Acunetix, 164, 170

adaptive security configurations, with GenAI, 38

advanced persistent threats (see APTs)

adversarial ML attacks, 223

adversarial training, 49, 51

AFL (American Fuzzy Lop), 165

AI (artificial intelligence), 46-49

  adaptive learning and improvement, 48

  AI-enabled security MVP, 134, 136, 140

  collaboration across teams, 48

  Continuous Monitoring and Response, 34-37, 48

  Continuous Security culture, 59

  Continuous Security technologies, 87-96

  emerging trends

    deception technology, 256, 259

    security orchestration, 255, 259

    threat intelligence platforms, 256, 259

    user activity monitoring, 253, 258

  enhanced threat intelligence, 48

  limitations and pitfalls, 49-52

  maturity level roles

    Level 1 – Initial, 56

    Level 2 – Managed, 56

    Level 3 – Defined, 57

    Level 4 – Quantitatively Managed, 58

    Level 5 – Optimized, 58

  overreliance on, 143

  proactive threat detection, prevention, and mitigation, 45, 47

  real-time incident response, 47

  secure supply chain management, 91

  security workflow automation, 47

  sustaining technologies, 97-100

  team topologies, 74

  tool sprawl, 145

  transformation tools and templates, 131, 139-142

  workloads in security-sensitive environments, 223-226

air traffic control, 210

alert fatigue

  cognitive overload and burnout, 254

  DevSecOps, 189

  overwhelming volume, 27

  reducing, 31, 48, 50

algorithmic trading, cyberattacks on, 203

Alibaba, 212, 221

alignment (see Team Alignment step)

Amazon, 212

Amazon Web Services (AWS), 199

American Fuzzy Lop (AFL), 165

Anchore Grype, 163

Anomali ThreatStream, 153

anomaly detection, 85-86, 91, 216

Apache JMeter, 169

Apache Struts framework, 163

API security testing, 168

application transformation scorecards, 109-110

APSM platform, xi

APTs (advanced persistent threats)

  evolving nature of, 28

  financial institutions, 203

  lateral movement, 90

  rise of, 4

organizational friction, xi
OSS-Fuzz, Google, 165
OT (operational technology), 209
overloaded platform team topology, 77, 81
OWASP Threat Dragon, 167
OWASP ZAP, 160, 164

P

PaC (Policy as Code), 127, 152, 190, 254, 259
Palo Alto Cortex XDR, 67
Palo Alto Cortex XSOAR, 175
Palo Alto Networks, 201, 224
Palo Alto Prisma Cloud, 168, 201
PAM (privileged access management), 156
patch and update management, 193
    AI role in, 45
    importance of, 29
patient safety, 206
payment card fraud, 212
payment processors, 204
payment system attacks, 203
PayPal, 204, 212, 224
PCI DSS (Payment Card Industry Data Security
    Standard), 14, 26, 170, 203, 231-232
penetration testing automation (automated
    pentesting), 37, 89, 166
Pentera, 166
people dimension
    AI-driven security culture, 59
    automated and adaptive security testing, 61
    Continuous Security monitoring and pre-
        dictive compliance, 62
    emerging trends, 253, 258
    feedback loops and continuous evolution,
        62
    integrated security lifecycle, 60
    intelligent incident response, 61
    intelligent security awareness and training,
        60
    Level 1 – Initial, 53, 56
    Level 2 – Managed, 54, 56
    Level 3 – Defined, 54, 57
    Level 4 – Quantitatively Managed, 54, 57
    Level 5 – Optimized, 55, 58
    observability design, 239
    proactive security risk intelligence, 61
percentage of applications fully integrated met-
    ric, 230, 234

percentage of security processes automated
    metric, 234, 236
percentage of security vulnerabilities detected
    metric, 234
percentage of systems audited and fully compli-
    ant metric, 231, 236
Pfizer, 207
Phantom, Splunk, 175
pharmaceutical sector, 205-208
    improvements through ICS practices, 207
    real-world organizations, 207
    security concerns, 206
phishing attacks, 12
PII (personally identifiable information), 85
pillars of practice, 59-63
    AI-driven Continuous Security culture, 59
    automated and adaptive security testing, 61
    awareness and training, 60
    continuous monitoring and predictive com-
        pliance, 62
    gap assessments, 116
    integrated security lifecycle, 60
    intelligent incident response, 61
    proactive security risk intelligence, 61
    security feedback loops and continuous evo-
        lution, 62
pilot phase, of replacement decisions, 99
PJM Interconnection, 209
platform engineering, 174
platform team for security and AI topology, 75,
    80
Plutora, 173
PoC (proof-of-concept), 105, 123-124, 184
Policy as Code (PaC), 127, 152, 190, 254, 259
polymorphic malware, 12
portfolio management, 129
Postman Security Testing, 168
pre-deployment security, 18
predictive compliance modeling, 255, 259
predictive ML (see ML)
predictive security analytics, 86
Prisma Cloud, Palo Alto, 168, 201
privacy
    AI technologies and, 51, 96
    concern over adoption of emerging trends,
        258
    GenAI, 85
    healthcare security, 206
privileged access management (PAM), 156

About the Author

Marc Hornbeek, widely recognized as "DevOps-the-Gray," founder, CEO, and principal consultant at Engineering DevOps Consulting (*https://engineeringdevops.com*), is a seasoned technology expert, author, consultant, and thought leader in the fields of continuous testing, DevOps, DevSecOps, Intelligent Continuous Security, and site reliability engineering (SRE). With over four decades of experience in engineering, security, and IT operations, Marc has become one of the most respected voices in the DevOps and cybersecurity communities. His extensive background spans software development, network engineering, systems security, and enterprise digital transformations, making him a sought-after expert for organizations looking to scale and optimize their security, software delivery, and operations practices.

Throughout his career, Marc has held leadership roles at major enterprises, technology firms, manufacturers, service providers, and government agencies, helping to design and implement highly resilient, secure, and automated IT infrastructures. His hands-on experience has allowed him to pioneer methodologies that integrate AI-driven automation, risk-based security management, and continuous compliance enforcement into modern DevSecOps and SecOps practices. He has advised numerous Fortune 500 companies on their digital transformation journeys, guiding them in breaking down organizational silos, enhancing security automation, and adopting intelligent, data-driven security strategies.

Marc is the author of *Engineering DevOps* (BookBaby, 2019), a widely regarded book that provides a structured and engineering-based approach to DevOps transformation, helping organizations develop scalable, resilient, and highly automated software delivery pipelines. He is also the author of *Continuous Testing, Quality, Security, and Feedback* (Packt, 2024), which explores the fundamental role of continuous testing in ensuring software reliability, security, and quality across the DevOps lifecycle. His deep expertise in Intelligent Continuous Security has led to the development of cutting-edge strategies that unify DevSecOps and SecOps into a seamless, end-to-end security framework.

Marc is a regular blogger and speaker on major websites, including DevOps.com (*https://devops.com*), Security Boulevard (*https://securityboulevard.com*), Techstrong.ai (*https://techstrong.ai*), Platform Engineering (*https://platformengineering.com*), and Cloud Native Now (*https://cloudnativenow.com*). Beyond his writing and consulting work, Marc is a frequent speaker, trainer, and mentor, actively contributing to industry-leading conferences and events such as DevOps Enterprise Summit, DevOps World, Velocity, and cybersecurity forums.

He serves as a course author and instructor for DevOps, DevSecOps, SRE, and security certification programs, including those offered by the DevOps Institute, PeopleCert, and DASA. His dedication to thought leadership and knowledge sharing has influenced the way security professionals, engineers, and executives approach AI-powered security automation, threat modeling, and Zero Trust architectures.

Marc is an IEEE Outstanding Engineer and an IEEE Life Member. He holds engineering and business degrees, numerous certifications, and industry awards. As a consultant, Marc continues to work with organizations worldwide, helping them implement, sustain, and evolve DevOps, DevSecOps, SRE, and ICS practices that enable them to proactively detect, prevent, and mitigate security threats in real time. His unique ability to bridge engineering disciplines with security-first thinking ensures that businesses can achieve both robust security postures and accelerated software innovation.

When he's not writing, speaking, or consulting, Marc enjoys sharing his knowledge with the next generation of DevOps and security professionals, staying actively engaged in community-driven initiatives, research, and mentoring programs (helpful tools and other relevant information can be found at his website, Engineering DevOps Consulting (*https://engineeringdevops.com*)). His passion for engineering excellence, security resilience, and intelligent automation continues to shape the future of Intelligent Continuous Security and its impact on enterprises worldwide.

Colophon

The animal on the cover of *Intelligent Continuous Security* is an Indochinese leopard (*Panthera pardus delacouri*). A subspecies of leopard native to Southeast Asia, the Indochinese leopard is found primarily in fragmented forest habitats across Laos, Cambodia, Thailand, Vietnam, and parts of Myanmar. This elusive predator prefers dense tropical and subtropical forests, often in mountainous or hilly terrain.

The Indochinese leopard is slightly smaller than its African relatives, with males typically weighing between 110–132 pounds and females between 66–88 pounds. Their short, dense fur is covered with distinctive rosettes. These solitary and nocturnal carnivores primarily feed on medium-sized prey such as deer, wild boar, and monkeys. Their lifespan in the wild is usually 12–15 years. Due to poaching for skins and traditional medicine, along with habitat fragmentation, the Indochinese leopard is listed as Critically Endangered by the International Union for Conservation of Nature (IUCN), with only a few hundred believed to remain in the wild.

Many of the animals on O'Reilly covers are endangered; all of them are important to the world.

The cover illustration is by José Marzan Jr., based on a black-and-white engraving from *Meyers Kleines Lexicon*. The series design is by Edie Freedman, Ellie Volckhausen, and Karen Montgomery. The cover fonts are Gilroy Semibold and Guardian Sans. The text font is Adobe Minion Pro; the heading font is Adobe Myriad Condensed; and the code font is Dalton Maag's Ubuntu Mono.

O'REILLY®

Learn from experts.
Become one yourself.

60,000+ titles | Live events with experts | Role-based courses
Interactive learning | Certification preparation

**Try the O'Reilly learning platform
free for 10 days.**

www.ingramcontent.com/pod-product-compliance
Lightning Source LLC
Chambersburg PA
CBHW080931220326
41598CB00034B/5750